The Emperor's Guest

分

抑 留 者 名 票

収容所 Camp		爪哇 II　32474
収容年月日 Date Interned		昭和 19年 2 月 29 日　(III)
氏　名 Name		BOZUWA, Gerard Gijsbert.
番　號 No.		
生年月日 Date of Birth		1926-2-16.
國　籍 Nationality		蘭
本籍地 Place of Origin		DJAKARTA, Java.
身分職業 Position or Occupation		Scholier.　生
抑留前ノ住所又ハ居所 Address before Internment		Houtmanstraat 43, BANDOENG, Java.
父ノ名 Father's name		Gerard Gijsbert.
通報先 Destination of Report		Mevr.M.BOZUWA-VAN STRIJ,Houtmanstraat 43,BANDOENG, Java.
母ノ名 Mother's name		VAN STRIJ, Marie.
特技 Speciality		
妻(夫)ノ名 Wife's (Husband's) name		
特記事項 Remarks		23139/W3 S.S. Plancius 1-12-45

The Emperor's Guest

Coming of Age behind Barbed Wire during WW II in Indonesia

Titia Bozuwa

Triple Tulip Press
Sanbornville, N.H.

Published by Triple Tulip Press
2717 Wakefield Road
Sanbornville, N.H. 03872

In the interest of protecting the privacy of individuals whose real identities are not central to the story told here, certain names have been altered in several instances.

ISBN 9780975482544
LCCN 2009932936

Editor: Sue Wheeler
Line Editor: Elizabeth Barrett
Cover Design: Norman Royle
Cover picture supplied by NIOD – Nederlands Instituut voor Oorlogsdocumentatie
Printing: The Sheridan Press, Hanover, P.A.

For:
Gijs and Janneke

In memory of Vader and Moeder Bozuwa

Also by Titia Bozuwa

Joan, A Mother's Memoir (2000)
In the Shadow of the Cathedral (2004)
Wings of Change (2007)

Acknowledgements

I wish to thank Gijs from the bottom of my heart for his grace in allowing me to delve into the painful memories of his adolescence without restrictions. Together, we were able to match his recollections with the historical facts my research brought out in harmonious cooperation.

His sister Janneke was invaluable in filling in the blanks with her enviable capacity to remember events into the smallest details. It was a joy to work with her to make sure this would indeed be a true story.

Sue Wheeler, again, gave unselfishly of her time and expertise to make sure the story flowed without excess information and anecdotal side trips. I am immensely grateful for her characteristic enthusiasm and support.

I also want to thank Elizabeth Barrett for the excellent job line-editing the manuscript.

Our son Paul worked hard on the technical aspects of turning the story into a book, and I thank him for his efforts, as well as his wife Colleen, who came up with the sub title. My granddaughter Johanna was the first to read the finished manuscript and I thank her for her wise remarks and enthusiasm.

A special thanks goes to my distant cousin Theo Wetsclaar, who tirelessly researched the archives in The Hague. He provided valuable information.

Norman Royle created a compelling book cover from the picture my brother Herman secured from N.I.O.D. (the Dutch Institute for War Documentation). Norman was wonderful to work with.

I thank Jim Murfy for helping me getting the manuscript from my computer to the printer, a task beyond my technical expertise.

During the long process, several people read parts of the book. I appreciate the comments and encouragement they gave me to go on with what at times seemed an impossible task. They are:

The attendees of the Twin Farms Writers Workshops, Sherry Bryant, who would even brave a snow storm to listen to the next chapter, Mary and Flagg Avery, Jan and Mimi Havinga, Maggie Kennedy, and Helen Bradley.

My heartfelt gratitude goes out to all.

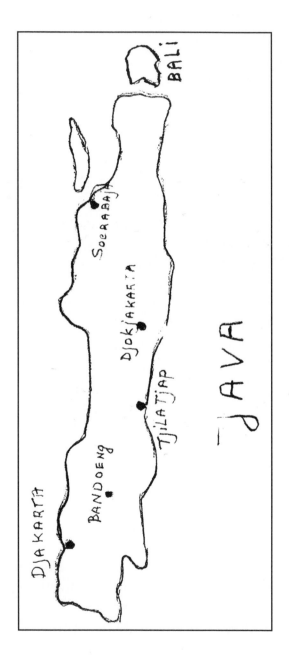

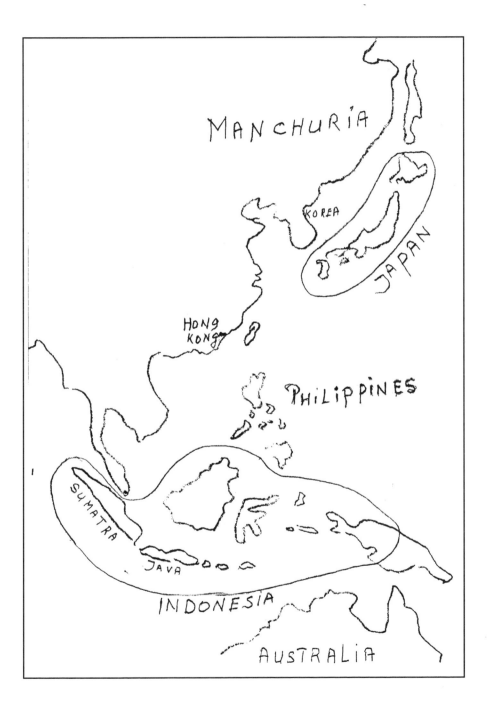

Chapter 1

"Come on, Soepardi, let me drive!" Gijs begged.

A smile spread over Soepardi's face. Several teeth were missing, and the ones that were left had turned almost as brown from smoking as his face was from birth. His smile was impenetrable and mysterious. Soepardi kept polishing the black hood of the car until the metal resembled a mirror. His *Tuan's* imposing six-seater cabriolet was his pride. In it, he drove Captain Bozuwa every morning at dawn to the naval air base in Soerabaja.

Gijs had been after Soepardi for weeks, months even, dying to get behind the wheel of his father's Chrysler. Exasperated by Soepardi's silent resistance, he decided to bribe him, taking note that Mascots were his favorite brand of cigarettes.

Today it finally worked. Soepardi drove to the city's outskirts and switched seats with him. During Sunday road trips with his family, Gijs had closely followed the motions from his jump seat in the back as Soepardi started, shifted, accelerated and put on the brakes. Now, proudly sitting behind the wheel, he felt a flush of power and accomplishment. His father didn't know how to drive a car. It really wasn't all that hard to make this big chunk of steel do what he wanted.

With the roof down he could smell *sateh* being barbecued by the side of the road, but he didn't dare look at the native who sat fanning the fire with a folded newspaper. He concentrated on keeping the car straight or Soepardi would tell him to stop. If he even so much as scratched his father's car, Soepardi would get into undeserved trouble.

Gijs sped up a bit. The wind ruffled his hair. The experience of driving, feeling the motion and hearing the hum of the motor, was absolutely thrilling. If only he were eighteen, he could get his driver's license, but he wasn't even sixteen yet. Two years from now, his father's four-year-tour of duty in the Dutch East Indies would end and they would return to Holland, where they'd never owned a car. Maybe, though, his father would have to stay longer. They certainly couldn't return to Holland if it was still occupied by Hitler and Nazi Germany.

He turned the wheel to make a right turn onto a road that led to the bridge, from where he'd be able to see the harbor. He'd been to the harbor many times. His father was commander of the naval air base, but after the Japanese bombed Pearl Harbor, he seemed too preoccupied to think of taking Gijs to the base with him. Coming home from the base that fateful day in December, he said only that the Japanese were prowling in the neighborhood. The next day, America declared war on Japan.

"Be careful on the bridge," Soepardi warned. "Don't let the rumble scare you, but slow down."

"Am I going too fast?"

"Not yet," Soepardi said with that peculiar smile, his usually supple body looking as stiff as his starched white shirt.

Gijs pressed the clutch to the floor with his left foot and reached for the stick with his right hand.

"Don't forget to double-clutch," Soepardi said.

He carefully shifted down twice and eased the car onto the bridge. Soepardi was right about the rumble. It was louder than he'd thought. He had never paid attention to it before. The tires sang and echoed against the metal sides of the bridge. Such a fierce noise! More like screeching and droning.

Soepardi yelled, "Stop!", so Gijs jammed his foot on the brake. Had he done something wrong with the shifting? Had he ruined the engine? Soepardi pointed at the harbor. There was such a racket around and above him, Gijs felt like ducking his head. A whistling, dark shadow sailed over their car and the foul smell of diesel smoke filled their nostrils.

"Oh my God," Gijs said.

All traffic on the bridge had come to a dead stop.

Bombs fell out of screeching planes and rained on the ships and yards. Before he could count how many planes, they pulled up and away toward the ocean. Within a minute all that was left were vapor trails in the sky and gaping craters in the earth.

Next to him Soepardi was jabbering in Maleis. Gijs had learned some words in Maleis, but not enough to understand an agitated native. He tapped Soepardi's arm and raised his eyebrows.

"Move over," Soepardi said when he realized Gijs didn't understand him. He took over the wheel and sped the car toward home so fast that Gijs didn't have time to see if the big hangars that housed his father's planes were hit. And where was his father? Soepardi seemed to hold the same thought, because he was driving like a maniac, his usual laid-back demeanor now evaporated.

The car roof was still down. The palm trees by the side of the road blurred into pointed blades. For a confusing, chilling second they looked like bayonets, like the ones he'd seen mounted on the guns of Japanese soldiers in a news journal about the war in China. Seeing bombs fall out of airplanes was different. It seemed like all people had done in the two months since Pearl Harbor was engage in the luxury of theorizing about a war that was imminent. "What if?" had changed into "Now what?" Today, seeing planes overhead with a red circle on a white rectangle painted on their wings and sides, was a stark reality. No wonder his father had been so distracted lately. He knew.

The sun stood high in the sky, creating blinding spots of light on the pavement through the tall tamarind and palm trees. Native people dotted the landscape, some napping, leaning against wide tree trunks, while others hunched over tiny stoves, fanning fires. Gijs wondered if they'd even heard the bombing and if they were worried about what had happened to their city and what this would mean to their lives. The mixture of the everyday cooking smells and the sweet smell of gardenias distracted him from his own dark thoughts. It seemed to take forever to get back home, even with Soepardi's lead foot on the accelerator.

Gijs ran into the house. His mother stood with the telephone to her ear while she held the cord curled around her fingers. Thank God, he heard her say. That, at least, was encouraging.

A breeze billowed a net curtain in the open window. His mother's tall and erect body was silhouetted against the light that fell into the living room from the wide veranda, where Owi was rearranging the chairs after he'd swept the tile floor. It was eerily quiet. Just the clock on the white wall made its insistent ticking sounds.

"Yes, we'll have to wait and see what your orders are going to be," Gijs heard his mother say. Then she put the phone back in its cradle.

"Moeder, who was that? Is Vader all right?"

"Yes, he's fine. His part of the harbor was spared."

"I saw the bombs fall on the harbor," Gijs blurted, and then realized he'd given away his secret trip with Soepardi. His mother, the telephone cord still curled around her index finger, fixed her blue eyes on him without seeing him. His heart beat a little slower. His father was safe.

In 1940—two months before Germany invaded Holland—his family had left for his father's third tour of duty in the Dutch East Indies. Europe was in turmoil. The Nazis were busy rearranging its borders, starting with Poland. Within months their black ink had splashed over the map, until most of Europe looked like an amorphous blot, bleeding into its far reaches. Gijs, his parents and his five-years-older sister Janneke had traveled by train to Genoa in Italy, where they would board the ss *Johan van Oldenbarneveld*. On the way, while the train stopped in Paris, vendors ran along the platform waving newspapers with the disturbing headline: Germany invades Norway. The rest of the train trip, through the entire length of France, was spent with all the shades pulled. The French didn't take any chances. They were already at war with Germany. It was a spooky trip, sitting in a blinded train for hours and hours.

Once aboard the luxurious liner to the Dutch East Indies, the war had seemed like a mirage. The daily routine aboard was carefully programmed to give the passengers blissful amnesia. Surely, officers like his father knew a Pacific war was a possibility; civil servants wondered how they would govern the Dutch East Indies if communications with the motherland were broken; planters knew they would soon be back in the jungle without the niceties of a dance floor and beautifully dressed women in their arms. But the crew was bent on making it easier to tune out those concerns. The passengers were entertained from morning till night with games, shows and exquisite food for a whole month. Champagne flowed like an endless river.

Two years had passed since that carefree journey.

As they sat at the dining room table that evening, his father still in his white uniform, Owi moved around like a shadow, serving them their meal.

"I expect that this attack will start the ABDA on Java," Vader said.

They all knew what that meant. The American, British, Dutch and Australian governments had united their territories—the Philippines, Malaysia, the Dutch East Indies and Australia—for defense purposes and had brought the military forces under one allied command, commonly referred to by its acronym: ABDA. The one-eyed British field marshal, Sir Archibald Wavell, was its appointed supreme commander.

A silence fell around the table. Gijs mashed the boiled potatoes on his plate with his fork. His mother didn't serve the typical Indonesian *rijsttafel*. Only rarely did she allow their *kokkie* to prepare native dishes. She was petrified that food from the markets might be spoiled. If she wanted to serve chicken, she asked the vendor to kill it before her own eyes. They drank canned milk imported from Holland.

"The Japanese are now in Thailand," Vader said. "Hong Kong fell on Christmas Day. They will try to take Borneo. It's where the oil is." He sighed. He hadn't said more than what they'd already read in the newspapers, but it was clear that he meant to warn them.

A few days later, his father came home early for the midday meal.

"Helfrich called me this morning," he said. Rear Admiral Helfrich was the commander of the Royal Dutch Navy in the Dutch East Indies. "He wants me to report to Bandoeng. Wavell has arrived. ABDA's headquarters have been set up there, and he's put me in charge of the Allied Reconnaissance Division."

"How soon?" Moeder asked.

"Immediately."

"Does this mean we're all going to Bandoeng?" Gijs asked.

"It means that we are leaving from here in three days."

Vader pushed his napkin out of its silver ring, which was engraved with his initials, spread it over his lap and took up his knife and fork, a signal for the rest of the family to do likewise.

"Me too? Then I have to give up working?" Janneke asked. She served in the Women's Volunteer Corps, driving and repairing big trucks to replace the drivers who'd been called up in the mobilization. Gijs had snickered the first time she'd come home in a khaki uniform, black grease under her fingernails. The image didn't fit the one he had of his sister, five years older than he. It was impossible to think of Janneke's slender hands bolting on tires.

"We'll see," her father said.

Janneke looked stricken. Jan, her fiancé, was at sea, serving on a submarine. They'd just celebrated their engagement and she was anxiously awaiting his return to Soerabaja. Vader looked up at her. From the moment he'd come off the street, he'd appeared preoccupied, his face set in deep lines. There seemed to be something he wanted to say to her, but he remained silent.

Moeder took the news with deliberate calm. Gijs wasn't surprised. His family wasn't given to a show of emotions. That was frowned upon. The life of a navy officer was guided by strict codes of behavior.

Vader and Moeder Bozuwa

Certain things one just didn't do. They wouldn't pass muster, like wearing a bright red tie to dinner or sporting a racy dress at an official event. The navy liked its officers to stand ramrod straight, their spouses with proper hats and white gloves beside them.

Before Jan Schippers, a young officer, could ask for Janneke's hand, he'd had to ask permission from his commander first. Officers were expected to marry women who did honor to the navy. Janneke had passed the test. Or maybe her father had, because of his rank.

Yet Gijs read from his mother's face that she didn't take this "pack up and go" order lightly. Her nostrils flared, something he'd noticed she did when she was holding off stress within herself. She'd hardly touched her food and was already folding up her napkin.

"We have work to do," she said, and pushed her chair from the table.

When Vader got up from the table, Owi started to clear the dishes. Vader took Gijs into his office, to where a large map hung on the wall. He swept his right hand over it until he found Japan and pushed a thumbtack in the island of Kioesjoe, its most southerly point. He fastened a string to the thumbtack; the other end he tied around his fountain pen.

"Look where that drops to, Gijs," he said as he let the string slip from his fingers. When the pen stopped swinging from left to right, from Thailand to the Marshall Islands, then on its slowed-down swing from Sumatra to New Guinea, he said, "If the Japanese succeed in taking the Philippines, their way to our colonies will be free. We have to stop them."

Gijs looked at the plumb string that extended from Japan to the island of Ambon. It had fallen neatly between the Philippines on one side and the various groups of islands that were already in the hands of the Japanese on the other side. Vader had shown him what was at stake, and the message was clear. The war was progressing at an alarming rate. Japan now ruled an area many times the size of its own island nation. Would strong men like his father be able to stop the Japanese? He didn't know of anyone who truly believed that Java, this rich jewel of an island, might be squeezed from the Dutch crown.

After he'd made his point, Vader told Gijs to ask Janneke to come in.

"You can stay here a week longer after we close the house," Vader said when Janneke joined them.

"Is Jan coming back?"

"I cannot tell you the details and I don't want you to talk about it. Ask your friend Ton Perks if you can stay with her and give her a reason, like you want to help her with the baby." Ton Perks was a navy officer's wife.

Janneke didn't ask for more information. The rules of the navy were that once at sea, a war ship's location and destination were secret. Her father was dead serious. That was not hard to see. Janneke turned uncharacteristically quiet, but the color had come back to her cheeks. Gijs was sure his sister was exploding with anticipation.

Two days to close the house and one day to travel. Since they lived in a rented house, at least they didn't have to find a buyer in a hurry. Of their belongings, they could take only what they could carry. A friend who worked for a shipping company told Moeder she could store what she couldn't bring in one of his warehouses on the harbor. Knowing the harbor could be bombed again, this was risky, but it was the only reasonable solution.

It seemed to Gijs that, in spite of the threat of war, his mother was in her element. His father depended on her to make the right decisions on domestic issues, and moving was something she had done many times before. She considered it part of being an officer's wife. Every four years it was the same. Pack and unpack, either within Holland or sailing to the Indies. Gijs had been born in Batavia in the Dutch East Indies, brought back to Holland in a basket, returned to the tropical islands when he was six, and then again, this last time, when he was fourteen. Their furniture in Holland had gone into storage, and Moeder furnished their homes in the tropics with furniture from the secondhand market that thrived on the regular back-and-forth of navy families. Chairs, sofas, wardrobes traveled from house to house, from hand to hand. An exception was the fashionable furniture in Gijs's room. He was very proud of his Gispen desk and his chair, with its gleaming steel frame and woven seat that his parents had bought especially for him. The simple, strong design looked masculine and modern. He hated to see it being wrapped in brown paper and carried to the big van that stood parked in the yard all day.

Moeder charged ahead like a train coursing to a certain destination, even though she had no idea what their living situation would be in Bandoeng or for how long. Without hesitation she told the movers what to pack—most of it—and what to leave. Gijs saw her standing wistfully in front of the tea table with its delicate porcelain teacups and saucers. Her slender hands held up a small tortoiseshell box that contained the silver teaspoons she had inherited from her mother. She opened it, counted the spoons, hesitated for a moment, and then put them with a small pile of things she would take with her.

More than furniture was left behind. Moeder gave all the servants two months' salary and sent them on their way. Soepardi had already left in the Chrysler, filled to the roof with things Moeder felt she could not do without. His orders were to drive the car to Bandoeng and return by train. But telling Owi and his wife Mina the news of their sudden move had been heart wrenching. Two years earlier Gijs's family had spotted Owi and Mina on the pier when they disembarked. In bare feet and wrapped in colorful sarongs, Owi and Mina had waited for their *Tuan*, having heard rumors that Captain Bozuwa was coming back to Soerabaja. Owi had offered his services, saying he and Mina would terminate their present employ to serve the Bozuwa family again. He worked as the *djongos* and Mina as the *baboe,* in charge of the household chores. A *kokkie* to do the cooking and a *kebon* to take care of the gardens had come with them. Owi and Mina, who were married, lived in the *bijgebouwen,* modest servant quarters behind the main house.

When they walked out of the house, and out of their lives with the Bozuwas, Gijs felt the sudden urge to comfort them. All the wretched feelings the bombardment had aroused—thoughts of the looming war, knowing he would lose his friends at school, and having to give up the first room that had been truly his—all these unexpected losses culminated in a deep sadness toward Owi and Mina. With a feeling of foreboding, Gijs watched two natives, who had demanded so little for themselves and served them with such loyalty, bowed to him and his family. A middle-aged couple with their dark brown eyes and brown skin, small in stature, their straight hair as black as coal, had been as much a part of him as his own white skin. Every day, Mina had awakened him at 5 AM with a cheerful greeting, picked up the clothes he dropped on the floor, and protected him in every way she could. They had made the Bozuwas—four tall, blue-eyed, blond people—their life, eclipsing their own. Did they have children? He didn't even know. His heart ached. Where would they go? Back to the *dessa* where they'd come from?

His parents might not approve, he knew, but he didn't care. Before Mina walked away, he hugged her. When he let go, her eyes looked like black coffee as they filled with tears.

Chapter 2

"Happy birthday."

This was not the voice he'd learned to expect first thing in the morning, when he lay curled up with his *goeling*, before Java's unforgiving sun had turned into a fireball.

Through the netting of the *klamboe* he saw his mother standing at the foot of his bed, fully dressed.

"You are now sixteen, *jongen*." She paused to let this important fact sink in. "We have a present for you, but first we have to get ourselves to the station. Vader will meet us there. Janneke is making breakfast."

It was the sixteenth of February 1942, his sixteenth birthday, and he had to spend it on a train for over twelve hours. As a first thought of the day, Gijs didn't find it an appealing prospect.

"Sorry to rush you, but trains don't wait," Moeder said.

There was no arguing that, so he got up and put on the clothes he'd put out the night before on top of his bulging leather suitcase, since his chair had disappeared into the moving van. Janneke, as much a mother to him as Moeder, had mostly decided what he should be taking with him to Bandoeng.

"Will you see Jan?" Gijs asked his sister, as she set some slices of bread on the bare table. The silver breadbasket was in storage.

"I hope so, but Vader can't tell me anything. You know the navy's rule: Don't mention the whereabouts of a ship unless it's moored in plain sight. I hope Jan will call before the week is over."

"Does he know where to call if you stay with Ton Perks?"

"I've left messages everywhere." She said this calmly. It always amazed him that she could get all worked up about coffee spilled on the rug or whatever, but tough things like not knowing if she would see Jan before the end of the war didn't seem to throw her into a tizzy.

A taxi drove up, and again the Bozuwa family closed the door on a rented house. At the station they spotted Vader, in civilian clothes, pacing up and down the platform. Porters carried their suitcases and trunks to a first class compartment.

"I will send you a signal when you have to come to Bandoeng," Vader called to Janneke, who remained on the platform.

"I'll wait for Jan and then I'll come."

"You will come when I call you. These are dangerous times, Janneke."

"Yes, Vader."

She was in love. Within two months she would turn twenty-one.

The whistle blew, and the train slowly pulled out of the station. Gijs stuck his head out of the window to wave at his sister, who was easy to identify. She stood a head taller than most of the crowd milling on the platform, and her blond hair stood out like a bright moon in a dark sky.

As the train rumbled over a bridge near the harbor, Gijs spotted the huge aluminum hangar that was part of the naval air base. He started to say something to Vader, but thought better of it. It might not make him happy to be reminded of having to trade his post for a delicate leadership position among foreigners. British and Dutch navy men had a long history of rivalry that went back to the sixteenth century, when both countries fiercely competed for profitable trade routes. Would they cooperate in their joint fight against the Japanese?

Gijs craned his neck to see if planes were on the field next to the hangar, but didn't see any. They must be in the air, searching for Japanese warships. Every morning during his Christmas vacation he'd climbed into the backseat of the Chrysler when Soepardi drove his father to the base. At the base, Vader had assigned a man named Willem to look after him. A tall, burly petty officer, Willem didn't take flak from anybody.

"Here's a cloth and polish," Willem told him one day. "I want you to polish every bit of brass on this speedboat till you can see your own face in it."

Gijs saw more than his own face. The sweat beads on his forehead picked up rays of sun and looked like a string of pearls as he peered into the brass horn. It had been worth it, though. Willem had allowed him to join the sailors when they took "his" boat and roared over the water to pick up a seaplane's crew that had just landed in the harbor after a reconnaissance flight. A nimble pilot jumped down from the wing of the Dornier into the speedboat, a thrilling sight. One day Gijs would be serving in the Royal Dutch Navy himself, as an officer like his father.

Their train left Soerabaja behind, turning it into a memory for the rest of their lives. Huffing and puffing the train wound its way through the lush scenery of Java, revealing a more rural way of life than he was used to. The rich and abundant growth of ferns and trees didn't match the paltry living conditions of the natives in the *kampongs* they passed. He watched as three young boys carried water buckets that dangled in perfect balance on either end of long bamboo sticks resting on their narrow shoulders. Farther along the track an old woman stood barefoot in a *kali* as she washed her clothes, and an old wrinkled man sat in his *toko* shaded by a fragile roof of dried leaves, the wobbly bamboo counter straining under his bounty of aubergines and *laboepoetih*. These people had to work hard for the things he took for granted, like water coming out of a tap, and he wondered if Mina and Owi were on their way back to this hardscrabble way of life. No wonder they had cried when they said good-bye, even if they lived only on the fringes of the world that the white folks had created for themselves.

The brakes screeched, and the train shuddered to a stop at the next city. Frightened natives, who wanted to get back to the *dessas* they hailed from, packed the platform. The prevailing wind of power would soon blow from another direction, and they could see it coming. Close to his window a young mother stood with a baby in a *slendang* on her back while a basket with live, cackling chickens hung from her arm. Men sat huddled around overflowing reed suitcases. These sights and the cacophony of voices, mothers calling their children, men arguing in Maleis about what train to take, the complete chaos below his window increased his own sense of displacement.

It seemed like his family's big moves always started on his birthday, like on his fourteenth, in 1940, when they pulled the door shut on their rented house in Den Helder. It had snowed that day. Moeder had worn a fur coat. Today his clothes were damp and clung to his body in the sweltering heat.

"Moeder," he said, "you had a present for me."

She looked apologetic. Vader peeked around the edge of the letter he was reading and smiled. He put the letter back in his attaché case while Moeder rummaged through her leather handbag. A velvety box appeared with the name of the best jeweler in Soerabaja imprinted on the top in gold letters. Jewelry? For him? He pushed the tiny brass knob on the side and, as the box sprang open, he saw the glitter of a silver watch. He removed it from the lever that held it in place. A Swiss watch with a wide leather band.

"Oh, thank you!" He almost shouted it.

"Well, this is an important birthday, *jongen*," Vader said. "Sixteen!"

Gijs immediately put it on his wrist.

"Here, hold it in my bag where it's dark and you'll see what's special about it," Moeder said.

"Oh, look at that!" he said. The numbers and the hands were fluorescent.

"Yes, I thought you'd like that," Moeder said.

The train clattered on.

The last leg of the trip took them through rice paddies that glistened under the ever-present sun, terraced into the Preanger Mountains like a shuffled deck of cards. Mighty steel bridges spanned ravines;

brooks rushed in free fall to their deepest point. The air cooled as they neared Bandoeng, the first city he would live in that didn't have a harbor.

Without the slightest regret they got out of the hot, unventilated train and called for a taxi to bring them to the Grand Hotel Preanger. Gijs liked Bandoeng at first sight. The boulevards were wide and lined with impressive government buildings that sparkled in the setting sun. The biggest one, Vader pointed out, was the Department of Defense. Military trucks bustled along the streets. The city was clearly preparing for war. Every face he looked into reflected the gravity of the situation, and fat headlines screamed from the newspaper stands by the side of the road.

Their hotel was exclusively populated with officers in uniform. Wherever Gijs went, he found small groups of them in the hallways and lounges, whispering in English, Maleis and Dutch. The bombardment in Soerabaja had been ample proof for him of the danger, but here the prospect of war hit him harder. It didn't seem a distant threat anymore.

Gijs couldn't see himself hanging around the hotel all day. He asked the bell captain to show him the way to the LBD headquarters (Anti-Aircraft Defense). He had volunteered for the LBD back in Soerabaja. All scouts—and he was a sea scout—had been encouraged to serve.

"What is your name, young man?" a bespectacled office clerk, who sat behind a desk that was hardly visible for all the papers and telephone wires, asked him.

"Gijs Bozuwa."

"Your age?'

"Sixteen."

The man looked him up and down. "Have you done anything like this before?"

"Yes, sir, in Soerabaja as a sea scout. I got here yesterday."

"You can join a group that is patrolling the outskirts of the city. This is serious business, you understand? The next week will be crucial. You're late coming into this, but we can use any young man who's got his head screwed on right."

With that warning he was dismissed and sent to another civil servant, who provided him with a uniform shirt and an armband to put over its sleeve. He was told to present himself at six the next morning.

Gijs was relieved he didn't have to feel utterly useless anymore. The city was buzzing with rumors and he didn't want to sit on his hands. Nobody was talking about going to school, and he wasn't going to bring it up.

Back at the hotel he told Moeder what he'd done. She approved, and a smile appeared on Vader's wan face when he came in late that evening and saw the LBD band on Gijs's shirt. It seemed to please him. His father was a man of action.

Singapore had fallen that day. Moeder wrung her hands at hearing the news. Singapore was the last British stronghold. Now the road to the Dutch East Indies lay wide open. Gijs remembered the map his father had shown him back in Soerabaja. Japanese troops had already set foot on Sumatra, Vader said, and they were marching toward Palembang, the all-important oil harbor there.

As he told them this bad news, they were sitting on the veranda of the hotel, being served tea by a *djongos*. The air was cool and a pleasant breeze ruffled Moeder's dress to above her knee. She didn't notice.

"Can we hold on?" she asked. "Do we have enough troops?"

Vader shrugged. He probably didn't want to scare her. The area they had to defend was as big as all of Europe, and they only had an army of 35,000 professionals and 25,000 men hastily called into service. Twenty tanks ... fifty-four cannons ...

"When you consider the amount of shoreline that is involved," he finally said, "I think the battle will be fought on the seas."

Gijs could tell his father didn't have much faith in the ability of the army to fend off the well-equipped Japanese. The Dutch government had set aside 200 million guilders for weapons, but only ten percent of the orders had been filled. Worse, a shipment of Hurricane and Kittyhawk fighters had arrived a few weeks ago, but only the rumps were on the ship. The wings were supposed to have come on a separate ship, but that one got torpedoed. This news had been all over the radio and the papers.

"I alerted Janneke that she has to leave Soerabaja immediately," Vader said. "Telephone connections have been broken, but I got a message to her through a chain of military radios. There will only be a few more trains leaving from there."

Gijs watched his father pull a small cigar from a silver etui. The *djongos*, ever watchful, reached over with a cigarette lighter. Vader drew in the smoke and let it come out in small circles, watching them as they dissipated in the air, one by one. He looked tired and thoughtful. It would be one of the most vivid images that Gijs would hold onto during the coming years: his father sitting in a *rotan* armchair in his white navy uniform, blowing the bluish cigar smoke into the darkness of a tropical night.

Chapter 3

The next morning, Gijs walked over to the LBD headquarters and reported for duty in his new uniform shirt. The others had come on their bikes. He looked around to see if he could hitch a ride.

"Hello, I am Pieter Donk." A young man with blond hair and steady blue eyes stuck out his hand. He was tall and probably a year or so older than Gijs.

"I am Gijs Bozuwa." Gijs shook the hand held out to him.

"Would you like to join me? I have a motorcycle with a sidecar."

Gijs couldn't believe his luck. Before he knew it, he was viewing the world from a low, slanted position, going at breakneck speed over the boulevard and expecting his buttocks to scrape the road surface any minute. After the initial shock, he noticed that Pieter Donk was quite adept at handling the bike, so he settled into his seat with a bit more confidence.

The city was coming to life. Not the kind of awakening he'd been used to in Soerabaja, where children biked to school, himself included; where vendors ambled with their small stoves on *pikoulans* under the tamarind trees; where men in white linen suits were being driven to their offices. Here and now, the army dominated the scene, its troops on the move to set up defensive positions. On the best of days traffic was chaotic on Java. He was used to the undisciplined weaving of pedestrians, bikers, *bedjahs,* and automobiles. Today, the usual chaos was joined by an invisible component. Fear. Every truck filled with soldiers was like a wagging finger: remember, this is about WAR. As Gijs watched them pass, he couldn't help think of Vader's prophecy that the war would be decided on the seas. His brave pilots flew out daily to find the positions of the Japanese fleet. They fished scores of drowning sailors out of the water at great personal risk. Their Dornier planes could land with their bellies on water. Still, the Japanese, Vader said, had a great advantage. They had a well-stocked air force to locate the enemy's vessels, commercial as well as navy. They sent bombers, their infamous Zeros, after them. Already they had sunk two great British battleships, the *Prince of Wales* and the *Repulse*. Winston Churchill had heard the news with tears in his eyes. So it said in the papers.

Gijs wondered what kind of information was available to Pieter Donk. Did he believe the newspapers that kept telling the public that the island of Java was impregnable? Was Pieter's father an army officer? Time would tell. The motorcycle made too much noise to carry on a conversation.

They stopped in a residential area. Gijs wormed himself out of what had seemed like a baby's cradle and stretched his cramped limbs. None of the others had caught up to Pieter's fast motorbike.

"What are we supposed to do?" Gijs asked.

"See if people have followed instructions for total blackout and for outfitting a bomb shelter. We'll wait for the others."

"Have you lived in Bandoeng long?"

"Long enough to know my way around," Pieter said. "We came from Holland five years ago. First we lived in Batavia. My father was transferred to Bandoeng two years ago."

"Is he in the army?"

"No, he's the principal of a high school here. How about you?"

"I was born in Batavia, but my father is in the navy, so we moved back and forth between Holland and the Indies. He was just transferred from Soerabaja. We only got here a few days ago."

"Is he with the ABDA?"

"Yes."

"What does your dad think of our chances in the war?"

Gijs hesitated. Pieter leaned back against his bike and pulled a pack of cigarettes from his shirt pocket.

"Smoke?"

"No, thanks."

Pieter didn't seem to be in a rush for an answer. He struck a match and cupped his hand to protect the flame from the breeze with deliberate and confident motions. Gijs felt himself relax in his presence.

"Vader thinks the war will be decided on the seas."

"Because he is in the navy?"

"Not entirely." Gijs wanted to be cautious. "He is with the Navy Reconnaissance. Many ships have been torpedoed in the last two months. He says the Japanese have superiority in the air."

"He's probably right." Pieter took a long drag from his cigarette. "Not a comfortable thought, is it?"

The rest of the group arrived, and they started to knock on doors and do the job they were told to do. They found infractions galore. How could people treat the blackout order as a bagatelle? Did they really think there was no way the Japanese could come close enough to send planes to bomb Bandoeng? At the hotel, the atmosphere among the officers had convinced him that war on Java—and probably defeat—was inevitable. Some of the people whose doors they knocked on acted as if there weren't a cloud on the horizon, no danger in sight. Gijs found it awkward, as a teenager, to reproach adults who'd decided to stick their heads in the sand.

A few days later, on the twenty-second of February, Vader came back to the hotel and told them that he expected the ABDA to dissolve. A large Japanese fleet was on its way, taking a course directly aimed at Java. He said they could not expect more English or American troops to help them defend the island. What was on the ground already—and outside of the Dutch, that was mostly Australians—would stay. Churchill, he said, had sent a telegram to Sir Archibald Wavell, the supreme commander of the ABDA, that read: "Java should be defended to the last by all combatant troops on the island."

Moeder put her hands to her face in a gesture of dismay and fear.

"No one to the rescue! What will we do?"

"Our last and only chance will be a battle on the sea."

"Will it be enough?"

"God only knows, Rietje," Vader said, and put his hand on her shoulder. Gijs suspected he knew more than he could say.

On his way to the LBD headquarters the next morning, Gijs looked at the paper's headlines as he passed the newspaper stand. Nowhere did it say that the ABDA would be disbanded. Instead, the articles sounded like pep talks. The gap between what he heard out of his father's mouth and what he saw in black and white in the newspapers was so huge, he wondered if the Dutch Information Service was getting close to telling lies.

At the LBD building Pieter Donk was already present with his magnificent motorcycle. A group had formed around him.

"What are people worried about?" he overheard one of them saying.

"What reason do you have not to be worried, Hans?" Pieter asked.

"The Japanese will never set foot on Java," the boy named Hans said with great aplomb. Gijs took him in. A head shorter than Pieter, he stuck out his chin in defiance.

"Are you sure? There's evidence to the contrary," Pieter said. "How about Singapore? And they've already taken Bali! Java is in a vice."

"We have a strong defense. Where do you think all these trucks are driving all these soldiers? They will defend the shoreline. You wait and see! Those Japs won't have a chance to get on land." Hans was getting agitated.

"Who's pumping all that good news into you?" someone else asked. "You're spending too much time reading the papers."

"Is your old man in the army?" a boy who'd just arrived asked Hans. Gijs remembered him from the day before. His name was Wouter, and he was memorable for a scar above his right eyebrow.

"My father is a captain in the artillery," Hans said, puffing his chest in a vain attempt to look taller.

Gijs hoped nobody would ask what *his* father did. He looked over to Pieter and raised his eyebrows. The conversation could only deteriorate to no one's benefit.

"Okay, time to get going," Pieter said. It seemed to come naturally to him to take the lead. "We have to check house to house." He started up his bike and gestured Gijs to join him.

That evening, after he came home from knocking on many, many doors, his mother told him the Governor General would be speaking over the radio any moment. The Dutch-speaking guests had already assembled around a radio in the lobby, and Vader joined them just as Jonkheer Tjarda van Starkenborg started to speak.

"We know that Java's coastline is long, that the enemy can attack us on several sides, and that additions to our equipment would be very welcome, but also that our navy lauds the aggressive principle … It gives fortitude to realize that every day that passes can bring new, favorable developments … Do not forget that the eye of the world is upon us. I address these words to all of you: there are moments that distinguish themselves from everyday life; there are events that will stand out in the row of events, which together form the chain of history. We stand before such moments and events."

Gijs looked at his parents, who leaned forward in their chairs, totally absorbed. When the governor talked about solidarity with the natives and about not leaving their posts, Moeder nodded in agreement.

"A hard battle is awaiting us. We will fight it with all the powers given us. May God bless you and me." These words ended the broadcast.

The lobby was eerily quiet. The Governor General had established himself as an upright man and a capable administrator. Fully aware of these laudable qualities, the audience didn't doubt his honesty and the seriousness of the moment. Gijs wondered if Hans, the artillery captain's son, was also listening. And what was the GG, as he was popularly called, hinting at when he spoke of the "aggressive principle"? It could only mean a battle.

Chapter 4

Pieter Donk came over to the hotel and sent a *djongos* up to the Bozuwa quarters with a message. Would Gijs like to go for a ride on his motorcycle, just for the fun of it? It was very early in the morning, well before they had to present themselves for LBD duty. Gijs was flattered by the offer. His father had already left for ABDA headquarters. The hotel was draped in tension, and he was dying to get away from the oppression he felt all around. He was ready for some relief, no matter how short-lived it would be.

Pieter pushed his foot down on the starting pedal, while Gijs seated himself in the sidecar. They drove through the city as fast as traffic allowed. Pieter came to a stop in back of the Technical Institute, which was surrounded by a generous parking lot.

"Shall I teach you how to drive this rig?"

"Are you sure you want to do that?"

"Sure," Pieter said. "I'll show you how to get the sidecar up in the air."

"Up in the air?"

"Yes. If you lean hard into the curve, the sidecar's wheels lose contact with the road." Pieter sounded very confident.

He got his bike up to speed and raced around the parking lot. As the sidecar lifted into the air, Gijs felt as if he were sitting in a Ferris wheel. This guy didn't joke around.

Pieter stopped, got off, and gestured to Gijs to take over. He managed to get the motorbike going. Gingerly at first. Pieter was now the passenger in the sidecar.

"Faster," Pieter shouted in his ear.

Gijs accelerated, but he couldn't get the wheels of the sidecar up in the air on the first try. He looked at Pieter, who gestured that he should throw his body weight into the curve. It took some nerve to follow his orders, but somehow he trusted this Pieter Donk. It worked.

After a half hour of tearing around, Pieter said they'd better go to work.

At the LBD Headquarters Gijs and Pieter stared at the headline in the newspaper: "Flagship HMS *de Ruyter* sunk." The ink was barely dry.

On the 27 and 28 of February, 1942, a fierce battle had been fought and lost. It would go into history as the battle in the Java Sea. Rear Admiral Karel Doorman had drowned, along with eight hundred fifty of the sailors under his command, Indonesian as well as Dutch.

That was not all the bad news. The Japanese invasion fleet that Karel Doorman had wanted to intercept had set foot on Java late last night. Fifty-five thousand soldiers had come ashore at four different locations on Java's northern coast.

This battle at sea must have been "the aggressive principle" the Governor General had hinted at in his radio address. Gijs was almost sure his father had known about it beforehand.

"We're sunk," the clerk said, when Gijs and Pieter walked in. "The Japs have landed at Eretan Wetan and I bet they'll run straight to Kalidjati."

Kalidjati was a big airfield forty kilometers from Bandoeng.

"Not only that," the clerk said. "Wavell left. We've been abandoned."

"Is there anything we can do?" Gijs asked, though he felt silly offering help in view of the magnitude of these bad tidings.

"Go tell anyone you meet to make sure they know where the nearest bomb shelter is. They'll soon need them."

The clerk put his elbows on the desk and rested his head in his hands, looking exasperated and defeated. Gijs and Pieter felt inadequate consoling a despondent adult they barely knew, and they tiptoed out of the office. Once outside, they ran into Hans, who blocked their path with his bike. Hans looked pale, and his demeanor had noticeably changed from just a few days ago, when he had so boisterously proclaimed that the Japanese would never set foot on the island.

"Did you hear the news?" Hans said. "They've landed!"

"Yes, we just heard," Pieter said.

"Did you ever hear what those Japanese soldiers do? They murder, they burn villages, and they torture."

"Where did you hear that?" Gijs asked.

"Well, that's what they did in China."

"Don't believe everything you hear, Hans," Pieter said, trying to calm him down. Hans was plainly scared, but Gijs couldn't blame him. He had heard those stories too.

"My father is in the army," Hans said with a catch in his throat.

"Good for him! You must be proud of him. He's doing his duty," Gijs said.

"Is your father in the army?" Hans asked Gijs.

"No, he is in the navy."

"I hope he wasn't on *De Ruyter*?"

"No, don't worry. He is alive and well. Let's go and check on bomb shelters. We might as well do something while we still can."

The three of them walked off to the center of the city where they found traffic in a snarl. People lugging heavy suitcases seemed to walk around in a daze. It made for a bizarre sight.

"Where do all these people come from?" Pieter asked a vendor at a newspaper stand.

"They're coming in droves from the railroad station," the man said. "They're fleeing Batavia. There's talk of closing our city."

This last part of the news worried Gijs. Had Janneke followed Vader's orders to come to Bandoeng immediately? What if she was too late? He kept these worries to himself, but his mood had changed drastically from the early morning excitement of riding a bike with a sidecar in the air. Just looking into the faces of the people who poured like an unstoppable stream of lava out of the railroad station was enough to see that something terrifying was afoot. Their dazed looks told the story of a sudden breakdown in the order the Dutch had so effectively established over the years that they had governed the island. The rulers had been turned into evacuees, carrying just a few of their earthly possessions without a clue of where they would end up.

"I can't stand this," Hans said. Sweat beads dripped from his forehead.

"It's tough, I agree," Pieter said. "We'd better go and do what we're told. There's not much sense in standing around."

"I am going home," Hans said. He jumped on his bicycle and disappeared in the opposite direction.

"Oh well," Pieter said. "We'll have to do without him. Let's get my bike and go to the outskirts."

They knocked on many doors and rang many bells. Whoever answered the door was either agitated like the clerk at the LBD desk, or in a panic like Hans, or completely disbelieving of the news. It couldn't happen to them. Not here, not now. Pieter and Gijs tried to calm the worriers and light a fire under the disbelievers. With maps that had been given to them by the LBD, they pointed out where the nearest bomb shelters were. The exciting start of the day had already turned into a memory of a lifestyle that would soon cease to exist. They were tired and discouraged at the end of the day. Pieter rode his bike with less verve, carefully picking his path in a traffic pattern that was hardly recognizable from even two days ago. Bandoeng was clearly a city under siege. They said good-bye in front of the hotel. When would they meet again?

Coming into his family's living quarters, he found Janneke lying on his bed. She'd made it! His heart leaped. From the looks of her, though, he realized she'd pulled it off at a price. Her flushed face indicated a high fever and her cough sounded awful. Moeder was mothering her with hot tea and aspirin. She'd had an exhausting trip with her friend Ton Perks and Ton's little baby in a reed basket. The train had been filled beyond capacity. People were packed in without any ventilation and in oppressive heat. Ton and the baby would not have been allowed into Bandoeng since she could not claim a certain address, so a family member had met them at another station before they reached the city and driven her and the baby to his house. Janneke had managed to talk herself into Bandoeng. The rumors about the authorities closing the city were evidently true.

Between coughs she told Gijs, "I will tell you more later," then sank into a feverish sleep. Moeder said she had a temperature of 103 degrees.

Events were rapidly closing in on them. Vader came to bed in the middle of the night. The next morning they sat down for breakfast in the palm-lined dining hall without Janneke, who still ran a fever. Gijs noticed Captain Wagner, an American Air Force officer, making his way to their table. Vader got up and invited the captain to join them. After he seated himself, Captain Wagner said, "It looks like it's all over here. I am getting out."

"Where to?" Vader asked.

"Australia." The captain looked at Moeder. "I could take you and your children on my plane."

His parents looked at each other across the table. In one sentence Captain Wagner had compelled them to make a life-changing decision. The defeat of the Dutch army, even with the little bit of help from their allies, was not a question anymore. Surrender to the Japanese was more than a probability. What came to Gijs's mind immediately was the address over the radio by the GG, when he had urged Dutch citizens to show solidarity with the native population and to remain at their posts. His message had been clear: they should not abandon the native people and the country. It would lead to chaos. If doctors and teachers fled, the healthcare and education systems would be in shambles. If the Dutch engineers left, the infrastructure would collapse. To leave or not to leave was an ethical decision, and Gijs remembered how his mother had nodded in agreement when the GG had come to that part of his address. During the last weeks, but especially the last few days, he'd overheard his parents criticizing pilots who packed their planes with their wife and kids—their household goods even—and flew them to Australia.

Gijs sat quietly and waited for their response while his thoughts roamed over the possibilities. Australia? Maybe even America? Exciting, but it wasn't up to him. Nobody asked for his opinion.

Vader looked at his plate and took a deep breath.

"I don't know yet what my orders will be," he said. "Whatever they may be, Rietje, you have to make your own decision."

A *djongos* walked over to refresh their teacups. Moeder reached for the sugar bowl and with a gesture devoid of thought, she twirled the sugar cube around and around with her spoon, staring into the eddy she created inside the porcelain cup. Then she looked up, glanced at Vader, and said in a resolute voice, "I thank you for your offer, Captain, but I will not take you up on it."

Vader looked at her intently, perhaps wondering if he should talk her out of her decision. Apparently, he decided not to. Gijs held his breath. Good-bye, Australia! Good-bye, America!

"I will not leave," Moeder said, and with those four words sealed their fate for the rest of their lives.

Gijs looked at both of his parents. They were solid people. He had a lot to live up to in his life.

A *djongos* came over to pull Moeder's chair back when she folded her napkin and excused herself to go and take care of Janneke. She walked out of the dining room to the lobby, ramrod straight, her head held high. She wasn't athletic—she did not play any sport— and there was even a stiffness about her, but she was an elegant, awe-inspiring woman, Gijs thought, as he watched her make her way through the maze of tables. He never admired her more than at that instant. His mother didn't talk out of two sides of her mouth. Never.

Chapter 5

Everything pointed to change. A sea of change. Life in the Indies would never be the same. That much was clear. What was unclear was what it would be like to have the Japanese in charge. Gijs made himself no illusions, even as he tried to ban from his mind all he'd heard and read about the brutality and torture that had been part of the Japanese conquest of China.

On the first of March, his family moved into a house on the Jan Steenlaan that belonged to a friend of his parents, Mr. Kroese, a colonel in the army. Kroese had been ordered to leave for Australia a few days earlier. Before the city of Bandoeng had closed its gates, Soepardi had delivered their Chrysler and then returned to where he'd come from, which was God knows where, but in some *dessa*. Gijs had not been present when Soepardi left, reportedly with tears in his eyes. He would have liked to thank Soepardi for teaching him to drive, but then, he couldn't have done that in front of his mother.

Janneke was the only one in the family who could drive a car *and* had a license, so, sick or not, she drove Moeder and Gijs to their new address.

Night had already fallen when he heard his father's familiar whistle outside. He scrambled out of bed to open the front door and saw Vader's white uniform starkly outlined by the lamp in the front hall against the pitch black of the night. The city had cut off electricity to the streetlights, and his new neighborhood seemed to strictly adhere to the blackout ordinances. The street looked as spooky as the jungle in its utter darkness. From his bed he'd had to guess at every sound below his window.

They all gathered in the living room, sitting on the rented chairs around the rented coffee table in the rented house.

"I have come to say good-bye," Vader said.

"What's happening?" Moeder asked.

"I have been ordered to destroy every naval air base on the island and then take my planes to safety."

He told them of the heated debate between Admiral Helfrich and the British Rear Admiral Pallisader earlier that morning. Helfrich had been determined to fight to the last ship and the last man, even though most of the fleet he commanded had been sunk in the battle of the Java Sea. The British and American navy commanders preferred to bring the little that was left to Australia or Ceylon. Helfrich was furious. After all, he'd told the British admiral, "My navy has done more to help you defend Malakka and to protect your convoys than your fleet has ever done for the defense of the Dutch East Indies." But Admiral Pallisader maintained that his orders from London were to direct His Majesty's ships to India.

The ABDA Commando had been disbanded at 10 AM. Vader had just put Admiral Helfrich on one of his Catalina seaplanes to Ceylon under the cover of darkness.

Moeder had anticipated this outcome, and now here it was.

"Then this is the end," she said. It was a sober conclusion, stated without obvious emotion.

"I'm afraid you're right, Rietje," Vader said. "I don't expect the army to be able to hold them off much longer. Think of it this way. If you would project the north shore of Java onto the map of Europe, it would equal the distance between Paris and Madrid. Our army simply cannot defend the entire coastline. We have to be realistic. It won't be long and they'll take Batavia."

"What should we do?" Janneke asked.

"Stay here." Vader looked around the house. "The Allies have to regroup. We will fly the planes to Ceylon. Then we'll go to Australia and launch our attack to take Java and the other islands back. It may take a while, but we will do it."

It was a solemn moment. Vader had served in the Royal Dutch Navy since before the First World War. He knew what was expected of

him: total loyalty to his queen and country. He was as used to following orders as giving them. Moeder, at his side for most of those years,
was well versed in what sacrifices were expected of the military and
their families. For Janneke and Gijs, who had followed their father to
wherever he was stationed, this was the first big test. Their father away
at sea was nothing new to them, but Vader leaving Java while they
had to stay behind in the face of war and probably defeat left them
gulping for air. They knew better than to show their emotions. Their
parents would not appreciate it. Besides, it would just make it harder
to say good-bye. They embraced each other with hardly a word.

Outside, a chauffeur was waiting in the idling car, its headlights
turned off. Just before settling himself into the backseat, Vader
turned to Gijs and said, " Take good care of your mother and sister.
You are now the man of the house."

The car drove away into the darkness.

After a restless night, Gijs woke up in his new room, surrounded
by unopened suitcases. It was hot and muggy. That at least felt
familiar. He heard Moeder's and Janneke's voices downstairs and
the sound of furniture being shoved around. Wherever they found
themselves, Moeder and Janneke would rearrange the furniture.
Today, they probably did it to keep their minds off other things.
He wondered what his father was doing right that minute. What
did it mean when Vader said he had to destroy the bases? There had
been talk of the "scorched-earth policy," and the Dutch engineers
had already torched oil fields on Borneo before they left their posts.
The Japanese would not be able to just walk in and start pumping
oil. Apparently, his father was going to see to it they couldn't use the
bases either.

When he got downstairs, Moeder and Janneke sat waiting for
him at the dining table. A *djongos* stood silent, ready to serve breakfast, and he heard noises in the kitchen. A *djongos* and a *baboe* must
have come with the house.

A few aimless days passed. Gijs found a bicycle in the garage. It
probably belonged to the colonel. He couldn't wait to jump on it

and get out. It oppressed him to just sit and listen to rumors being passed around. Every shred of news, every rumor was shared. The neighbor on the right had rung the bell, introduced himself, and told Moeder that Dutch troops had retreated from Bantam. The neighbor on the left showed Gijs a newspaper with the headline, "Japanese Troops Advancing to Bandoeng." The air was thick with unspoken anxiety. At least if he went downtown, he might run into Pieter Donk.

Once there, however, he realized there was no getting away from the feeling of impending doom. The scene of military trucks trying to get through chaotic traffic jams and hundreds of citizens criss-crossing the roads reminded him of animals scurrying in all directions before a thunderstorm. He turned around and went home.

Janneke sat on the veranda in a rocking chair, still looking very pale and nursing herself back to health. He let himself fall into the chair next to her. It dawned on him that he knew nothing about her last days in Soerabaja.

"Did you get to see Jan after all?" he asked.

"Yes," she said, without looking up.

"That's good," Gijs said. He didn't know what else to say. Janneke had always lived in other circles. At their ages, five years made a huge difference. When they still lived in Den Helder, the city where the Royal Naval Academy was located, her social scene was with the naval cadets. He remembered her in evening gowns on the arms of handsome young men, dressed in resplendent uniforms. Jan had been one of those, and Gijs had been in awe of his future brother-in-law, who showed him around the submarine he was serving on as the youngest officer.

"Could Jan get time off to see you?" he tried.

"No. We saw each other in the sentry room because he was on guard duty. He asked a friend to stand in for him for an hour. Not the most romantic place to say good-bye." She gave a short laugh. "We promised to write as often as we could. That was about it, but at least we saw each other."

"You must have at least kissed him!" Gijs dared to say.

"Anything else you want to know?" Janneke asked.

They were shaken out of their depressed moods by an improbable apparition: a car with government license plates stopped in front of the house. Their father stepped out and briskly walked up the path. Janneke and Gijs got out of their chairs and rushed to him. The family gathered inside. Vader told them he had indeed destroyed all the naval air bases on Java, and then had taken his planes on the journey to Ceylon. They had landed in Tjilatjap, an important harbor on the south shore of Java, to take on fuel before they could start on the long haul over the ocean. But the Japanese had already bombed it and destroyed the fuel storage. His airplane had turned around and he'd returned to Bandoeng.

"What will happen now?" Moeder asked. She sat on the edge of her chair, her hands tightly clenched.

Thoughts of his father not being able to escape in time from Java flashed through Gijs's mind. If he couldn't make it out, he would surely become a prisoner of war, and what if the Japanese found out he was the one who had ordered the destruction of every naval air base on the island? They would not be kind to him.

"My orders are to get to Ceylon. I will have to get there by ship. There are still a few merchant marine ships. What is left of the naval command here in Bandoeng is trying to organize a last ditch effort to escape. I will send you a message once we have boarded."

"Gerard, I took all our money out of the bank this morning," Moeder said. She grabbed her pocket book and opened a bulging envelope. "Here, take this."

"No, Rietje, you will need it more than I."

Moeder got up and stuffed a good portion of the paper money in his breast pocket. "You never know how you may need this," she said.

Vader protested, but let his wife button up the pocket on his white uniform shirt.

"I have to leave," he said.

The first time they'd said good-bye, they were confident Vader would fly to Ceylon and on to Australia. This second time left them measuring the uncertain odds. There were no words for their feelings of foreboding. There was no way to predict what would happen to any one of them in the immediate future.

"Yes," Moeder said. "You'd better get on your way."

They embraced each other.

Seconds later, Vader stepped again into a waiting car. As he waved, Gijs felt as if a heavy stone had fallen hard on his stomach.

On March fifth, the radio greeted its listeners with the news that Batavia, the capital, had fallen into the hands of the enemy. It sent a shiver through Bandoeng's population. If it had been that easy to take the capital, how fast would the Japanese make it to Kalidjati, the big airport to its south? The Governor General and his entire cabinet and staff had moved from Batavia to Bandoeng, to the relative safety of the Preanger Plateau. It had to be the Japanese strategic goal to get to Bandoeng as fast as they could.

That afternoon the sirens started to wail and the air filled with the drone of engines. Moeder told the servants that they should come with them to seek shelter, but they adamantly refused. Just as he led his mother and sister into the nearest air-raid shelter, Gijs saw red balls painted on the undersides of low-flying airplanes as they dived toward targets in the city's center. The Japanese were close enough to send bombers to Bandoeng. The airport at Kalidjati must have fallen into their hands.

Back at the house they found the servants under the old *waringin* tree in the backyard, squatting between the aerial prop roots that had grown into thick woody trunks. In Hindu culture it was a divine tree. Sitting under it would fulfill their wishes. Their beliefs had been vindicated. They went back to work.

The next three days would always remain a blur in Gijs's memory; shifting sensations of fear, panic, responsibility, excitement, anger. Some happenings receded into mere commonplace, while others stood out, like the expressions on the faces of the fearful citizens. But being an optimist by nature, he never felt doom.

One of those vague memories was about being with a group—most probably the people of the LBD—in an open truck on a busy road, caught among military vehicles ferrying fresh troops to the front and bringing the wounded back. Japanese planes swooped overhead and fired on the slow-moving traffic. The truck Gijs was in ditched itself on the side of the road, and everyone jumped out and crawled underneath for protection. How he got there and how he got back was hard to explain later in his life. But it did happen. Absolutely. It was one the many chaotic moments of those last colonial days, which were marked by inefficient defense and iron Japanese determination to conquer all of Southeast Asia. Lt. General Hitoshi Imamura, following the example of what Hitler did to the city of Rotterdam in Holland, let it be known that Bandoeng would be obliterated if the Dutch government did not surrender. His ultimatum: surrender before 10 AM on March 7, or else.

Japanese bombers circled nonstop over the city in a nerve-wrecking drone.

Chapter 6

At the end of the day, on March 7, 1942, Radio Bandoeng concluded its broadcast with these words: "We close now. Fare well. Till better times. Long live the Queen!"

"It's all over," Moeder said calmly, after they'd listened to the last gasp of the familiar radio station.

A click. Then silence. The radio was dead.

The next day, at 6:20 PM, Lt. General ter Poorten signed the Japanese conditions of surrender of the Dutch-Indonesian forces.

Would Vader have made it out of Java in time? There was no way to find an answer. But an answer did arrive a few days later in the form of a surprise visit from a good friend of the family, Jan Kuyper, who headed shipping inspection on Java. The news was devastating. Vader and several other officers and authorities had managed to board the ss *Poelau Bras*, a merchant ship, the night of the seventh. It had been the last ship to leave from Wijnkoops Baai. A Japanese Zero spotted it the next morning from the air, and came back with bombers. They sank the *Poelau Bras*. Mr. Kuyper told them that Vader was not on the list of survivors.

"But," Mr. Kuyper added immediately, "don't give up hope. This is only a temporary list. There is always the possibility that he survived if he made it to one of the lifeboats. When I know more I will let you know. You can count on that. Keep up your hopes!"

Moeder thanked Mr. Kuyper, although the message he brought was not something to be thankful for. Still, better to be told by a friend than by a complete stranger.

Gijs swallowed hard. Thoughts of his father being trapped inside the ship on its way down to the floor of the Indian Ocean were unbearable. He tried to focus on imagining Vader swimming and reaching a lifeboat. At fifty-two, Vader was a strong man, an excellent swimmer, and in good shape.

After she'd taken in the news, Moeder suddenly said, "This is the second time."

"The second time?"

"Yes. The first time was in the North Sea off the coast of England during WW I. He was the youngest officer on a destroyer when a German U-boat came up beside them. It signaled they wanted to board. In those days that was done with flags. So, the German commander came on board and was received in the captain's lounge. After they'd enjoyed a glass of sherry together, the German said to his host that he was terribly sorry, but he had to sink his ship. He gave them enough time to get out in a sloop. It was November and the water was frigid. The crew rowed the sloop to England where they sat out the war."

"Were you married then?" Gijs asked.

"No, not yet, but we knew we would be after the war was over."

"Moeder, it doesn't make sense at all that the German wanted to sink a Dutch ship. Holland was neutral in the First World War."

"You're right, and that fact was brought up, of course. The German replied to this that he was sorry, his orders were to blow them up."

"Crazy," Gijs said. "The whole world is crazy."

"I know, I know. That's the world we live in. We'll just have to do the best we can and not have ourselves brought down to the same level of insanity. See it as a test."

His mother, he knew, would fight any injustice, swallow her pride with a fierce self-discipline, and never give into despair. Even though, right now, he felt a rising anger at the Japanese for torpedoing the ship his father was on, mixed with fears for the worst, he also knew that giving voice to those thoughts would not be tolerated. Moeder herself didn't show any signs of falling apart.

"Your father survived the first time. I have good hope he may have pulled it off again."

Moeder said this after she'd looked hard at him. Always on the positive side, Gijs thought. It was effective self-protection. Was she willing herself not to give in to despair, or did she really think Vader could have survived? He guessed the first, and he was grateful. It would be much harder to be the man of the house with a despondent mother on his hands.

Janneke was not at home at the time of Mr. Kuyper's visit. She worked at a soup kitchen downtown. Bandoeng was filled with aimless and homeless people who were getting hungry, because the normal food supply had slowed to a trickle. Crops grown in the countryside could not find their way into the city's markets. The infrastructure was wrecked. Janneke washed and diced all the vegetables the soup kitchen could get its hands on. She was not alone. Many young women had shown up to help. She might, Gijs thought, even be having a good time.

He jumped on his bike—he'd claimed it as his own since there was no way Colonel Kroese could return now—and rode downtown. Immediately he heard the rumor that the Japanese troops were going to make their entry into Bandoeng. People thronged along the Dagoweg, a main artery through the city. It was eerily quiet. Many of the people lining the road were natives. They were as fearful as they were curious. Finally, a white horse came into view, carrying an officer with medals on his chest that glistened in the morning sun. The crowd was impressed. The horse moved with a steady, stately gate over the pavement. Less impressive was what followed. Short men marched four abreast, dressed in dirty khaki uniforms with puttees around their bowed legs, many wearing round spectacles that reflected the sun like the medals on their commander's chest. They wore cotton caps with a visor in front and a sort of bib hanging from the back to protect their necks from the tropical sun. The spectators were underwhelmed.

Gijs stood holding his bike in the middle of a group of boys his age.

"Is this the army that beat the KNIL?" one of them whispered.

"Hard to believe, isn't it?" another answered, but none of them wanted to further the conversation. The other boys' fathers might be serving in the army, and it would be tough to admit that these small men in their shabby uniforms had crushed the Dutch-Indonesian army.

Behind the walking soldiers appeared another contingent on bicycles. So far only the white horse had looked impressive and powerful, capable of conquering an entire archipelago.

Gijs looked into the faces of the natives who stood beside him, searching for clues of what this invasion meant to them. They had been bombarded with the Japanese propaganda slogan of "Asia for the Asiatic." Would they see the Japanese as liberators who would replace the *Tuan belanda* in their lives? If so, they didn't show any delight. Their faces were closed, their body language mute, and their thoughts unfathomable.

The crowd dispersed gradually and quietly. He didn't feel like going back to the house. What was the point? Janneke was at the soup kitchen. Moeder was busy creating a home. He was a stranger to the servants. It wasn't like it had been in Soerabaja, when he could hang out with Soepardi and watch him polish the car, or go out and kick a soccer ball around with his friends. Suddenly it hit him: his life had changed drastically. A new city, a new house, no school, no friends, no father, and everything topsy-turvy. The realization stuck like a fishbone in his throat. He jumped back on his bike and spurted down the road, away from his own thoughts. It was just the way it was, he told himself.

The Dagoweg lay before him like a wide ribbon, patterned by the shade of tall trees on both sides. This must be the neighborhood of the movers and the shakers in this city, judging from the well-kept, stately houses. He began to slow his getaway pace and took in the surroundings. During the barely three weeks since he'd moved here, he'd seen Bandoeng mostly from the perspective of the low sidecar of a motorcycle, weaving in and out of army trucks. The rest of the time had been spent in bomb shelters or inside their house. It had become tiresome to get in and out of those crowded, dark shelters toward the end. They'd reasoned that, maybe, the holy tree in the backyard, where the servants sat silently on their haunches, would protect them as well.

What was this city like? One good thing about it was its mild climate. That aspect alone made a sharp contrast to Soerabaja. When they'd disembarked from the train, it had struck him what a difference it made to be on a plateau, seven hundred yards above sea level.

By now he'd slowed to a crawl, taking in the beauty of the spacious parks, colorful gardens with shrubs with bright yellow and red flowers and remarkably tall trees waving their crowns over the roof of City Hall. He admired the fountain in Pieters Park. Gradually, the fishbone in his throat became unstuck as he took in the sights and cruised along Bragastreet, devoted to fancy shops and exclusive restaurants. Soerabaja was a port city, bustling with commerce and a lively harbor. He used to stand on a bridge over the harbor, watching the traffic of fishing boats. Some, like the native *prauw*, were big enough to house a whole family underneath their thatched roofs of *atap*, the woven leaves of the nipa palm. The endless movement of small and large boats was like watching a flock of quacking ducks paddling around in a pond. Soerabaja had been noisy and colorful in a different way than this more sophisticated place. Somewhat like the difference between Rotterdam and The Hague. His memories of Soerabaja were of neighborhoods of the rich and poor closer together; of the smell of sweat as well as of fruits, like the juicy, tempting mango, and the flowering shrubs on his path to school.

His reveries were interrupted. Down the road—he didn't know exactly where he was—something unusual and frightening was happening. In front of a government building a Japanese soldier approached a boy, the bayonet on his gun pointing at the boy's chest. The sentry—Gijs later understood that's what he was— screamed at the boy, who, of course, had no idea what was being said, but who decided to immediately dismount from his bike.

There he stood, still as a statue, bike in hand. This did not seem to satisfy the sentry. Gijs also got off his bike and watched from a safe distance as the sentry grabbed the boy's necktie and pulled his head down, screaming *"Dai Nippon."* Although he didn't understand the words, he did get the full meaning: bow for a Japanese sentry. The boy was let go.

Since he wasn't ready yet to bow, Gijs decided to turn around and avoid passing buildings with sentries in front. The Japanese were rapidly occupying every government building.

Eventually, he found his way back home. A black official-looking car stood parked in front. For a second he thought it might be Vader. His heart jumped into his throat. Just as quickly, though, the realization that that was impossible set in. It was out of the question that Vader would have returned home, if he hadn't drowned. The Japanese would arrest him immediately. But this car looked very official. Had somebody come to notify Moeder that Vader was lost at sea? Oh my God … Please … NO.

With lead in his shoes he entered the house. In the living room he found his mother entertaining a woman he vaguely recognized but couldn't put a name to. He was introduced to Mrs. Helfrich, the wife of the vice admiral. He remembered—a little late—seeing her in the Grand Hotel Preanger where the entire staff of the ABDA command had been quartered. Her husband had made it out of Java in time to escape the surrender.

Mrs. Helfrich was here to stay, he was told, with two of her children. The older children stayed with various friends in Bandoeng. Her real home had been the official residence of the vice admiral in Batavia. Of course, she could not return there. Neither could she stay in the hotel. The Japanese had already taken it over. She was at her wit's end. Her chauffeur had told her that Captain Bozuwa's wife had rented a house and suggested that maybe she could move in with her.

Mrs. Helfrich would occupy the upstairs floor. The chauffeur, whose name was Moestar, would also stay.

This was better news than Gijs had expected. His mood lightened at the thought of boys almost his age would be moving in. He didn't know them yet, but whatever they turned out to be like, it was better than being alone with his mother and sister.

Gijs and the two women were distracted by something happening out in the street. Moestar, who'd stayed in the car during the negotiations, came in to warn them that a troop of soldiers was marching down the street. They hastened to the veranda. Tall men in Japanese uniforms marched smartly, four abreast, down the Jan Steenlaan. These men were husky, Asian-looking. They radiated strength and power. A total opposite of what he'd witnessed earlier that morning.

"Koreans," Moestar said.

Chapter 7

A few days after the Koreans had marched through their street, Gijs stood idle on the veranda. He didn't think he would ever have such thoughts, but he was beginning to long for school. The street he lived on was residential and sedate, made up of almost identical white houses with neat front yards behind low concrete walls. Some walls were painted white; others were left their natural dull gray. Disregard the hot sun, the fauna and flora all around, and you could make yourself believe you were back in a provincial Dutch town where everything was as neatly in its place as in a meticulous tailor's sewing box.

Without any particular direction of thought, he gazed down the street. Something was moving. As it came closer, he saw it was a person. Not a *belanda* like himself or a native, who would be dressed in a colorful sarong from the waist down. Gijs trained his eyes on something that sparked in the bright sun on the person's chest. Buttons on a uniform. It couldn't be a Dutch military. Janneke had reported seeing Dutch soldiers packed into Dutch army trucks driven by Japanese military, on their way to POW camps.

Closer up, Gijs saw that the man was one of those Korean soldiers who'd marched through their street a few days ago. He was scrutinizing each house. The man's gaze fixed upon him—an unabashed, aggressive look that gave Gijs a chill. The soldier crossed the street and came straight at him. Thank God the women were inside. His father's last words rang in his ears. His eyes still fixed upon him, the soldier stepped over the low wall near the street, crossed the lawn, and jumped with ease up unto the veranda. The bulk of his body was imposing and he was very tall. The top buttons of his khaki uniform had been left unbuttoned. With less than a foot between them, Gijs's eyes were level with the bushy dark hair that bulged out of the man's shirt.

"Watchie, watchie," the soldier said.

Gijs pretended not to know what he meant and shrugged for an answer. The soldier shoved up the sleeve of his uniform shirt, revealing a row of watches stacked up on his arm.

Gijs furiously thought about what to do. Should he just hand over his precious birthday present that he'd barely worn for a month? The soldier grabbed Gijs's wrist and tapped on the crystal of his Swiss watch with his index finger. Thinking of the women inside, he felt he had no choice. He took the watch off and handed it over. It was added to the looter's collection. Satisfied, the thief pulled down his uniform sleeve, jumped over the side of the veranda, and went on his way.

Gijs fell back in a chair. A rush of adrenaline coursed furiously through his body. When he was a little kid in Soerabaja and came home with an empty bag, having lost all his marbles, he would cry. Playing with the Indos in the schoolyard had been tough. They were just so much better at shooting marbles; they never seemed to miss. His mother would always investigate, and if there had been foul play involved, there would be retribution. If not, he was told to get used to losing and stop crying about it.

What had just happened was a clear case of foul play. Retribution? What recourse was there when confronted with a looting soldier who was part of a conquering army? None. If he'd learned anything that day, that was it. The boy with the bayonet pointed at his chest had bowed. Now he had given up his watch. Not heroic, but what choice did they have?

He went inside and told his mother and Mrs. Helfrich what had just happened. Without saying a word, Moeder walked to the front door and locked it. Mrs. Helfrich turned white, but she didn't utter a word either. Frightening stories of looting, killing, and raping by Japanese soldiers during their war with China had made the rounds months before the war started on Java. Was this the start of more to come?

To get everyone's thoughts refocused, Gijs said, "Mrs. Helfrich, why are Koreans in the Japanese army?"

"Because Japan annexed Korea," Mrs. Helfrich said.

"Why was that?"

"Do you have an atlas? Then I can show you and you'll understand it better."

"Moeder, do we have an atlas here?"

"No, I haven't come across one among the things I unpacked."

"Well, then," Mrs. Helfrich said, "take a piece of paper and place Japan on the right side of the page. It's a series of islands, running from north to south. Then leave some room on the left for the Sea of Japan. To the left of that is Korea, which shares a long border with China. Korea is like an appendix hanging from the mainland."

Gijs was following her instructions on the back of an envelope.

"Show me what you did," Mrs. Helfrich said.

"You made Japan too large. You were probably thinking it was the size of our Indies. Believe it or not, the Dutch East Indies is about four times the size of Japan. Isn't that a galling thought? That a country one-fourth the size can just sweep it up?"

Mrs. Helfrich was getting visibly agitated. "The history of Korea is like that of our own country. China, Japan, and even Russia did to Korea what Germany and France tried to do to Holland over many centuries. Japan won out over its rivals. I think it was in 1910 when they annexed it."

"Did the Koreans become Japanese citizens?"

"Think more of it like what happened to Austria when Hitler annexed it. He took over the governing and he could make Austrians serve in his army. I suspect that's what is happening to the Koreans. They probably don't like it at all that they have to fight in this war on the Japanese side."

One late afternoon, a few days after the watch incident, the Bozuwas and the Helfrichs were sitting on the veranda. It was just before supper. The smell of onions frying in the kitchen mingled with the sweetness of tropical flowers. The air in the Indies was always full, Gijs thought. It was probably the heat that brought out so many smells, sweet or foul, of every living thing. They could be rotting plants as well as blooming ones; or food being cooked outside; or the smell of animal manure or putrid water in the *kali* that streamed nearby.

It was then that Mr. Kuyper walked up the driveway.

"I have news, Rietje," he called to Moeder before he'd reached the veranda.

Moeder quickly got out of her chair to greet him. He reached inside his shirt pocket and produced a tiny, crumpled piece of paper and handed it to her. A tense silence descended onto the veranda. Although Gijs was dying to know what the paper said, he didn't dare ask. There was as much chance that that small piece of paper contained good news as devastating news. Moeder seemed to have difficulty making out what was written on it.

"Sumatra?"

"Yes, that's right. He made it to one of the lifeboats that landed on Sumatra."

"So is he alive?" Gijs could not contain himself any longer. "Moeder, what does it say?"

"From what I see here," she said, "Vader is alive and in a prison in Palembang on Sumatra."

Gijs and Janneke jumped up from their chairs. "He's alive!"

"How did you get this message?" Moeder asked.

"Gerard must have hastily scribbled this down and given it to a native," Mr. Kuyper said. "The man somehow made it across the channel to Java. He carried the message inside a bandage on his leg."

"Thank God he's alive," Moeder said, "but I worry what the Japs will do to him."

"Just hold on to the thought that he survived, Rietje," Mr. Kuyper said.

They offered him a glass of Dutch *jenever*, which they'd found in a cabinet. Neither Moeder, Mrs. Helfrich, nor Janneke drank *jenever*. Not many women did. So they told him he could keep the rest of what was in the bottle and invited him to dinner.

Gijs liked the idea of a man at the table who knew his father and who was still fully engaged with everyday life. He had a multitude of questions about many things, and as soon as he thought it was polite to interrupt the conversation among the adults, he fired them off.

"Mr. Kuyper, have you discovered any more details about the sinking of the *Poelau Bras*?"

"All we know is that it left Java at Wijnkoops Baai in the evening of March seven, with three hundred passengers on board. About fifty of those were crew members. Then there was a group made up of navy officers like your father and important civilians like Mr. Colijn, who was the manager of the refinery in Tarakan on Borneo, and other Shell people."

"Mr. Colijn? A relative of the prime minister?" Gijs asked.

"Yes, his son. And I believe his three daughters were also on board."

"I wonder if they made it," Moeder mused to herself.

"How far out to sea were they?" Gijs asked.

"Six bells off Java."

"Bells?"

"That's a nautical measurement of distance on the seas," Mr. Kuyper said. " Overnight, they'd gone full steam to get to an area that would be outside the operating radius of the Japanese. "

"Where did the planes come from? It couldn't be from Kalidjati," Janneke said.

"From the Japanese aircraft carrier *Hiryu*. In daylight. The next morning."

"How many lifeboats did it have?" Gijs asked. He might as well get all the details. He didn't know why, but he wanted to know as much about it as he could. This was his chance.

"There were seven lifeboats. Three made it down. Each could hold fifty-three people. In all, there were one hundred sixteen survivors. That's all I can tell you, Gijs," Mr. Kuyper said. "One day we will know more, but first we will have to win this wretched war."

The *djongos* came in to clear the plates, and the conversation died down. It was better not to discuss political matters in front of a native. The three women in the room were only too aware that the Japanese had let it be known—even before the war—that they wanted to be seen as the liberators from the colonial yoke.

They got up from the table and returned to the veranda. Mr. Kuyper seated himself in the comfortable chair his father would have occupied. It suited him well. His body build and his demeanor were not unlike his father's.

The conversation turned to what to expect from the Japanese occupation.

"General Imamura posted copies of a proclamation everywhere. You can't miss it." Mr. Kuyper said.

" I've been mostly housebound," Moeder said. "I haven't seen it. What does it say?"

"They just put it up. It is addressed to the Indonesian population. The gist of it is that the Japanese have come here to lay the groundwork for a mutual existence and mutual prosperity. You know the slogans: 'A joint defense of Greater Asia,' 'Asia for the Asians,' and so forth. What was interesting is that it suggests they can together overthrow the previous regime—that's us—which had acted under the influence of America and Great Britain."

"Sure, the Brits told us what to do. They led us by the hand," Mrs. Helfrich said defiantly.

Gijs was sure the admiral had given his wife an earful about how the Brits had let them down in the end.

"Another remarkable sentence in it," Mr. Kuyper said, "is that the Indonesians and Japanese share the same ancestors and are of the same race. That was a surprise to me. I've never thought a Japanese and an Indo look much alike, except for the color of their skin. Their eyes are set at different angles. However that may be, the proclamation says the Japanese came to end the centuries-long oppression of the Indonesian people."

"Rebel-rousing," Janneke said.

"The proclamation ends with a warning. The Japanese army acts under strict discipline. Work can continue, but just don't do anything suspicious or you will be punished according to military laws and regulations. I'm sure that goes for us as well."

Mr. Kuyper took a deep breath. It was quiet on the veranda as his words sank in. It had turned dark. Close to the equator they had equal amounts of light and dark year-round. In Holland, it would have already turned dark in the latter part of the afternoon. Gijs wondered how he came up with such an unimportant fact at this particular moment. The frogs were giving their familiar evening concert, and he felt a certain comfort in seeing a salamander hurry across the wall, its legs spread out wide and navigating its path with its long tail. Mrs. Helfrich was the first to speak.

"The fact that this is so specifically addressed to the natives makes me wonder what's in store for us."

"There was no proclamation for the *belandas*. We'll have to look at their deeds before we can know what their plans are," Mr. Kuyper said.

"One thing I found out already," Gijs said. "We have to bow for the guards."

"Yes, that's true. A guard represents the emperor, that's why. The entire Japanese society is organized around the idea that the emperor is holy. It's even written in their constitution. His holiness is an indisputable fact. They won't let us forget it."

"Can white people continue to work?" Moeder asked.

"So far, most of them do. The Japanese did imprison the highest-ranking authorities in Batavia, because they refused to declare under oath that they would obey all the commands of the Japanese army. The Governor General is locked up in a prison, here in Bandoeng. But the essential people, the ones who keep things running, can stay at their jobs. Not at the same salary!"

"As wives of navy officers we won't receive a cent, I'm sure," Moeder said. "I took my money out of the bank first thing after the Japs set foot on Java. Now I hear they've closed the banks."

"They'll turn us into paupers," Janneke said.

"Let's wait and see." Mr. Kuyper got up. "At this point there's no telling what they want from us."

They said good-bye. And never saw him again.

Chapter 8

Ton Perks moved in with her baby. The family she'd stayed with after she moved from Soerabaja lost their house to a Japanese officer who wanted it for himself, and she had no place to go. Janneke was delighted. The house on the Jan Steenlaan stretched like an elastic band. Built for one family, it now held three tightly within its walls.

One day in May, Janneke drove Moeder and Mrs. Helfrich to the bank downtown. The banks had reopened, and they wanted to see if their husbands' monthly salaries had been deposited in their accounts. They returned in a state of agitation.

"We waited all this time to have the banks reopen," Mrs. Helfrich said. "How long was it? Two months? And now they have the gall to tell us that we will only have one month's worth of navy salary forthcoming and after that we can't withdraw from our own bank accounts!" Mrs. Helfrich was furious.

"We are non-Asians and non-Asians will not be helped at the bank," Moeder said.

"Who are the non-Asians besides the Dutch?" Gijs asked.

"Chinese, Arabs, every European national, and the Americans and Brits, of course, but that was a given. All of us are enemy subjects! We finally found out what we have in common with the Arabs and the Chinese." Janneke said this sarcastically. It wasn't like her, but Gijs knew she was more than a little angry..

"What will we do? How can we live?" Ton asked.

"We'll have to do with less," Moeder said. "I took out all our money before the surrender. Don't worry, Ton. We'll survive. We will put all our pennies together."

Meanwhile, Gijs felt lost. No school. There was a shortage of teachers, and teaching in the Dutch language was forbidden — even in homes. Those who'd been called up as reservists had later been taken prisoner, but Moeder figured out a way for Gijs, Jan, Lex, and other children in the neighborhood to get lessons from a few teachers she'd recruited. Learning on the sly was done in various homes that weren't as crowded as hers, and the teachers took their chances.

Among the students was a girl named Annie, blond, cheerful, and pretty. Gijs was immediately drawn to her, and he contrived to do his homework at her place, just up the hill from his. At the very least, it was a place to go. They had a good time, but Moeder worried about this romantic awakening in her son.

"Gijs, I think you are spending too much time with Annie. You can do your homework just as well here."

"Moeder, what's wrong with studying with someone else? She is smart and a real help."

"That may be. I just don't think it's proper."

"Come on, Moeder, there's nothing improper about it." Gijs didn't think that putting his arm around Annie while leaning over a textbook, or occasionally planting a furtive kiss on her cheek, was improper.

He heard the same reproach every time he came back from Annie's house, but he decided not to get pushed out of a good time. Had Moeder forgotten what *she* wanted when she was sixteen? Stories about her youth had always seemed painful and restricted to him. Her father had died when she was twelve. She'd been the youngest of four children, who had been strict with her.

Janneke rescued him.

"Moeder, Annie is a nice girl and her family is very nice as well, if that means anything."

The episode came to a natural end. The teachers gradually disappeared. Men between the ages of seventeen and sixty who didn't work were imprisoned. Not all at once. The Japanese worked furiously to find enough places for locking them up. Running out of prisons, they began to convert empty schools. The authorities gave no advance notice of arrests. An Indonesian police officer or a Japanese soldier would knock on the door and take the man of the house. Since it seemed a rather random process, all men waited with fear in their hearts for that dreaded knock on the door, waited for their own turn to be taken away.

On the veranda of the Jan Steenlaan. Front row l. to r. Mrs. Helfrich, Moeder, Janneke with Ton's baby. Back row l. to r. Jan Helfrich, Gijs, Lex Helfrich

Sometime in May, as they were sitting on the veranda, a military car stopped in their street. Curious and slightly concerned, Gijs and Jan Helfrich climbed over the veranda wall and watched through a screen of pointed palm leaves in their front yard. Two Japanese officers stepped out and walked up to the house across the street. A Dutch couple lived there. Gijs didn't know more about them than that the husband was an engineer and worked for the city. He seemed to still have a job, because he left early on his bicycle every morning. Moments later, the officers walked out, and the woman of the house ran across the street. She was crying.

"We have to move! They give us twenty-four hours to get out. What am I to do?"

Moeder invited her in. Janneke made her a cup of coffee.

"Do you have family or friends here in Bandoeng?" Moeder asked.

" All of our family is in Holland. We have friends here, of course. But that's no small thing to ask of a friend, don't you think? What an invasion of privacy! Also, we wouldn't be able to take all our stuff with us. What in God's name will we do with the furniture and everything else we own?"

Her blue eyes filled with tears again while she plucked nervously at her cotton dress.

"I would offer to take you in, but we're already living here with three families," Moeder said. "You can use our phone. Call the best friend you have. Your home isn't the first one that's been requisitioned by the Japs. It's happening all over. The only way we will get through this mess is by helping each other."

By the afternoon, the neighbor had found a friend who would take them in, and Gijs and Jan helped move as much of their belongings as time allowed.

Twenty-four hours later, on the dot, a van pulled up. It unloaded, among other things, a baby grand piano.

"I bet they stole that from another house," Jan said. "What military travels with a piano on its back?"

"Yes, I bet somebody's missing a piano tonight," Gijs said.

The new owners of their neighbor's home were not military men. They were civil servants who had been trained back in Tokyo. Their job was to follow the military and gradually take over the running of the conquered territories, the infrastructure as well as the banks and plantations. *Economen*—economists—they were called.

Soon, sonatas by Mozart, Chopin, and Bach flowed through the Jan Steenlaan from an open window across the street. One of the *economen* apparently was a pianist. It was beautiful to listen to. The man had a sensitive touch. Mesmerized, the various members of Gijs's home sat on the veranda and let the notes transport their minds to better days, when music was part of a more normal way of life.

The moment the music faded into the dark of the night, they all realized that no matter how elegant, the music was not in sync with what they had experienced thus far from this pianist's compatriots. The takeover of the house had been anything but sensitive or elegant.

Gijs's best friend these days was Colonel Kroese's bike. On it he coasted down the hill toward the center of town in search of contemporaries. They weren't hard to find. On the corners of intersecting arteries through the city, he could count on finding a group of loafers like himself. The Japanese authorities had closed institutions that reeked of Western culture, like schools and movie theaters. Leaning on their bikes, they congregated, swapped stories, smoked cigarettes, and shot marbles. The one constant in their changing world was their physical environment. The city of Bandoeng was as beautiful as ever. They could put their bikes on the lawn in the spacious Pieters Park and find blissful shade under tall deciduous trees. Squatted in a circle around a hole they'd dug in the moist soil, they shot marbles with fanatical precision. They weren't so much out to win from each other. It was the Japanese they wanted to beat. In this game they could exercise their own free wills.

Gijs kept hoping he would run into Pieter Donk somewhere. How stupid of him not to have taken his address down when they said good-bye in front of the Grand Preanger Hotel. That time seemed years ago. Would Pieter still have his motorcycle? He doubted it. The Japanese confiscated what they liked and motorcycles were probably high on their list.

Finally one day in early August, he saw a figure walk under the huge trees around City Hall. Tall, blond, and strong, he looked like Pieter. Gijs pushed hard on his bike's pedals and caught up with him.

"Pieter! It's you! I have been looking all over for you."

"Hey, Gijs, how are you? Where have you been? I went to the Preanger Hotel, but when I saw the Japanese flag flying in front, I figured you were not inside."

"We couldn't stay, so we moved to the Jan Steenlaan. I see you're walking. Where is your motorbike?"

"In our garage. I'd like to hang onto it for a little longer. One day it's bound to go the way of so many things these days. You know how it is."

"Too bad. It's a neat rig," Gijs said.

"What's happened in your life since those days in March?" Pieter asked.

"We moved and have taken in two other families since. It's getting to be close quarters."

They'd stopped under a tree. It was late morning and the heat was building. Gijs put his bike down and they sat on the grass. Pieter reached in his shirt pocket and produced a pack of Mascot cigarettes, as he'd done the first time they met.

"Now that there's no school, what does your father do?" Gijs asked.

"Waiting to be interned. It's bound to happen." Pieter hesitated, probably weighing if he should ask Gijs about his father.

"My father got out on the *Poelau Bras* on March seven," Gijs volunteered.

Pieter gave him a sharp look. He seemed to be aware what had happened to the *Poelau Bras*.

"He made it to a lifeboat," Gijs said quickly. "We got a message that he was taken prisoner on Sumatra. We haven't heard since."

A slight breeze was picking up, rustling the abundant leaves overhead. Patches of light and shadow chased each other over the lawns and paths around them, while Pieter and Gijs stretched their legs and digested each other's news.

"Isn't it amazing how it seems like nothing changed?" Pieter said, letting out inhaled smoke as he spoke. "It's deceiving. Just look around. Plenty of natives in their sarongs and on bare feet, but where are the Chinese? It's what you don't see that makes you realize things aren't as they used to be. Have you noticed there are fewer men in their white suits bicycling through the streets?"

Gijs looked around. In front of City Hall stood a Japanese sentry.

"How long do you think before the Allies kick the Japs out? Some people say in a couple of months," Gijs said.

"I have no idea. Sometimes I think it's the Japanese who plant those rumors. Just to keep us off balance," Pieter said.

"Somebody told me that in the press they talk about separating the Allied civilians. Have you heard anything about that?"

"Yes, vaguely. I do know that they're waging a propaganda campaign against us. Anything Dutch is no good. That's the message. It gets to be so you feel funny being Dutch. I had to register back in April, like everybody else over 17. Boy, did I hate having to swear that I would obey all Japanese laws and rules."

"Yes, my mother and sister had to do the same. They didn't like it either."

As they walked down the street, Gijs asked, "Do you have a piece of paper so I can write down your address?"

It turned out they lived in the same neighborhood. Gijs tore the piece of notepaper in two and they each wrote down their addresses.

"Let's stay in touch," Pieter said.

Chapter 9

Sometimes a wicked rumor turns into a stone hard fact. It had seemed like a far-fetched idea to set apart the seventy thousand white people who lived on Java from the native population, especially if you considered that in the Bandoeng area alone, there were twenty-seven thousand Europeans. When the Japanese army, immediately following its victory, had seized schools and government buildings and turned them into prisons for POWs, the citizenry could justify that action as part of waging war. Even imprisoning the enemy's high-ranking authorities was acceptable. But locking up every man, woman, and child with a white skin? This radical course of action didn't seem likely, and it hadn't crossed many minds.

Pieter Donk was the first to raise the possibility that, crazy or not, internment could happen. He'd biked over to the Jan Steenlaan for a visit. He found Gijs in a shed in back of the house, where he'd set up a sort of laboratory. There was still a chemistry teacher around who showed a small group of students in his neighborhood how to perform certain lab tests. Moeder wasn't crazy about the idea. Someday, she was certain, those kids would blow up the place.

Pieter sat on a stool, watching Gijs put some liquid in a test tube. He struck up a Mascot, took a long drag from the cigarette, and stated that life was going to change. Drastically.

"How do you mean?" Gijs asked.

"I was visiting a friend on the Houtmanstraat and he told me that the Japanese plan to turn the entire Tjihapit district behind his house into a camp."

"That doesn't make sense," Gijs said. "How can you make a camp out of a residential area?"

"You put a fence around it and a sentry post at the end of one street and you have a camp. On my way back I saw workers building a sentry post."

"Is that what they're doing? Who is going into that camp?"

"All of us!" Pieter said. "It's rumored they'll put all European women and children there."

"That's an insane idea. What good would that do?"

"Well, for one thing, they'd have us in one place. That makes it easier to police us."

"They're doing a good job of it now! I doubt that's the only reason," Gijs said. "There's got to be more to it than that."

Pieter took another drag from his cigarette and crossed his long legs to get more comfortable on the hard wooden stool.

"They'd probably just as soon drive us all into the ocean," he said. "They don't want us here."

"'Asia for the Asians.' You've got a point." Gijs added some fluid to what he already had in the test tube. As he swirled the contents, the liquid turned an intense blue.

"Yes, Asia for the Asians and Indonesia for the Japs!" Pieter said. "Let's face it: for all their high-minded talk about shared prosperity, it's our oil they need."

"I remember my father saying the same thing," Gijs said. "I wish the Allies would hurry up and drive the Japs out. Some say in a couple of months they could be here."

"I heard those rumors too. Hard to know who starts them. Seeing is believing. It may take the Allies a while to replace all those lost ships."

Pieter was not given to building castles out of air. He was a realist. Gijs looked over as Pieter balanced himself on the kitchen stool, smoking his cigarette. Had he come to warn Gijs of what might lie ahead? From the moment they'd met, Pieter had come across as steady and straightforward. As they made the rounds together in the residential neighborhoods of Bandoeng for the LBD, Pieter had reminded him of his own father. It had seemed to come so naturally to him to be diplomatic with the uncooperative women and reassuring with the fearful.

"How soon do you think this is all going to happen?" Gijs asked.

"As soon as they can get it all organized, I suppose. If it is their intention to get us out of the way, then they'll probably say, the sooner the better!"

"They'll have quite a time to persuade the women to give up their homes."

"It won't be voluntary, I'm sure. Look at what happens when a Japanese officer wants a nice house. He tells the owners to get out and fast, and he doesn't leave the impression that he lies awake about it at night."

"True. I saw that across the street."

"They'll give it a twist, of course, like this is for our own protection," Pieter said. "But protection from whom? The natives? So far, there hasn't been any rebellion against the white population. I think the natives are simply dumbfounded at what they see happening to us. Just as they couldn't believe that the Dutch army would fight only for a few days and then give up. Yet they don't seem to relish the thought of our downfall."

Pieter lifted himself off the high stool and stretched, getting ready to leave. Gijs threw out the blue liquid in his test tube on a bare spot in the garden. "Come again," he said. "With better news next time!"

On his way to the front door, Gijs walked by the kitchen window and sniffed the appetizing aromas of whatever *kokkie* was preparing for the midday meal. The working life in the Indies lasted from the very early morning, when it was still cool, till the sun climbed to its highest point in the sky. In Soerabaja the heat and the humidity had become unbearable around noon. Instead of fighting the punishing heat, a daily routine had evolved that avoided the hottest hours of the day. Business and schooling was tended to in the mornings, and the workers and students went home at one in the afternoon. After the midday meal, most went to bed under the *klamboe* till it cooled off. In Bandoeng the mercury didn't climb quite so high, but the pattern of daily life was the same. In the afternoon, the white population rested while their servants squatted in the yard to smoke a cigarette or share in a whispered gossip.

Moeder had started a routine of her own. It regarded the menu. Only twice a week did she allow *kokkie* to cook her native cuisine. On Sunday they had *rijsttafel*, which meant rice with a great variety of condiments, most of them hot to the tongue. On Wednesdays they ate *bami*, a native noodle dish. The remaining days *kokkie* cooked the Dutch staples of meat, vegetables, and potatoes, which Gijs preferred. When it was *rijsttafel* day, he just picked at the rice because his mother forced him.

The sounds of commotion inside the house made him wonder what was going on. He walked around to the front of the house, where the door was open. The front door was always open, allowing the air to circulate. Closed doors and windows in the Indies meant a hot house. Nobody bothered to carry a house key. The *djongos* would squat on the front step in front of the open door and remain there till his *Tuan* returned.

He found Moeder and Mrs. Helfrich going through all the closets. Several bottles of liquor that Colonel Kroese had left behind stood on the coffee table.

"What are you doing that for?" he asked.

"We're going to flush it down the toilet. All of it," Moeder said.

"Isn't that a bit drastic?" Gijs said. "Why are you so eager to get rid of it?"

"Because," Mrs. Helfrich said, "we've just been advised that we better not have hard liquor around. The Japs have a way of wandering into houses, usually drunk, and making it clear they want more. They don't just take your house. They can also walk in and drink your whiskey! We don't want drunk Japs in our house!"

"I won't miss the whiskey," Moeder said, "but a drunken Japanese soldier can do much harm. With four women in this house, we don't want to take any chances."

Gijs carried the bottles off to the WC. Emptying two bottles at the same time caused interesting color changes. It reminded of the lab tests he performed in the shed behind the house, but seeing the contents swirling slowly in the ceramic bowl didn't entice him to take a sip.

As usual, Moeder had made a wise decision. Hardly a month later, a Japanese officer walked into the house without ringing the bell or announcing himself. He carried a pistol in his right hand and treated it like a baton, swirling it around. He didn't seem to be drunk. It was unclear what he was after. He found the women sitting in the living room. Ton was feeding her baby. The officer walked around as if he owned the place, pointing at this and that, all the time twirling his revolver.

"You will have to leave this house soon. You all have to get out," he said in Maleis.

The women remained in frozen silence. Moeder was the only one standing, and she'd taken on a haughty posture. She looked straight into the officer's eyes, which emanated cruelty and indifference.

Suddenly, the officer stopped and stood still in front of a framed picture of Vader in full uniform. The revolver stopped twirling. He looked at Moeder and said to her in Maleis, "Good." Then he turned on his heels and left the house.

"What was that all about?" Janneke said as she regained her composure. They were in a state of shock and disbelief, sitting in their chairs like statues.

Mrs. Helfrich looked over at Vader's picture and said, "Thank you, Gerard. You saved us."

"Saved us?" Janneke asked.

"I remember my husband telling me about the Japanese military, that they will never surrender or let themselves be taken prisoner. They fight and if all else fails, they commit suicide. Surrender brings shame onto their family and their ancestors."

"I don't understand what that has to do with Vader," Janneke said.

"Well, the way I see it," Mrs. Helfrich said, "this officer knew the Dutch Navy fought to the end. They respect that. The army surrendered, but not the navy. That's why I'm so worried they won't treat the POWs well. Their cultural attitude is to look down on them."

They talked some more about the unexpected visit, about their fears of what to expect or what lay ahead for them. Janneke could still drive a car, though she mostly rode her bike to the soup kitchen every day. They could still go shopping in the Bragastreet and send *kokkie* to the *pasar* to buy food, but the unsettling feeling crept in that maybe the rumors Pieter Donk had heard were true, especially since the Japanese officer had said they would all soon have to leave the house. What would they do if they were ordered to get out? Did they have a contingency plan? A dark feeling came over them, as if they stood in the hovering shadow of a bird of prey.

Then came a call from a good friend, Mrs. van Straaten, who lived on the Houtmanstraat, the same street Pieter's friend lived on, the one who said the Japanese were building an internment camp.

"It's getting obvious that the street we live on will be the border of an internment camp from the front of our house to most of what's behind us," Mrs. van Straaten said.

"Are you sure?" Moeder said. "The whole Tjihapit area?"

"That's how it's shaping up. Look, I live in a very big house. It seems to me that if we're going to be forced to live together— many families to one house they say—we might as well choose our housemates!"

"Yes, that would be preferable," Moeder said carefully.

"I know you are living at the Jan Steenlaan with Ton Perks and Mrs. Helfrich. Why don't you all move over now, before you're forced to?" Mrs. van Straaten said. "I have some other people on my list. We can all fit into this sprawling place and help each other."

Under the present circumstances, Mrs. van Straaten's words were like manna from heaven. Of course! They would beat the Japanese to it!

When it turned dark, Moeder asked everyone, except the servants, to come to the veranda. There was nothing unusual about this. It was the best place to be when night fell. The sun went under at around six o'clock. A stirring in the air sent some blissful cooling over them as they sat in the comfortable *rotan* chairs. The *econonoom* across the street had taken up position behind his stolen piano, and the notes of a Mozart sonata floated through the still night. Moeder used this background distraction to broach the subject of moving. Lowering her voice, she passed on the invitation from Nel van Straaten to come and live in her home on the Houtmanstraat. An uncharacteristic silence fell over the veranda. Mrs. Helfrich said she would like to live in the same house with all of her children again. For months now, they had been spread out over various places. Janneke thought it was a realistic plan. There was no sense in pretending the internment wasn't going to happen. This way they would have time to do a decent job of moving. Ton agreed as well.

So it happened.

The furniture of all three families had been put in storage. They didn't own enough to need to hire a mover, yet what they did own was more than they could carry.

Gijs biked over to Pieter's and told him of their plan.

Pieter said he knew of a big cart. "I'll see if I can talk this old man I know out of it, or maybe just borrow it for a while."

What he came up with was a cart that had not been designed with motorized or even real horsepower in mind. Its rectangular loading platform extended in equal lengths—front and rear—from two high wooden wheels. For the *koelie* who would pull it, two long shafts extended from one end of the cart. For the *koelie* who would push it, two shafts extended from the other end. Gijs studied the contraption that had obviously been made for native farmers.

"This looks like a push me-pull you," he said.

"Yes." Pieter laughed. "We'll have to do some practicing to keep it in balance."

Thus started their brief moving career. After they'd carted the cargo from the Jan Steenlaan to Mrs. van Straaten's, other women beseeched them. Everybody was on the move. Pieter and Gijs learned to spare their backs by placing the front legs of heavy pieces on a small carpet and dragging it around. Cabinets, chairs, chests of drawers, they all got a ride on their magic carpet. The most difficult part proved to be going downhill with a full load. Gijs, up front, raised the shafts to let the load shift its weight toward the back. That slowed the cart down. Going uphill was Pieter's specialty, pushing the cart from behind.

The days of boredom were over. They had a full-time job, and for the rest of their lives they would know how to move furniture.

The official order from the Japanese authorities for them to present themselves in Camp Tjihapit had not yet arrived. In September, Moeder dismissed the servants of Colonel Kroese and gave them two months' worth of salary.

Janneke got behind the steering wheel of the Chrysler and drove the three women and the baby to Mrs. van Straaten's home. After they unloaded the last minute things they'd taken, she maneuvered the car into a secluded part of the large yard, opened the hood, took out the distributor, and threw it far into the bushes.

Gijs heard her chuckle as she put the keys in her pocketbook and walked into the house that would be her prison for untold years to come.

Chapter 10

Day by day, person by person, Nel van Straaten's house filled until forty-six people lived within its walls. With one family to a room, it became home to an enormous family without a father, but with no lack of mothers and siblings, from diaper stage to juniors in high school. Gijs was the oldest boy. He wondered how he should regard himself. Was he the oldest boy who could be ordered around, or was he the man of the house? But it became clear quickly that the women were in charge, especially his mother. First, they divided the housekeeping tasks among them. The good days were over, the days in which every conceivable household chore was performed by a *kokkie*, a *djongos*, a *baboe,* or a *kebon.* Undaunted, they rolled up their sleeves. In Holland they would have had, at the most, one servant. They knew how to cook and they knew how to do laundry and clean. It was an eye-popping sight, the first time Gijs saw the wife of the admiral sweeping the kitchen floor.

Across the street was a big building, once the Military Academy, which had been taken over by Japanese military. Sitting in rocking chairs on the veranda, Gijs and some of his newly acquired siblings watched Japanese soldiers training in bayonet charges. The bayonets had been left off the guns, but the purpose of the exercise was clear. Gijs and the other boys sat in fearful silence, listening to the incomprehensible orders of the commanding officer, who shouted at the soldiers, their sweaty, glistening bodies naked from the waist up. If the performance of one man didn't suit the officer, he would haul that soldier to the front of the line and whack him hard on the side of his face. One of the younger boys on the veranda whispered that his father had received a similar hard blow because he'd refused to sign the oath that he would obey all the rules and regulations of the

Japanese Army. The kid's face contorted as he watched the beating on the other side of the street. His father had been interned immediately afterward.

Every boy's father on that veranda had been taken away into some form of detention. If they were military, they'd been declared POWs and taken to prisons. If they were teachers, shopkeepers, bankers, or civil servants, they were sent to a man's civil internment camp. If they were engineers, plantation managers, or worked other useful professions that kept the infrastructure going, they were still at home. But for how long? The trained *economen* were rapidly taking over their tasks.

Gijs jumped off the veranda and motioned the others to do the same. Watching the beatings didn't do much for their morale. If the Japanese treated their own like that, what would they do to the *belandas*? Better to enlist the boys for the yard work he'd been ordered to do and keep their minds occupied.

The van Straatens' yard was wide and deep, filled with trees and flower borders. What Gijs knew of gardening was only what he'd observed. When he came home from school in Soerabaja, he'd spent many hours watching the *kebon* working. He'd never held a rake or a hoe in his own hands. But if Mrs. Helfrich could sweep the floor, he could find a rake to clean up the debris that had accumulated around the base of the tall trees, which looked to him as old as the universe. He didn't know what any of the trees were called, except for the palm trees. Those were the only ones he could tell apart.

The boys came with rakes and a cart they'd found in the shed.

"Let's go for it," Gijs said to them. "We have to get this yard cleaned up."

They worked till they had blisters on their hands.

"This looked so easy when our *kebon* did it," one of them said, looking for a place to sit in the shade and rest.

Crumpled, crisp leaves crackled under their sandals. All around them was growth, some of it wanted, most of it unwanted. The heat and the seasonal drenching rains encouraged rapid spreading.

It seemed that for every new leaf that grew on a branch, three had already fallen to the ground. Without an organizing human hand, a yard could rapidly turn into chaos. Gijs leaned on his rake under the shade of a palm tree, whose trunk was at least six feet around. A tough vine had wound its way to the top, sprouting elongated leaves with brilliant flowers at their tips. Here and there its tentacles had crept into the bark, where it was devoured by the widening tree trunk. Both the vine and the tree seemed to survive this intense, symbiotic embrace. He'd never paid much attention to growing things.

"Hello Gijs," a voice behind him said.

"Hey, Pieter, how are you?"

"Could be better, could be worse."

"What happened?"

"They came for my father," Pieter said. "And if that wasn't heart-breaking enough, they told us to get out of the house. You know, the twenty-four hour routine."

"Can I help you move? Do you know where you're going?"

"That would be great. I'll get the cart. You know where I live. My mother is packing and discarding. We'll be living somewhere here in Camp Tjihapit."

Gijs told the boys to quit working and walked back to the house to announce he was going to help Pieter.

The familiar cart stood in their yard, and Pieter's mother, her blond hair wet with perspiration, stood next to it, instructing Pieter and a younger boy—presumably Pieter's brother—what to load and what to leave. She paused a moment as Pieter introduced Gijs. Her friendly blue eyes, accentuated by tiny wrinkles, gave the impression of a cheerful personality. Yet they revealed a deep weariness as well.

"Thank you, Gijs," she said. "We can use all the help we can get. The Japs certainly like to spring surprises on us, don't they? Of course, we could see this coming, but when it happens, it's still a shock. Your mother was smart to get the moving over with before she was forced to."

"We were lucky to be asked to join Mrs. van Straaten. She was really the wise one," Gijs said.

Pieter and Gijs worked like a team of oxen without a driver. They pulled the farmer's cart back and forth between the Donks' old home and their new one, straight through the day, ignoring lunchtime and the customary siesta. Robert, the smaller brother, probably fourteen years old, helped unload and carry their things into the new house, where three other families already lived.

Gijs peeked into the garage to see if the motorcycle was still there. It wasn't. Along with Pieter's father, the Japanese had taken it. Why not? They considered people and things as their own property. The spoils of the victors. For Gijs, the absence of that wonderful bike highlighted the Japanese's arrogant attitude. He observed within himself that it didn't surprise him anymore. In only eight months he'd been brainwashed to accept that people disappeared, that their possessions were fair game, and that they, the *belandas*, were despicable and needed to be put out of sight.

At six, when the sun was done with the day, Pieter and Gijs, with Robert in tow, returned the cart to its owner. A shriveled old man sat on the stoop of a house, a cigarette dangling from his lips. Until recently, he'd been the caretaker of the house. Pieter slipped his watch off his wrist and put it in the man's hand without saying a word. The old man looked up at him, also silent, his dark brown eyes moist with affection. His calloused hands fingered the watch. Words seemed superfluous to the understanding between them.

On the way back to Pieter's house, Gijs asked how he knew the man.

"He once saved my life. He was our neighbor's *kebon*. Before that, he worked in the *sawahs*. Anyway, he saved my life when he saw a poisonous snake approaching me from behind. It got dangerously close. He jumped over the fence and killed the snake with a hatchet."

They walked on, not speaking, the silence almost palpable. Gijs thought he knew how Pieter and Robert felt—angry and alone, the way he had felt when he'd thought his own father had drowned. Their minds had to be on the past twenty-four hours: their father, their precious belongings, Pieter's motorbike, the old native friend, their home, all of it gone.

Gradually, the Tjihapit area of Bandoeng began to look like a camp. Like a noose around a neck, a fence of woven bamboo—*gedek,* it was called—enveloped the entire area, with a strand of barbed wire on top. Their first-row seat for watching military exercises was taken away by the *gedek*. More important to the Japanese, the natives walking in the Houtmanstraat could not see the *belandas*. Out of sight, out of mind. In that sense, Camp Tjihapit resembled a leper colony.

The Japanese commander let it be known that he wanted to deal with his captives through only one person, and it would have to be done in Maleis. Whoever among them was chosen had to be fluent in the native language. The leaders among them surfaced quickly. By Christmas, a camp leader with a knack for leading and negotiating was chosen. An organization to steer the roughly seven thousand mothers and children into a functioning community was born in a painful, drawn-out delivery.

Tasks, like running a central washing room and kitchen, were doled out. Young boys who'd only seen servants wash sheets found themselves hard at work wringing them out. Older boys, like Gijs and Pieter, were told to take on the heavy lifting jobs. Ordered around by bossy women—Girl Scout leader types—they were told to climb on a roof and fix a leak, or carry sacks of rice to the *goedang*, where food for the central kitchen was kept.

Other things were going on as well.

"Wim says he's 'done it' with Anneke's mother," one of the older boys, whose name was Dirk, said to Gijs and Pieter. The three boys were pushing a cart filled to the brim with trash that needed to be disposed of.

The way Dirk said it made Gijs look up at him. Dirk's expression was a curious mixture of delight in the gossip and poorly hidden admiration for the deed.

"Keep that stuff to yourself, Dirk," Picter said, and waved him off.

"If jerks like Wim keep that up, they'll send us away," Gijs said to Pieter.

"Yes, I wouldn't be surprised."

Unbeknown to them, the Japanese authorities agreed with Gijs's prescient remark. They saw the presence of adolescent boys as sexually undesirable in a women's camp. They hatched plans to heave them over to the men's camps. In the Japanese culture a boy of sixteen was regarded a man, but they computed a person's age differently. A human being, in their view, was one year old at birth. In the Dutch way of counting, the same boy would be fifteen and in no way seen as an adult.

In January 1943, a little slip of paper was delivered at Pieter's new home. The sender was the Japanese camp commander. It ordered Pieter to show up at the gate at a certain date and time, and specified what he was allowed to take with him.

What it didn't state was why or where he was going.

Chapter 11

That little piece of paper with its telex message set their lives on a radically different path. Gijs received his notice two days after his seventeenth birthday, in February 1943. Pieter had left two weeks earlier. Put on a truck. Destination unknown. Now it was Gijs's turn.

Moeder and Janneke saw to it that he had all he was allowed to take, which wasn't much: a folding cot, a blanket, a rolled-up mat called a *tikar*, three sets of underwear, three pairs of shorts, three shirts, toilet articles, and a fork, a spoon, and a small aluminum pan that could also serve as a plate. A knife, books, and pens and pencils were not allowed. At the last moment, Janneke slipped some pencils and three notebooks into his leather suitcase.

On the designated day and at the designated hour, Gijs stood at the gate with about ten other boys. His enlarged family had come along to say good-bye. Taken together with the other boys' mothers and siblings, they formed a crowd. Pieter's mother was among them. She asked if he would take a note for Pieter in case he went to the same camp.

Tears … Last-minute advice … Gijs let it all wash over him. He had mixed emotions. On the plus side, the Japanese considered him a man, which was distinctly different from being a big boy or the oldest boy. He was going to a man's camp. That he was sure of. On the minus side, he hated to leave his mother and sister behind, unprotected, even though the Japanese deceptively called the Tjihapit Camp a "Protected District."

Moeder stood ramrod straight beside him, seething inside, he was sure, that the Japanese were doing this to her son, but too proud to show it. The very fact that she couldn't go up to the commandant and tell him that it was against international laws and agreements to intern civilians sparked her motherly instincts. As a mother, she was powerless to prevent the rupture of her family. The Japanese were in charge. No matter how authoritative she might be by nature, there was nothing she could do or say to keep Gijs under her wing.

Janneke and Gijs

Janneke kept up a cheerful banter to distract him. As long as he'd lived, she'd protected him. When he was little, she would get him to school, dragging him along by his arm if his shorter legs couldn't keep pace. She would defend him, right or wrong. God, he would miss her.

The gate opened. Names were called out, one after the other. The sergeant came quickly to the B of Bozuwa. He felt his mother's embrace.

"Keep your chin up, *jongen*. Write us. Be strong," she said.

"Yes, Moeder."

Janneke tried to hide her tears. Bozuwas don't cry. Gijs quickly put his arms around her.

"I will miss you!" he said. "Take good care of Moeder and write!"

He waved at the others and stepped through the gate. He caught a last glance of his mother and sister standing close together. After everyone was accounted for, the gate slammed shut. There was no use guessing when he would see them again. Trying to look into the future was like looking through a frosted window.

An Indonesian sergeant in a Japanese uniform—such soldiers were called *heiho*—gave instructions in Maleis. Gijs didn't get it all, so he asked the boy next to him what they were supposed to do.

"We have to go into the camp's office in alphabetical order," the boy said, "then bow and wait there."

Inside the office, he found a Japanese lieutenant sitting behind a metal desk. Gijs bowed and waited. The officer looked at a list, put a Japanese character next to what Gijs assumed was his own name, nodded, and motioned him to go on outside. An open army truck stood parked in the street. Everyone's luggage had been dumped in a heap next to it.

Seated across from one another on wooden benches, their *barang* stowed between their knees, they rumbled through the streets. He didn't know any of the other boys by name, and only a few by face. He remembered surviving a day of laundry detail with one of them. It was the hardest job he'd had to do in the Tjihapit Camp; all day they'd scrubbed and rinsed, rinsed, and rinsed again, while the ladies-in-charge were standing by, chewing over rumors. Rumors galore! The forced integration led to high tensions in some homes. Gijs overheard the gossip about one woman who got so fed up with the poor behavior of someone else's kids in her house, she took a plate and smashed it on the mother's head.

Some of the streets the truck took them through he recognized, but he hadn't lived in Bandoeng long enough to know exactly where he was. Always attracted to the unknown, Gijs settled into the idea that he was on an adventure. After months of living among women, he welcomed the diversion.

They stopped at an office building.

"Do you suppose this is it?" the boy next to him said. "It doesn't look like a camp at all."

"What is a camp supposed to look like?" Gijs said. "For all we know, they turn office buildings into prisons."

Topographische Dienst, it said in big letters over the entrance at the Bangkastraat.

"Ah, a government office. I wonder why we're stopping here," his neighbor on the wooden bench said.

The *heiho* ordered them off the truck and told them to sort out their belongings. They shouldered the bulky rolls that held their cots, blanket, and mattress together with rope. Loaded up like pack mules, they were goaded into the courtyard. It was instantly clear that this was where they would stay. Men their fathers' ages, all in shorts, some with bare chests, looked up with curiosity as they entered. Would they find a son or other relative among the new-comers? Gijs wondered. There were no outburst of joyful recogni-tion, so he guessed not.

One of the Dutchmen, who seemed to be the elected leader among them, stepped forward.

"Give your name and we will tell you which room you are assigned to."

"My name is Gijs Bozuwa."

The leader wrote his name on a list, put an x in front of it, and told him to take his *barang* to room six.

Room six looked more like a barrack than an office. The walls, once hung with topographic maps of Java, looked as white and bare as sheets on a windless day, drying on a laundry line. Gijs guessed he shared the room with seven others, from the looks of seven cots with suitcases and bags stowed underneath that stood perpendicular to the longest wall.

"This is your *tempat*, Gijs," a friendly gentleman said to him, and pointed to the end of the row where he could unroll his cot and blanket. A strip of roughly five by nine feet would be his own little place in the world, providing enough room for him to sit and sleep. A narrow path separated him from the next man's *tempat*. No wonder so many men walked outside in the courtyard. Who would want to spend twenty-four hours here?

The newcomers were told to assemble in the courtyard. The midday meal had already been served. There would be roll call twice a day, wake-up call at 6 AM, lights out at 10 PM. Breakfast at 8 AM. Midday meal at noon. Evening meal at 5 PM. Mornings were for chores.

After they'd listened to the recital of basic rules, the boys huddled together on the steps of the covered gallery. Still feeling the sting of the good-byes, they hadn't talked much on the truck. Gijs missed the common ground some of the others shared by having gone to school together in Bandoeng.

"What's your name?" one of them asked.

"Gijs Bozuwa," he answered for the third time that day.

"My name is Frits. Where do you come from, Gijs?"

"I've lived all over the place. My father is in the navy. We lived in Soerabaja, but he got transferred to Bandoeng just before the Japs landed on Java. Where's your home? Rather, where was your home?" Gijs asked.

"I lived on a coffee plantation in the Preanger Mountains," Frits said. "My father was the manager there, but he was replaced by an *econoom*. I had hoped to find him here. Do you know where your father is?"

"Not exactly. Last we heard about him was last April. He was being held in a prison on Sumatra. That's what we were told."

Their identities came from their fathers' professions. The son of a schoolteacher, a banker, an officer, a preacher, a government worker, a planter, a retailer, that's who you were. They didn't realize it yet, but from now on their fathers' positions in life would no longer be in play. Instead, they were transformed into *tawanans* with a number, equalized by their guards who didn't care about their backgrounds, only that they had white skin and were Westerners. When their hair was cut down to their very scalps, for sanitary reasons, they even looked alike. One distinction remained. It was easy to tell which boys were born and raised in the Indies, because their speech was laced with Malaysian words.

Time for roll call. In rows of twenty, the *tawanans* assembled in the courtyard, waiting for the *heiho* who was the camp's commander. After they'd waited for fifteen minutes in formation, he finally appeared, dressed in a Japanese uniform, followed by two armed soldiers. Their Dutch leader called out, "*Ki wo tsuke,*" and everybody around him hastily stood at attention. "*Keirei,*" and they all bowed. "*Naore,*" and they straightened up.

The next order was "*Bango.*" Gijs had no idea what it meant. He was supposed to do something, but what? The first man in his row said, "*Iti.*" The second one said, "*Ni.*" When it was his turn, his neighbor whispered, "*Roku,*" so he repeated it. He got it. He had to learn to count in Japanese. The last order was "*Bakarre,*" and that meant they could all get lost.

His stomach was rumbling. Dinner had been one miserly piece of bread, and his stomach felt hollow as he stretched out on his cot. By the light of one 60-watt bulb that hung by a wire from the ceiling, the man next to him sat reading from the Bible. He'd introduced himself as Father van Gasteren, pronouncing the first letter of his last name with a soft *G*, which made Gijs conclude the man must have been born in either the Dutch province of Brabant or Limburg, where they spoke with a distinct dialect. He was a priest who looked about ten years older than Gijs. He had dark hair and was short of stature.

At ten, the lights went out. The next morning, the booming voice of the room's leader, Mr. van Dam, woke them at six. The priest next to him got on his knees beside his cot and mumbled a prayer. The other six gentlemen stretched, yawned, and got their towels out. It seemed best to follow them. In a large men's room, they took turns putting their heads under the cold-water faucet. Gijs was last.

Roll call came next. Same routine, except this time they were given a list of chores to do after breakfast. Gijs and Frits got the toilet cleaning detail. Breakfast was a big disappointment: a weak cup of tea and a steamed rice cake. This was the very thing he'd always disliked. Rice. He passed it up and looked forward to the midday meal. To his horror it was rice again. This time it was adorned with a tiny piece of meat swimming in a mixture of overcooked vegetables. In his mind he heard his mother admonish him, yet he had a hard time making himself take a bite, in spite of being hungry after doing the chores on an empty stomach. At home, at least, *kokkie* had given the rice some flavor with *sambal* and other spicy stuff. As he picked at the rice with his fork, Frits asked if he didn't like rice.

"No. Never have. At home we ate mostly typical Dutch food."

"I don't think they'll feed us potatoes and roast beef here," Frits said.

"I never give up hope." Gijs was annoyed at Frits and shoved his portion onto Frits's plate. "You can have it," he said. Frits looked up at him, shook his head, and stuffed the food into his mouth.

Gijs went upstairs and lay down on his cot, tired, hungry, and out of tune with his surroundings. It was too bad, he thought, the Japanese hadn't sent him to the camp where Pieter Donk was. The boys here, who'd suddenly been elevated to the ranks of men, did not seem half as mature to him as Pieter, who usually tried to find solutions to the problems that had been heaped upon them since the Japanese won the war.

The murmur coming from the next cot over made him look up. Beads on a bracelet slipped one by one through Father van Gasteren's fingers as he recited words Gijs could barely hear. This intrigued him enough to take his mind off his loneliness. Even though his parents listed themselves as Protestant on official papers, they seldom set foot in a church. From their home in Soerabaja, the loud call to prayer could be heard daily, and he'd watched men take off their shoes and enter the domed building on his way to school. It was a church for Muslims, his father had said, in a tone that made him understand that it was not a place he should enter. It somehow was also understood, back when they were still living in Holland, that Protestants didn't enter Roman Catholic churches. He only had a vague idea of what any church, temple, or mosque looked like on the inside.

The next morning, after the same unpalatable breakfast, he noticed Father van Gasteren standing on a part of the gallery that encircled the courtyard. Adorned with a beautifully embroidered shawl, the priest spoke to a small group of men facing him. Because he wasn't sure if he was allowed to be there, Gijs stood at a distance and listened. He caught words like hope and God's eternal love. There were many motions involved in the ceremony. From a crude wooden table, the priest took a cup and let each of the men, who knelt before him, take a sip from the cup. As he did this, he spoke some words softly, the same for every man, but Gijs could not understand it, for the priest spoke in a language he'd never heard before.

The first week was not even over, and he felt weak and sick. When a doctor came to hold office hours, he presented himself with complaints of dizziness and cramps in his stomach. The doctor asked for his name, and when Gijs told him, he looked up and said, "I know your mother and sister! They live on the Houtmanstraat, right?"

"Yes, doctor. May I ask how you know them?"

"I am also in Tjihapit, but I am allowed to get out of the camp and help here and there."

"Will you tell them I am here, but please don't tell them I am not feeling well. They'll just worry," Gijs said.

Before the doctor answered, he first examined him and asked pertinent questions.

"Look, Gijs," he finally said, "you simply have to eat more. You say you don't like rice, but that's all you're going to get here. You just have to make yourself get over your aversion of whatever they serve you. It won't change. Most likely it will get worse." The doctor sighed and pushed his hand through his graying hair.

"It's a tough situation we're in, but this I can assure you. If you don't eat, you won't walk out of this camp or any other camp."

"Yes, doctor," Gijs said, painfully aware he sounded meek.

The doctor put his hand on his shoulder in a fatherly gesture. "Gijs, promise me you will eat rice from now on. I will tell your mother that you're in this camp and that you're doing fine."

Gijs left relieved. Being regarded overnight as an adult had its pitfalls. Maybe it was easier, after all, to be treated as a child and be told what to do, like eating what you don't like. From now on he would pretend he was eating potatoes when they placed a ball of rice in his pan.

Lunchtime had already passed, so he went up to room six where four of his roommates had rolled up their bedding and sat on the floor playing a game of bridge. Stretched out on his own cot, he tried to call up the image of his father. It disturbed him that he just couldn't get Vader's face into focus. The trappings like his crisp white uniform, his shiny black shoes, and gold insignia were clear, but the details of his face eluded him. If someone would ask him what color eyes his father had, he could immediately answer, blue. Still, he didn't see those blue, intelligent eyes on the screen of his mind. Where would Vader be now? Still in a prison in Palembang? Had the Japanese found out he'd disabled the naval air bases on Java?

Gijs shivered in spite of the afternoon heat that was building up in the room. A Christmas tree replaced the vague image of Vader. A Christmas tree in January, as he remembered it lying on the side-walk in front of their house in Den Helder, undone of its glitter and decorations, left to wither. Done and over with. Turned from center of attention into garbage.

"Gijs," a voice close to him said. When he opened his eyes, he saw Father van Gasteren standing over him.

"I saved you a piece of *tempeh*."

"Oh, thank you. That's very kind of you."

"You've got to eat, Gijs. I noticed you weren't standing in line for food."

"I went to see the doctor. He told me the same thing." Gijs straightened up and ate the *tempeh*. Did he just say that to this stranger? Even though he'd firmly made up his mind he wasn't going to tell anyone?

"Good move!" the priest said. "Our bodies seem unhappy with the food we put into it, don't they? The inescapable truth is that we can't fast our way out of our predicament. It won't get us back to our old lives, and anyway, the Japanese would just shrug their shoulders and say that it's our own doing."

Gijs wondered what the proper way to address a priest was. Others called him father, so he guessed he should do the same.

"Father, I heard you speak to a group on the gallery the other day. You spoke of hope. How can you preach about hope when we are in an internment camp and have no idea for how long, or what's up for us next?"

"As long as we have faith, we can have hope," Father van Gasteren said, sitting on the side of his cot. "Saint Paul wrote to the Romans: 'Let hope keep you joyful; in trouble stand firm; persist in prayer.'"

"That's a tall order," Gijs said. "I know very little of the Bible. My parents are Protestant, but they didn't go to church very often. Religion is something I am aware of, but it wasn't a part of my upbringing, although my parents live by strong principles."

"I am sure they do, and you can be sure their strong principles find their basis in the Christian faith, whether they realize it or not."

"Probably. I remember my mother telling me that her father was a deacon at their church in Dordrecht."

"Our faith, Protestant as well as Roman Catholic, is rooted in the same God, who sent us his son Jesus to make us understand not only his commands, but also his eternal love for us. The New Testament, which deals with Jesus's life, is filled with hope, love, and eternal wisdom. Here, take my Bible and read St. Matthew 5, 6, and 7.

To learn what Jesus taught, that sums it up the best. I think you will recognize many of your parents' principles in his words."

Gijs took the Bible and opened it on the page Father van Gasteren had found for him. It was the Sermon on the Mount.

"How blest are those who know that they are poor; the Kingdom of Heaven is theirs. How blessed are the sorrowful; they shall find consolation. How blest are those of a gentle spirit; they shall have the earth for their possession." Farther on he read, "How blessed are those whose hearts are pure; they shall see God. How blessed are the peacemakers; God shall call them his sons."

He leafed through the pages and found, "Those who are sad shall be given courage and comfort," and "You have heard it said, 'love your neighbor and hate your enemy.' Well, I say love your enemies as well, for God makes the sun rise for evil men as well as good, and sends his rain upon honest men as well as dishonest."

How did this work? When the Japanese officer had slapped the soldier hard on one side of his face, the soldier could do nothing more than stand there and take it, because he knew he was the subordinate. What if a guard slapped *him* in the face? Would he offer him the other cheek? Could he love a man who was the enemy of his country? *God expects a lot from us,* Gijs thought. Then again, an eye for an eye and a tooth for a tooth would never resolve a conflict. It would go on and on. Another eye for another eye. A vicious circle. He pondered another line: "Those who make peace shall be known as the sons of God." What would it mean to be a son of God?

"Thank you," Gijs said to Father van Gasteren as he handed him back his pocket Bible.

"You're welcome, Gijs."

From then on, Gijs regularly went to the early morning gatherings on the gallery, and each time he moved a little closer. Inch by inch, he blended into the group. Many questions welled up during the miniature mass, as the priest spoke in Latin and performed rituals Gijs did not understand, but it felt good to belong to a group, to hear words of encouragement, to feel that he wasn't alone with his questions, and that, probably, there was a God he hadn't been paying attention to, something far bigger than the Japanese Army, something far deeper than just eating and drinking.

"Don't let this experience break your spirit," Father van Gasteren said in his short sermon. "Your spirit is not for the Japanese to break. Your spirit belongs to God. Rise above the humiliations you have to endure, help one another, love one another, and recognize the power of God's love that surrounds you when you open your heart."

Gijs felt as if his whole way of thinking was put on a different path. It gave him strength to belong to a group of men who spoke of hope, of helping, of love. One evening, after the 60-watt bulb was turned off and the room was supposed to be quiet, he whispered to his neighbor, "Father, I want to become a Catholic."

"It is easier to see God through a barbed wire fence, Gijs, than through a stained glass window," Father van Gasteren whispered back. "This is not a good time for you to make such a momentous decision. Just know that God lives in you and will sustain you through these difficult times. Sleep well."

Chapter 12

He'd hardly been at the *Topographische Dienst* a month, when Mr. van Dam told them after roll call one morning that they had forty-five minutes to get packed. When a series of trucks appeared, Gijs and his fellow *tawanans* stood at attention in the courtyard with their *barang* heaped on the gallery floor.

"They never tell you where they will take you!" Mr. van Dam said under his breath. "They love to spring a surprise."

Gijs remembered Pieter's mother saying the same thing. "Would they bring us back to Tjihapit?" he asked.

"I doubt it. Don't get your hopes up," Mr. van Dam whispered.

Some people around him thought they knew where they were headed, but nobody really was certain. It was a relief to be in an open truck, to look around and be able to conclude that the world beyond the bamboo enclosure was still intact, as if they'd been living in a burrow and had just crawled out. The trucks took them from one corner of Bandoeng to another, until they stopped in front of a sprawling complex of buildings.

"Oh my God," Mr. van Dam said. "Don't tell me they will put us in a House of Correction!"

"Do you know where we are?" Gijs asked.

"Sure. This is *s'Lands Opvoedings Gesticht*, LOG for short. This is where the government puts boys-gone-astray. Some of them never learn, so part of it is a prison."

"Oh great!" Frits said. "We're going to prison."

In front of the tall gate with a Roman arch, Soekono, the Japanese man who was the camp's boss, awaited them. He told them to behave or else, and to sort out their belongings. They did as they were told. The gate opened, revealing a central yard. Gijs glimpsed a pigeon house in the middle, a human touch that briefly lifted his spirits. They shouldered their cots, mattresses, and blankets, took up their suitcases, and faced their new reality with sweat pouring off their faces.

Each man was assigned to a room in one of the many buildings. Gijs found his. It was located on the far end of the yard, opposite the gate. The room was already full with wall-to-wall cots. He stood with his bed and bedding on his shoulder, not knowing where to set them down. Less than two feet of space separated the cots; the middle path was one-and-a-half yards wide at the most.

"Don't worry. We will fit you in. We do it all the time," a voice behind him said.

Gijs did not turn around for fear he would knock over the man speaking to him.

"Just put your *barang* down on another cot for the time being," the voice continued.

He let it fall and turned. What he saw was a man a bit shorter than himself, with dark hair and a resolute mouth. When Gijs looked into his eyes, they seemed to match the kindness of his words. The man asked his name.

"Gijs Bozuwa."

"Welcome, Gijs. I am Hinten. They call me Paatje Hinten here. I will be your room commander. Now, let's see how we can fit you in." And the man started to shove cots closer together until there was enough space for Gijs. It made for even tighter quarters, but Paatje Hinten didn't seem to mind.

It was late morning. After he'd organized his meager possessions into a *tempat,* Gijs went out to investigate the place. Over the past month, he'd come to terms with the fact that his life had changed drastically. It still felt like an adventure. The biggest part of the adventure was that from now on, no one was responsible for him but himself. The doctor had brought that home to him, and the priest had put his parents' outlook on life in the context of Christian values. Father van Gasteren had made him understand that what he'd often experienced, with some resentment, as excessive discipline, was really the mirror of his parents' essential integrity and compassion. The examples his parents offered were firmly embedded in his mind. He found strength in the gained insight, and he was grateful to the priest for having clarified it.

The LOG camp was big. The main buildings on each side of the central yard were L-shaped. Four were freestanding. Overcrowding was the norm. Forty people or more to a room squeezed together, neatly positioned, cot to cot, like chocolates in a box. When he'd asked Paatje Hinten how many people were in the camp, he said it varied, but there were at least fifteen hundred.

"We'll have to hang them from the ceiling if they bring in more," he said.

What was called a room was more like a barrack with thin walls. The government hadn't built luxury hotels for young criminals. There were no WCs, but between the solid camp enclosure and the backsides of the buildings were sheds with wooden swing doors that hovered over a narrow stream. On each side of the stream Gijs noticed footsteps cast in concrete at regular intervals. The strong suggestion, when he looked at it closely, was to place your feet in the concrete forms, hunch over and relieve yourself. The trickling stream took care of the rest, by floating the excretions downstream. He watched as a fellow *tawanan* threw a bucket of water after his bowel movement to help the process along. The natives performed this most human act by the sides of the *kali* without any wooden enclosure to keep themselves out of sight. He'd seen it many times. No wonder the rivers looked dark brown. Without shame and without fear of disease, they used the rivers as their sinks as well as their toilets. He'd never dreamed he would have to follow their example. His mother would be horrified.

If going to the bathroom was not as it had been at home, washing up wasn't either. At morning call, his roommates trooped to the wash place behind one of the buildings. It was a small yard with a concrete floor. A crude, large table stood in the middle of the floor.

A pipe with a faucet stuck out of the ground next to a large tub with a spout that constantly drained from the bottom. Towels and washcloths hung from lines that had been randomly strung from the building's gutters. The sound of water splashing as the men took turns sticking their heads under the running faucet wiped the cobwebs from Gijs's mind. He'd spent a restless first night. Not just the man sleeping next to him, but several men around him ground their teeth in their sleep, and it had kept him awake. The prospect of spending the day with uptight men and listening to their grinding at night had obsessed him. Relief came when Paatje Hinten got everyone out of bed at seven.

At eight, Paatje shouted, "Out in front." Gijs followed his roommates—there wasn't one boy among them—to the corridor where they assembled for roll call. The procedure was the same as at the *Topografische Dienst*. They stood at attention, they bowed, they called out their number in Japanese, and then the inspecting officer, who went from building to building with three armed soldiers in tow, dismissed them.

One volunteer went to pick up breakfast and returned with a basket. He handed each man a banana leaf in which a ball of rice had been steamed, and a boiled duck egg. This was more generous than what he'd had at the other camp. Other food was in the basket. They looked like small tiles. Some men ate them, while others passed them over with a look on their faces of "you must be kidding." He got curious and asked his neighbor what it was.

"It's some native delicacy, if you can call it that," the man said.

"What's in it?" Gijs asked.

"God only knows. It tastes awful."

"It's made of steamed *sing-kong* and mixed with *goela-djawa*," Paatje said.

"You would know," the man said to Paatje. "You lived in the jungle." This was not said with admiration.

"Yes, I did, and it comes in good stead right now," Paatje said.

"What did you do in the jungle?" Gijs asked.

"I am a grade school teacher and I went into the hinterland to teach native children, in one of those way-out places on Java. I lived in the *kampong* and married a beautiful woman there. The Japs thought that was all good and well, but I had white skin, so I got marched off to this camp like all other white men."

The simplicity with which Paatje summed up his life was impressive. With one stroke he leveled the barriers by stating they were all white and that was why they were here. None of them had a special lever they could push to set them apart or get them out of internment. Gijs had never met anyone like Paatje.

The word *goela-djawa* had made his mouth water. It was derived from sugar cane, and Kokkie used to make the most wonderful dark brown pudding from it. He took his chances on the *sing-kon*. It was some sort of root in the ginger family of plants, Paatje said. It really wasn't bad.

After breakfast, on their way to outside to anywhere away from that overstuffed room, Paatje told Gijs he wanted to talk to him. Gijs followed him into the corridor.

"I wanted to tell you," Paatje said, "that there are several good teachers in this camp. The Japs have forbidden any form of education. You know that, of course. We're finding ways around it. The rule is that no more than five people may congregate, except for standing in line for food or roll call. So the teachers can only take on three or four pupils at a time. I think it would be a good idea for you to see if you can join. Contact Mr. van Meir. He teaches math. Good luck."

Gijs watched Paatje as he walked away. A strange nickname, Paatje. It meant little father. He wondered if someone had given the name to him in the jungle out of affection, or if his roommates had stuck it on him because he was indeed small and their boss. Regardless, he liked the man. It might be a good idea to take his advice. So much precious time had been lost already.

Gijs found Mr. van Meir sitting on his cot in room 26. He'd been the principal of a Bandoeng high school. He asked Gijs if he had any idea what he wanted to be. An officer in the navy, Gijs replied. Mr. van Meir arranged for him to join a three-pupil group studying astronomy, and added, "If you own something you can sit on, bring it."

"I have a canvas tripod," Gijs said.

In his first few days at the camp, Gijs discovered that boys his age had been sprinkled over the various rooms. That way they could be better supervised. He looked for Frits and found him at the other end of the camp. Like himself, he was the only boy in the room.

When he asked Frits how he was doing, the other boy quickly replied that he was bored.

"The men in my room can only think of playing bridge, and then afterward they accuse each other of making stupid mistakes. Boy, do they know how to hash and rehash! Sometimes I listen to them and wonder what they were like in real life."

"Real life?" Gijs said. "Maybe this is real life."

"What do you mean?"

"Most of these men were in positions of power. It's easier to hide your shortcomings when you're the boss and nobody can tell you to your face that you're a bastard."

"I guess so," Frits said. "When I stood in line for the midday meal yesterday, I saw somebody try to get an extra portion by intimidating the boy in front of him, but he was caught by an older gentlemen behind him, who really let him have it. Later, they told me the first man had been a prominent banker in Batavia. I was shocked."

"Yes, I bet," Gijs said. "Hey, did you know they play handball here at four in the afternoons? Let's get a little exercise that's more fun than cleaning toilets!"

Frits laughed. "See you at four, Gijs."

At one end of the yard there was room for playing handball. A mixture of boys and men had started a rather listless game. Gijs and Frits watched, mingling with the older men who leaned against the wall of one of the buildings, smoking cigarettes.

"How long have you been at LOG?" one of them asked.

"One week," Frits answered.

"I thought so," the man said. "You're still strapping young men. Those over there are beginning to show the lack of nourishment."

The curls of smoke from the man's cigarette tickled Gijs's nose. He moved on to another small group. These men were discussing the prospects of the Allies ending the war.

"A few more months and we'll be out," one man said. "Mark my words. The Americans are retaking the Philippines, and we'll be next."

Gijs was stunned. How could anyone say with conviction that they would be liberated soon? Did they have a radio in this camp? Where did these rumors come from? He listened to their suppositions, their complaints about the food, how unjust the Japs were, and so on. These men did not for a moment doubt that it had been their right to be masters of this land, and they had barely adjusted to the fact that the war had displaced that right. They fully expected it to be restored and their freedom regained, and they counted on the Allies to do it soon. Gijs wondered if they really believed these rumors, or if believing them was a way to keep going.

Frits elbowed him, and they joined the players for a while till mealtime, kicking the volleyball over an imaginary net.

As he was eating the evening meal on his cot, Gijs noticed that the man across from him was cutting the minuscule piece of meat on his plate with a knife. This was intriguing, because knives were not allowed at camp. The guards would have taken it away at arrival.

"How did you get that knife?" Gijs asked.

"I made it," the man said. His name was Piet.

"You made it? How?"

"That's a long story. In peacetime, there was a trade school here to teach the delinquents crafts. Everywhere I looked, I saw pieces of metal, wood, planks, and old tires. Stuff I could use to make things with. We found a piece of rails too. That served as an anvil. I put a thick piece of wire on it and flattened it into a blade with a railroad spike. For the handle I found a stick. So, now I have a knife!"

Piet held it up and waved it at Gijs as if it were a medal he'd won at the cattle show.

"That's impressive," Gijs said, and he meant it.

"If you think this is impressive, let me show you the eye glasses I made." He took off his spectacles and held them up.

"My frame broke and I was desperate. With another *tawanan* I found a piece of steel wire and we fashioned this beauty. It was quite a job, but we managed. See, we flattened the wire to make the nose pieces."

It didn't escape Gijs how cheerful the man seemed. Quite different from the somber tone he'd overheard at the ball field. People who had found something to do seemed happiest here. On his way back from playing handball, he'd taken his time and noticed that in room 33, the walls were hung with charcoal drawings. They depicted camp life and they were very good. Mr. Liesker was the artist. In peacetime he'd been the art teacher at a high school in Bandoeng. With the portraits he drew of people, he bartered for food or for repairs of worn sandals and clothes.

A few weeks went by. More boys arrived, younger than he had been when he was summoned back in February. The Japanese must be lowering the age threshold, he thought with disgust. The overcrowding got worse and the meals did not improve, in quality or quantity, but none of that was as hard to take as the lack of stimulus. The days crawled by at a snail's pace with the same routine of roll call twice a day and food being doled out at regular intervals. Gijs wondered if the Japanese guards knew that the worst punishment they doled out was boredom. He was thinking of taking up the game of bridge and was hunting for someone to teach him. Steady partners had already formed and it was hard to get in, but one day he came across Mr. van Dam, his previous room commandant, and he took the time to introduce Gijs to the game. The drawback of playing bridge was that he could only play it with older men, most of whom were depressed, but at least it was a way to spend time.

Then an epidemic of dysentery broke out. It raged through the camp. In his mind, Gijs heard his mother say, "Are you surprised?" No, of course not, he answered her. All his life his mother had warned against unsanitary conditions. She was petrified of them. That was why she never shopped at the *pasar* and why he hadn't been allowed to eat from the small stands by the side of the road, where natives cooked wonderfully smelling delicacies like sateh on a stick. He'd been jealous of his friends who'd stop on their way home from school in Soerabaja. For a few cents, they ordered a banana leaf with *nasi* rice and ate it leaning on their bikes.

It was no wonder, considering the way people had to relieve themselves in an open gutter, that at some point there would be an outbreak of inflamed guts and ferocious bouts of diarrhea. The only wonder was that it hadn't happened earlier. The epidemic created an untenable situation in the rooms. The nights became a cross to bear for everyone as men stumbled through the narrow paths between the cots on their way to the latrines, leaving a trail of what they could not keep in. The smell alone was enough to keep everyone awake.

The Dutch camp leadership decided to do something about the situation. The men with the worst cases would be brought to the sickbay near the camp's entrance, where the doctor's office was. The room commandants were told to provide volunteers to help care for these patients, who were getting too weak to help themselves.

Paatje Hinten called for attention during morning roll call, as they stood lined up in the corridor in front of their room, ten to a row. Gijs stood in the second row.

"Who will volunteer?" Paatje asked.

It was very quiet.

There were no takers.

Chapter 13

Paatje looked into the faces of his roommates, but all the men around Gijs stared down at their toes. These men, who had chosen him as their room commander, couldn't meet his eyes. Paatje didn't fit the model of men Gijs had met through his parents. His father's friends had mostly been officers with a sprinkling of successful colonialists, the kind of men he now shared intimate quarters with. Paatje Hinten, as far as he could tell, was not a typical colonialist. He'd gone into the jungle to teach the natives. He'd married a Javanese woman. Success in business had not been his aim in life. Yet it was Paatje who'd surfaced as the best choice when an effective room leader had to be chosen.

Again, Paatje put the request to the men. Again, dead quiet. Gijs began to feel very uncomfortable. He didn't know what to do. Was he old enough to help out in an infirmary? Doing what?

"All right, you lousy wimps," Paatje said, "if you're too selfish to go out and help others, then I don't want to be your room commandant any longer. I will go myself."

Gijs felt pressure building up in his chest. He couldn't stand the tension a moment longer.

"Then I will go with you!" he yelled to his own surprise.

Paatje turned around, because he'd already started on his way, and said, "Do you know what it means, Gijs?"

"I'll find out," Gijs said, and followed Paatje Hinten.

Together they walked over to the gate area where the doctor's office was, the infirmary next to it. A Dutch doctor in a white coat answered the door.

"We're volunteering," Paatje said simply.

The doctor looked them over and asked their names.

"Call me Paatje Hinten. Everybody else does. And this is Gijs Bozuwa."

"Mr. Hinten," the doctor started. Apparently, he had difficulty calling Paatje by his nickname. "I would like you to help me in the outpatient. There's a room where you can sleep. Gijs, how old are you?"

"I am seventeen, doctor."

"I need extra help in the ward. That means you will be emptying bedpans. Are you up to that task? Now is the time to say no. I would forgive you."

"It's probably not much worse than cleaning toilets and I've done quite a bit of that," Gijs said.

"All right, you will work with Keereweer. He is a medic. He will tell you what to do."

Paatje said he was going back to get his stuff and set it up in his new quarters, and suggested Gijs come along with him and do the same.

"The doctor didn't say anything about me sleeping here."

"I bet they'll want you close by. I would take my chances, if I were you," Paatje said.

Gijs thought it over. It was not terribly enticing to go back to that room filled with depressed, older men who played bridge all day. Besides, he was still angry with them for not helping out Paatje. Even if emptying bedpans were not something to look forward to, it would not be boring. He was ready for a change.

Keereweer was standing in front of the infirmary's door when they returned. He was tall and muscular, his head covered with wavy blond hair. Gijs immediately recognized in him the petty officers who served under his father. Competent, tough, authoritative, and unsophisticated, like Willem, who'd told him to polish the brass on the speedboat at the navy yard in Soerabaja. If he had learned anything in his life thus far, it was that orders are given and taken. No ifs or buts.

Keereweer looked at Gijs's *barang*.

"I see you have committed yourself. You don't even know what it's like!"

"Can't be worse than cleaning toilets," Gijs said.

"OK, you can sleep behind there," Keereweer said.

Gijs glanced into the ward. Twenty cots were lined up against the walls on both sides, with a path in the middle that was more generous than in the room he'd just vacated. On each cot lay a patient who looked sicker than anyone he'd ever seen. At the very end of the ward was a curtain. It separated two cots from the rest. Gijs stuffed his own folded cot under the one he was assigned. He would need it if the Japanese made him move to yet another camp.

"What I want you to do first," Keereweer said, "is watch me."

Gijs positioned himself so he could take in the entire ward. Keereweer went over to a patient who had called out for help. On his way he fetched a bedpan from a stack on the far end of the room. All of them were white enamel with a narrow blue rim. With more tenderness than Gijs had expected, Keereweer placed the pan underneath the man and waited till he was done. Just as tenderly, he moved him on his side, took the bedpan away, and washed the patient. So, that was what he would have to do. Well, he'd wanted change. He got it.

"Do you think you can handle this?" Keereweer asked.

"Sure," Gijs said bravely.

"Good. Follow me. I'll show you where to dump."

Carrying two bedpans, Keereweer kicked the door. It swung open on its two-way hinges. The WC was down the hall. Gijs noticed with relief that it had an honest to goodness ceramic toilet bowl that could be flushed. He spent the rest of the day walking back and forth with the bedpans Keereweer handed him. It was a smelly job, but not boring. Enough was going on in the infirmary to keep his mind on other things than flushing the toilet. The outpatient area next door was busy. The row of men waiting in line never seemed to thin out. At the very end of the building the infirmary was in, was the kitchen. Across from it was an outdoor kitchen with three army kitchen wagons parked to the side. It might not be a bad thing to live close to a kitchen, Gijs thought. Every job had its perks.

The next day, Keereweer put him to the test.

"Looking is learning. You are now ready to help these men yourself," Keereweer said. Gijs could not help but notice the wicked little smile that played around his mouth.

"Of course!" Gijs said, and returned the smile. He had begun to like Keereweer. Last night they'd played cards before they turned in.

The first patient he approached with a bedpan was too sick to know whether he was Keereweer or somebody else. The man kept his eyes closed while Gijs told him he would wash him. No response. Feeling very much like a novice, he threw back the sheet and lifted the patient up. He was appalled. The man was so thin, Gijs felt bones where he expected solid flesh.

A week passed. He got into the rhythm of maneuvering bedpans under grateful men and cleaning them up afterward. But he wondered why some patients could walk out relatively unscathed after a few days of care, while in others, the dysentery gripped them unrelentingly. He posed these questions to Keereweer.

"Because they came into camp with chronic diseases," he answered.

"Like what?"

"Like ulcers, emphysema, heart failure."

"Heart failure? If their heart fails, wouldn't they be dead by now?" Gijs asked.

"Call it a weak heart, then."

"How can you tell?"

"With a stethoscope. You can hear signs of fluid in the lung's basis, and you can tell by swelling of the ankles."

"What does fluid in the lungs have to do with heart disease?" Gijs asked.

"Because the heart is not pumping the blood around efficiently."

Gijs began to look at the patients differently after the word heart failure had fallen into the conversation. When he'd followed Paatje impulsively to the infirmary, he'd thought he would be scrubbing floors or some such thing. The dysentery was an epidemic. It would pass, like an outbreak of the flu in Holland. It had turned out differently, though. These men might die, an aspect of the job he hadn't foreseen. You went to an infirmary or a hospital to get better. The doctor who'd told him to eat rice or he wouldn't walk out of that camp had probably meant just that: when you don't eat, you die. At the time, it hadn't made him think of death. He'd thought of sickness. Would he be able to stand the sight of one of these men dying? Maybe he should quit. Maybe being bored was not as bad in comparison.

One of the patients called. "Water. Please give me water," he whispered.

Gijs got some, but the man could not get the glass to his mouth without help, so Gijs knelt beside the cot, raised the man's head, and poured some water into his mouth. Half of it spilled onto his neck, but the patient opened his eyes and said thank you.

How could he quit? For all its agony, its ghastly odors, its suffering, there was something about the ward that made him want to hang on. He thought of the conversation he'd had with Frits about real life. Their lives in a man's internment camp were nothing more than a juvenile fantasy. No school, no home, no family. That's what it had seemed like in the first few weeks, but here in the infirmary, it was different. The patients' suffering was real. Here there was work to do.

And then there was Keereweer.

"Good morning, gentlemen, here is your coffee. As black as the night and as sweet as a woman's love." Every morning he could be counted on to say this with cheer in his voice, as he kicked the swinging door open and walked in with a tray full of steaming cups of coffee.

The stories he told Gijs as they took a break for breakfast, sitting on their cots, were spicy. It wasn't hard to get him to talk. He was a marine, he said, and before the war he'd spent most of his time on war exercises in the jungle. He confessed he'd been "rough" with the native women. "I wasn't respectful, Gijs," he said. "I'm ashamed now that I look back on it, but that's what us soldiers did."

Cleaning their plates to the last kernel of rice while the patients, on the other side of the curtain, gave a flatulent concert, Keereweer would remark, "They may pass gas on the rim of my plate, but they're not allowed to spatter!"

This was man's talk. Even though he was considered a man by Japanese standards, when Gijs heard remarks like this, he knew he had a lot to learn before he could feel like a man. The men who'd served under his father had never talked to him this way.

It would be better, Gijs thought, not to tell Keereweer that his father was in the navy; that before the war every man would scramble onto the deck and salute when the whistle blew to announce the commander's arrival on board. He'd only been a kid then, walking behind Vader on the gangplank, but it had left a lasting impression. His father had authority, with golden stripes on his epaulettes to prove it, but Gijs had never seen that authority tested. Now his father had been reduced to the status of prisoner, as if the ship of authority had capsized. Yet Gijs was convinced that wherever Vader was—still on Sumatra or taken to some other place—Vader would always be in command of himself, no matter how his guards might try to cow him. "Don't let this break your spirits," Father van Gasteren had said. "Your spirits belong to God,"

Another memory popped up. He was back in Holland, in Den Helder, the navy base. Their house was on a canal. Mostly officers lived there. On the other side of the canal stood smaller houses, and behind them was an open field. From his bedroom window he could see boys playing soccer in the field. He didn't know them, but he was dying to play with them, so he walked over. He came home sweating, with dirty knees and shoes with grass stains, and had to answer his parents' questions about where he'd been. Playing soccer across the canal, he'd said. He was aghast when his father made him promise never to do that again. Officers' children didn't play with the children of petty officers, Vader said. Gijs asked why. "Because I say so," his father said. Gijs hadn't even known they were the sons of petty officers, and he couldn't see what difference it made. Not then, not now.

Here he was, sitting on Keereweer's cot while they ate their meager meals. How life had changed. The *heiho*, who walked around the yard with a wooden gun, preposterous in an ill-fitting Japanese uniform, had been given the authority to slap the faces of men, whose only sin was that they were white. He could beat them with his leather belt at the slightest provocation. What justice was there in that kind of authority? How had he earned it? At least Vader knew how to sail a ship, and Keereweer knew how to handle patients. They deserved to wear the mantle of authority.

Gijs looked around the small space he shared with Keereweer. His side cried out for some form of organization, even if he didn't own much of anything. Eating from a plate kept under your bed was like admitting your lifestyle had a taken a steep dive. If Piet had managed to fabricate a knife out of nothing, he might be able to help Gijs. He found Piet in the old workshop combing the floors for useful leftovers.

"Hey, Piet, can you help me put up some shelves? I mean, I don't have wood for shelves. Do you know where I can find some?"

"Hey, Gijs, how are you doing in that sickbay? Aren't you coming back to our room?"

"No, I don't think so. There's a lot to do down there."

"I don't see how somebody your age can enjoy being in that stink hole."

"Oh, you get used to it," Gijs said. He didn't want to insult Piet by saying that no way would he go back to that stodgy old room. "How is the room faring without Paatje?"

"We chose a new leader. A man who used to be in shipping. The Japs are giving us interesting assignments. Yesterday we were told to catch flies."

Catch flies? To eat?

"No! To stem the spread of dysentery. That's after we were told to take the WC doors off their hinges. That's the only privacy we had! Gone! The Japs are scared stiff of disease, so they give out these wacky orders. Okay, let's see what we can find in the way of wood. And nails, I presume?"

Piet looked behind a workbench, saying it was where he hid anything useful he found. He held up an irregularly shaped piece of wood and asked if it would work for Gijs.

"I think so," Gijs said.

They walked over to the infirmary together, Gijs holding the plank under his arm and Piet carrying a few nails and the railroad spike that served as hammer. It didn't take him long to fasten the wood to the wall above his cot.

"Well, I have to say this for your new home," Piet said. "You have more room than I have in mine, but, phew, I could not stand the smell or being with sick people all the time. Good luck, Gijs." Piet slapped him on the shoulder and left.

Gijs put on the shelf his fork and spoon beside the little pan that served as his plate. Moeder had given him Vader's razor and brush, even though when he left Tjihapit, he didn't have more than some fuzz on his cheeks. He ceremoniously laid those next to his toothbrush and what was left of his bar of soap. His three sets of underwear, shorts, and shirts he left in the suitcase, as well as the three notebooks and pencils Janneke had slipped in at the last moment. Better leave those out of sight, he thought.

Keereweer pulled the curtain back and motioned him to come out. A patient was stumbling into the ward, supported by a doctor.

"See if you can get some water into him," Keereweer said.

Gijs came back with a glass of water. As he approached the new patient, he recognized him. It was Mr. van Dam.

Chapter 14

The instant recognition of Mr. van Dam jolted Gijs. Until now, lifting a patient up on a bedpan and washing his behind afterward was simply an acceptable routine, an impersonal deed, bearable as long as there was no personal connection. A thin line separated caring and taking on someone else's suffering. So far, he'd been able to maintain a safe emotional distance, but Mr. van Dam was someone he knew and liked. It felt different.

"Keereweer," the doctor said. "This patient suffers from dysentery."

"We'll take good care of him, doctor," Keereweer said. "The usual?"

"Yes."

Gijs was told to make some strong tea. He knew getting water into a patient was difficult. Would strong tea be easier?

When Gijs returned with the tea, Keereweer was holding an instrument Gijs hadn't seen before. It resembled an injection needle with a blunt end.

"What's that?" he asked.

"That's to put the tea you just made into the patient," Keereweer said with his customary wicked smile. "You'll see."

He approached Mr. van Dam's cot and told him to roll over on his side.

"This is how we serve tea around here," he said. "Gijs, get a bedpan and a towel. All right, Mr. van Dam, just lift up your bum and we will fix you up with some tea. The best tea you ever had. Do you take it with or without sugar?"

Keereweer stuck the enema in Mr. van Dam's anus and pushed the liquid in. Mr. van Dam groaned..

"All for the good, Mr. van Dam. Hold on as long as you can. We want the tea to shake hands with your enemies inside before we let them all out into the wide world."

Watching, Gijs felt the pain he knew Mr. van Dam must be experiencing. He couldn't stand it and walked away, praying that Keereweer wouldn't call him back to do the cleaning up. As he sat down on his own cot and thought about how ill prepared he was to be this close to sickness and suffering, memories of being a patient himself flooded through him.

At the time Vader had been stationed in The Hague, as the aid to the Minister of Defense. A terrible earache in both ears had landed Gijs on the operating room table for a double mastoidectomy. When he came out, his head was wrapped in bandages with only an opening for his eyes. The pain was incredible. The doctor said to his parents, "He will probably be deaf, but at least he is not dead." The first thing he'd done was grab for his ears and yank at the bandages, so the nurses put stove pipes on his arms and tied them to the sides of his bed. Moeder was with him night and day, but he remembered how ill at ease Vader had been. It wasn't hard to see he wanted to get out of the sickroom as fast as he reasonably could, but he gave Gijs a wonderful thing to look forward to: he would fly over the hospital in a zeppelin. The nurses had to be convinced that their young patient was not hallucinating. Moeder told them that her husband was with a special party that had been invited to make the zeppelin's maiden trip. Only half-convinced, the nurses tucked him in a blanket and brought him to a large balcony. He was so excited when he saw the improbable flying monster that looked like a long, thick cigar, the nurses had to hold him down.

That was the only trip to a hospital he could remember. Nobody in his family had ever needed to be hospitalized. Both his parents hated disease. While Moeder was petrified of infection and contagion, Vader was irritated by it. But both believed disease was something you avoided. You didn't talk about. If he or Janneke coughed,

Vader would tell them to stop, even during a bout with the whooping cough.

Sitting on his cot, Gijs thought it over. He had a choice. He could say to Keereweer that he was sorry, but taking care of a patient he knew was more than he could bear and he would go back to his old room. There must be other people from other rooms who could volunteer, although there was no evidence of that. But could he bear to leave Keereweer and trade him for the roommates who wallowed in their own distress? A nagging feeling of guilt turned the question of choice into self-examination. Wouldn't he be a coward if he left? Looked at in that light, he knew he would stay.

Mr. van Dam didn't recognize him for several days. He was in another world with his eyes closed. The patient next to him fared even worse. Something besides dysentery had taken a hold of him and he was going downhill fast. Gijs dreaded the prospect of the man dying. He'd never seen a dead person before, and it was clear to him that this would be his first. The anticipation made him tense. The doctor had examined the patient and given Keereweer permission to administer some pain-killing medicine. When is that final moment? Gijs wondered. Dying, it had always seemed to him, was bound to be a violent event. You couldn't leave this life without putting up a fight, without kicking or screaming. On his way back from the WC with the bedpans, he noticed Keereweer standing next to the man's cot. He bent over, pulled the patient's right eyelid up, and touched the cornea with his index finger.

"That's how you can tell a patient has crossed over to the other side," he said. "If he were still alive, he would react."

Death had not stirred up the drama Gijs had expected. He looked at the man who'd "crossed over," and a great sadness suffused him. Who was this man and what sort of life had he led? Was he married? Did he have family? If he did, how would they find out he'd died, that he'd slipped away, lying on a cot among sick people without the solace and support of anyone? He felt remorse that he hadn't paid more attention, but how do you connect with someone who is

dying? He stood looking at the dead man's face for a while. It was neither peaceful nor agonized, neither old nor young. It looked utterly
exhausted. So many thoughts rushed at him, and even more questions.
Keereweer had said, "He's crossed over," in an offhand manner.
Did he believe in another side? Gijs missed Father van Gasteren,
who could have given him some clue, even though Gijs doubted
he could fully accept whatever the priest's explanation would have
been. Perhaps there wasn't any. You lived and you died. Who knew?

"We won't throw a sheet over him," Keereweer said. "That's disturbing for the others. Go next door and ask the doctor to come.
He has to pronounce him."

An hour later, a cart that looked uncannily like the one he'd used
with Pieter Donk stood parked at the gate. On the wooden planks
between the two very large wheels lay the wrapped body of the man
who'd crossed to the other side. As a Japanese guard wheeled the
cart away, a shiver raced down Gijs's spine. A life that had ended too
soon was being carted off by an indifferent foreign soldier. It could
happen to any of them. He wished he knew where his father was.
At least he could be sure that his mother and sister were in Tjihapit.
They'd written a postcard. It had been no more than a sign of life,
written in Maleis, as required by the Japanese authorities. Dutch
was a dead language, as far as they were concerned. Every card or
letter was censored.

Paatje Hinten spotted him and walked over.

"You look too serious for a seventeen year old, Gijs," he said.

"I know. I've never felt so serious in my life."

"You need to come up for some air."

"It got to me this afternoon, I guess." Gijs didn't feel like elaborat-
ing. Paatje didn't press further. "How's it going with you, Paatje?"

"All right. I don't think I'm cut out for doctor's assistant, but it
will do. I've started on a project in the off-hours. I'm working on
a World Council idea, a forum where all nations can mediate their
differences."

"Good God, that's quite an undertaking, Paatje."

"It's a better way of spending idle time than fuming about the Japs," Paatje said. "By the way, Gijs, I think you should go back to getting lessons. You've done your duty here."

"I don't want to go back to that room. No way."

"You don't have to. I'm sure you can stay in the infirmary, but you don't have to work all day. The worst of the dysentery epidemic is over now. You're seventeen. Don't let this time go by. Someday we'll get out of this mess and you'll have to find work that's more than carrying bedpans."

Later in the day, Mr. van Dam surprised Gijs when he went over to take care of him by saying, "How's your bridge game these days, Gijs?"

"Not very exciting, Mr. van Dam. My partners here aren't a terribly lively bunch."

Mr. van Dam smiled. "You thought I didn't know you were here, did you?"

"You seemed pretty unaware of anything around you. Are you feeling better? Can I get you something to eat?"

"That would be a miracle."

"I'll try to snatch some rice. We're next to the kitchens."

"I am glad there's a bonus to being a volunteer in the infirmary," Mr. van Dam said. "You look like you've done this work before."

"I do? Not even close," Gijs said.

He went to the outpatient section to ask Keereweer if Mr. van Dam was ready for some rice. Before he could ask, though, Keereweer told him he needed Gijs's help in pulling a tooth.

"What do you want me to do?"

"Hold his head."

Keereweer told Gijs to sit in a chair. A middle-aged man sat on the floor in front of him; Gijs was to hold his head in his lap and keep it still. Keereweer sat on another chair, a dental instrument in his hands.

"Sorry, Mr. Klaassen. You're not in a dentist's office, but don't worry, I'm real handy with this tool. Done it many times in the jungle."

With a fragment of a broken mirror, he looked in Mr. Klaassen's mouth.

" Okay, which tooth is it? Oh, it's a molar. That makes it easier. Oh, and I see you've got gold in it. The Japs love gold. You can use it to trade!"

He sprayed a stream of ethyl chloride into Mr. Klaassen's mouth, which would freeze it at least a little bit. Gijs expected a fight to hold the man's head still, but Keereweer was so fast, almost sneaky, that the molar came out with one firm yank.

"Here, Gijs, use this gauze to stop the bleeding. Press your finger hard on the hole."

Mr. Klaassen was given his valuable molar with the gold in it and told not to eat for the rest of the day.

"Leave that roast beef alone for a while!" Keereweer called after him.

"I'd really come to ask if Mr. van Dam can have some rice," Gijs said.

"Sure. Are you good at stealing? See if you can get somebody to give you some in the kitchen."

Gijs had walked by the kitchen many, many times on his way to emptying the bedpans. In all his life, he'd never held so much respect for what went on in a kitchen. The *tawanans* who worked there held the keys to the food supply for hundreds of men. Of the various chores that needed to be performed in the camp, helping in the kitchen was the plum everyone was after. The closer you could get to the source, the better. Working in the kitchen was definitely more fattening than keeping the rooms and toilets clean. As Gijs stood in the open kitchen door, he noticed a tall, muscular boy about his own age chopping vegetables. Memories of standing at the side of the swimming pool in Soerabaja flooded his mind, and with them a deep feeling of inadequacy. Because he was not allowed to swim with his head underwater ever since his mastoidectomy, whenever they went to the pool, his mother watched over him like a Doberman. To dunk someone's head underwater and hold it there for an uncomfortable while was his classmates' favorite pastime. He felt like a momma's boy, having to say he couldn't get into the pool with them.

The boy in front of him was not in a bathing suit, and swimming was not the issue here. It was just that working in the kitchen and having a well-fed body was more macho than carrying stinky bed-pans back and forth.

"Hello," he said. "Could you spare a little rice for a patient?"

"You're working in the infirmary, right? I've seen you walk by here," the boy said.

Gijs tried not to cringe. "They needed people to help out when the dysentery epidemic broke out."

After looking at him for a moment, the boy took the small bowl Gijs had brought and walked over to a huge cooking pot. He glanced around to see if anyone was watching, then he quickly lifted the lid and used the bowl as a scoop. It was done in less than a minute. As he returned the bowl to Gijs, he winked at him. Gijs knew not to profusely thank the boy lest he be caught by other *tawanans,* but a scoop of rice was a huge present. On his way back to Mr. van Dam with his trophy in his hand, he reflected that he'd unfairly pegged the boy. Couldn't a well-fed, macho boy have as much compassion as a skinny one?

That afternoon he set out to reconnect with his teacher. Unreal, he thought, that he, the pupil, was begging the teacher to give him schoolwork. He found Mr. van Meir sitting on his cot with a group of other men. They'd arranged their cots in a circle. He hesitated, uncertain if he should interrupt the conversation or come back another time. But Mr. van Meir gestured to him to join the group. He fell into the middle of a discussion about how they could get the Hungarian musicians among them give a concert. First, they would have to convince the Hungarians, and second, the Dutch camp commandant. Most importantly, they had to get permission from the Japanese camp commandant. Gijs was surprised to hear there were musicians from Hungary among them. Someone explained that they had fled Europe just before the war broke out, seeking out the Dutch East Indies in their flight from the Nazis. They'd played gypsy music in the hotels to make money. At least one of them had managed to bring his violin into the camp.

Gijs told them about the Japanese *econoom* who'd played classical music on the stolen piano across the street in the Jan Steenlaan. The Japanese liked classical music, he said. The group decided to risk failure. It was exciting for Gijs to be privy to such an uplifting conversation, and to know that not everyone had let his mind go into hibernation. Men with a plan had it over the many who gave into the boredom. Like Paatje Hinten, the eternal idealist, who was concocting a plan to save the world.

Gijs looked around the room. The walls were dotted with narrow shelves that carried some last lifelines to civilization, like a razor, a deck of cards, or tin cans of food with brand names he recognized, though he doubted the original products were still in them. Laundry lines had been woven back and forth between the walls, and their bath towels hung like flags over their heads.

When the group broke up, Mr. van Meir turned to him. "I understand you volunteered for infirmary duty. Can you restart your lessons? Astronomy, wasn't it? You should also do geometry."

Gijs set up a schedule with him.

"Do you still want to be a navy officer, Gijs, now that you have been exposed to medicine?"

"My memories of what the navy was like are more exciting, Mr. van Meir. I think I will stick to my original plan."

Was it the navy or was it sailing the oceans? He remembered how the Indian Ocean had stretched out like a seamless sheet of paper without end, when they entered it after sailing through the Suez Canal. The bow of the ship had sliced the surface like a pair of scissors. The trip on the *Johan van Oldenbarneveld* from Genoa to Soerabaja had been exciting. Vader had taken him to the captain's hut and explained the instruments that determined their course and location. At night he had pointed out the stars and constellations.

When instruments fail, Vader had said, you've got to know the firmament. He and his father had hung together over the railing, in the daytime and at night. In silence they'd absorbed the immensity of the sky and the sea, and he'd felt his father's reverence for it.

Gijs walked back to the infirmary, excited to start again the lessons that would get him closer to his goal of attending the Royal Naval Academy in Den Helder after the war, whenever that would be. After all, wars wouldn't go on forever.

Chapter 15

Gijs fell into a different routine. With the worst of the dysentery epidemic over, Keereweer limited Gijs's involvement to helping with the early morning chores so he could spend more time outside of the infirmary.

Fresh air filled his lungs as he walked over the center courtyard and stopped in front of the pigeon cage, which was the only entertaining and decorative part at the LOG camp. He chuckled to himself. The pigeons were engaged in the same kind of competition for food as the *tawanans*. If one encroached on another's turf, it would pick at the other or, in defeat, flutter indignantly to a higher roost. At least, Gijs thought, the birds were having more fun in their imprisonment. He noticed the concentrated look of an obviously female pigeon sitting on her eggs. He would have to come back and see if her effort produced babies. Walking on, he took heart in the simple fact that there was still a world out there, that there were still leaves on the trees and birds singing in the branches.

Back to his schooling, he reconnected with the other boys, who gossiped in between lessons about the goings-on in the camp. They'd had had fun a few nights earlier, and they were still giggling about it. Gijs asked what they had done.

"There is a man in our room we cannot stand," said a boy named Fred. "He doesn't take care of himself. He stinks. He doesn't wash his clothes. Really, he's not fit to be around."

"So, what did you do about it?" Gijs asked.

"You know they took the doors off the latrines, don't you, and you know we're supposed to clean up by throwing a bucket of water afterward? Well, it was dark and we waited till Mr. F made his way to the latrine. We'd put a full bucket of water close by, and when he was in a squatting position with his feet in the concrete footsteps, we threw the water over him."

"And then you ran, I bet," Gijs said.

"We sure did!"

"Did he find out who did it?"

"Not yet. The older men in our room had just as hard a time living with him, so they pretended to see nothing and hear nothing."

At the end of one lesson, the teacher told Gijs to take advantage of the library.

"A library? Here in the camp?"

"Yes, believe it or not. Some people brought books. It wasn't really allowed, like we weren't supposed to bring paper and pencil, but many risked it anyway."

"Haven't the guards found it out yet?" Gijs asked.

"No. If the Japs didn't find the books when they entered camp, they kept them. The guards seldom come into our rooms. After a few weeks everyone knew their own book by heart, they'd read it so many times! We got the idea of putting them all together and starting a sort of lending library."

Gijs was directed to the secret "book place" and looked through the collection of pocket books that were easy to hide. It was like being in a candy store. He thumbed through the detective novels by Agatha Christie. *Appointment with Death* didn't attract him. He'd already had his appointment with death. He decided on *Evil under the Sun*.

Life in camp was bearable with a book to read and his mind engaged with geometry and astronomy. The food was terrible and scarce, that wouldn't change, but Mr. van Meir and his roommates had got permission for the concert, and it was held one Sunday evening. When the Hungarian violinist took up his bow, a benign silence fell over his audience of *tawanans,* who had been without radio and gramophone for as long as they had been behind barbed wire. Even the Japanese commandant and a few guards lurking in the background were entranced by the pure, exquisite notes the violinist brought forth from his instrument. His music created in Gijs an intense yearning for a life that had been taken for granted and seemed lost forever. At the end, more than a few men's eyes were glistening with tears.

Shortly after that, something completely unexpected happened. Japanese soldiers discovered a sanatorium for tuberculosis patients high up in the Preanger Mountains. The patients who were white were arrested and brought to the LOG internment camp. Obviously, they needed to be isolated from the other patients. Where to put them? The infirmary was on one side of the gate, and on the other side was a room with *tawanans* who had been and probably still were Nazi sympathizers. Foreseeing nasty fights, the camp leadership had wisely chosen to separate the Nazi sympathizers from the general population. The TB patients were put in a room next to them.

Keereweer had his hands full. He needed help. Gijs volunteered. There was so much to do. The patients were weak and needed help with eating and washing. Since there was no known cure for tuberculosis, the Japanese doctor issued strict rules in handling these contagious patients. Keereweer got after Gijs at every turn to use extreme caution and wash his hands often. Gijs did his best not to get too emotionally involved, but it was hard not to empathize with these poor men who might survive if they were someplace with optimal conditions, like fresh mountain air and good food, the very things lacking at the LOG. Their ages ranged from early twenty to forties, but he only knew that from the medical charts. Just looking at them, they could be any age. Men suffering from malnutrition— and they were all around him—didn't look like these patients, with their sunken cheeks and hollow looks. Skin over bone. Wasted away.

One day, Gijs was caring for one of the patients. Mr. Kramer was extremely weak. Keereweer didn't give him more than a few days. As Gijs fluffed up his pillows and helped him into an upright position, Mr. Kramer suddenly got a coughing fit and threw up blood all over Gijs. Keereweer shouted at Gijs to run out and get to the faucet. Gijs ran as fast as he could. Undressing, he let the cold water run over his hands, his arms, and his chest. Then he washed his shorts and ran naked through the infirmary to his cot for clean clothes. When he got back to the TB room, Mr. Kramer had died.

Years later, when Gijs had to have a routine X-ray taken, a calcified lesion appeared, a result of his exposure, but he had remained asymptomatic.

Keereweer began to involve Gijs more in the outpatient work. Paatje, who was still helping out, was nonetheless getting deeper and deeper into designing the ideal forum for nations to settle their disputes. At one point he was desperate, because he'd run out of paper, so Gijs gave him two of the three notebooks Janneke had slipped into his suitcase. Paatje spent most of his days thinking and writing. Nobody bothered him. Despite his proximity to the Japanese commandant's office, he went about his pursuit undisturbed.

Once a week, the Japanese doctor appeared and discussed the medical charts with the Dutch doctor. He usually brought medicine with him, but it was never enough. The demand outstripped the supply by far, and it forced the Dutch doctor to make excruciatingly difficult decisions.

Keereweer taught Gijs how to give injections. Arthritis was a common ailment, and it was treated with a calcium shot.

"Okay, Gijs, here's what you do," Keereweer said as a patient dropped his shorts and exposed his behind. " Give me that pen so I can draw where the optimal spot is to give the injection on this gorgeous behind. See, you make a triangle between the top of the hipbone and the point where the buttocks come together, and then put it a third of the way down. That is the area you shoot into." As he talked, he threw the injection needle into the man's buttock. "You can't go slow. No pussyfooting around."

"Can't I learn the throwing part on an object first?" Gijs asked. It was a daunting prospect to willfully stick a needle into a man's buttocks.

"I practiced on an orange, but I wouldn't know how to get hold of an orange here. Just decide you're going to do it and get it over with. It will get easier and easier. You'll see."

The next patient didn't know he was a guinea pig. He dropped his shorts and thought Keereweer was standing behind him. Gijs drew a deep breath and threw the injection needle into the man's muscle as if he were playing darts. It worked wonderfully well. It was rather fun, he thought. From then on, Gijs gave the arthritis shots. He quickly became adept, and Keereweer thought it was time to teach him how to give intravenous injections.

"You're not afraid of blood, right?" he asked, as he asked a patient to make a fist after he'd put a tourniquet high up on the man's arm. "See these wormlike bulges? Worms are great for fishing and they're the best for drawing blood. Get your needle in line with the worm and let it go into it in that direction. Draw back a little to make sure you haven't come out the other end. You've got to see blood, because you want to be sure you get the stuff into his bloodstream and not into some subcutaneous tissue."

Beads of perspiration trickled down Gijs's neck, but he was intrigued enough to want to do it. You never knew, he told himself, how it might come in handy down the line to know how to give an infusion.

Eventually, the intense exposure to so much disease and the deficient diet caught up with Gijs. He came down with bacillary dysentery and fell deathly ill. The pain in his stomach was searing, his diarrhea a bloody mess. Keereweer put him on the ward so he could keep an eye on him. Paatje spent more time in the outpatient to help Keereweer out, but Gijs was unaware of that. Like Mr. van Dam, he lay with his eyes closed and wondered if he was dying.

The pain didn't let up, and he could tell that Keereweer was getting worried about him. He called in the Dutch doctor several times, but the doctor couldn't offer an effective cure, though he knew what the cure was. A German researcher had won the Nobel Prize in 1939 for developing a sulfa product that cured bacterial infections selectively.

It was not widely available. Only the Germans and Japanese could put their hands on it.

One day the Japanese doctor appeared at Gijs's bedside, the Dutch doctor and Keereweer behind him. The Japanese doctor examined him. Gijs had always found it hard to read a Japanese person's face, and he was too sick to concentrate on the doctor, but he felt warmth radiating toward him. There must be kind Japs, he thought groggily. He hoped the man was a doctor first and foremost, and had been put in an officer's uniform to be sent off to Java, just like the *economen*.

After the doctors left, Keereweer came back with a big smile on his face, as well as a glass of water and a pill.

"We got it, Gijs," he whispered in his ear.

"Huh?"

"Cibasol. Here, put it in your mouth and take a drink of water. This will make you better fast."

He was right. In a few days the pain subsided and Gijs could hold on to fluids. As he improved, he realized the enemy had saved him.

Thirteen years later, when he married a young woman from Holland, who'd spent the war years under German occupation, he found out that the same drug had saved her life. In her case, it was blood poisoning. An Austrian officer had given the medicine to her father, who was a pharmacist. Both their lives had been saved by their enemies, and they never forgot it.

Chapter 16

"At the gate tomorrow morning at 9 AM. With your belongings packed. All of you."

The *tawanans*, all fifteen hundred of them, bowed, straightened up, and were dismissed.

It was January 19, 1944.

An uncomfortable question hung over the courtyard. Where would they be taken now? Thus far, moving meant going from a small place to a bigger one. More people, less room, less food. Murmuring voices faded into the twilight as men scurried to their rooms to get ready.

Keereweer was sitting on his cot, stuffing his duffel bag.

"Be sure to take your valuables, Gijs. I don't believe in giving a generous tip for lousy service."

"Don't worry. I've put the family silver in my pocket."

"We'll leave them our fancy furniture," Keereweer said, as he pulled the straps on his bag tight.

"What about the patients?" Gijs asked.

"They'll leave before we do."

Gijs looked into the infirmary. They had fewer patients after the bout with dysentery had quieted down. He checked to see if their belongings were ready to be taken. When he reached under one cot, his glance fell on a leather suitcase that was plastered with stickers from places like Genoa, Italy, Zurich, Switzerland, Paris, and London, even a sticker of the steamship that had brought this patient to the Indies. The man lay on his back, staring at the ceiling. What was he thinking? Gijs wondered. Would he be going back on an ocean liner someday? Would any of them? It was too scary a thought to pursue.

He walked into the outpatient. Kecreweer was cleaning out the place.

"No sense leaving them things we could use later," he said. "Here, take this nifty instrument to pull teeth with and put it with your family silver. You never know how it might come in handy. There are two. I'll take the other."

Looking around, Gijs felt a bit of nostalgia pulling at his heart. He'd come here wondering what he'd done to himself by volunteering. The putrid smells had nearly driven him out. Seeing people sick and dying was horrible. Yet being part of the care giving had fascinated him enough to keep him there. Was it because even if he could not find good answers to why innocent people had to suffer and die at the hands of bullies, he could take it as long as there was something he could do about it? The tools for giving care that Keereweer had shown him were like a shield against his own feelings of vulnerability. They allowed him to do something positive in the face of misery. Like his father, he felt better if he could act. Philosophizing had its place in life, but he would rather be on the side of problem solving.

It was total bedlam in the courtyard the next morning. A heap of rolled up *tikars*, folded cots, and suitcases lay in front of the gate. In the middle of the courtyard the *tawanans* stood at attention in rows of ten for morning roll call. The rumbling of trucks lining up in the street drowned out the shouts of the Japanese commandant. One man was missing from room 32, and the room leader was called forward to account for his charge and given a hard whack in the face. He stumbled and almost fell over, but he quickly recovered.

Gijs stood in line with Paatje and Keereweer. It was important not to get separated, but there was no guarantee that the three of them would get onto the same truck. So far, they were lucky that they stood in the same row of ten, because the guards were moving prisoners onto the trucks in groups of ten. A father and son got separated that way. They pleaded with the guards, but all the father accomplished was getting poked in his ribs with the barrel of a gun.

"We're not in a good mood, this morning, are we?" Keereweer said under his breath.

"They're nervous," Paatje whispered back. "Moving fifteen hundred people in one day can't be easy." He had a way of looking at the other guy's problem first.

"Their own doing," Keereweer said. "I'll offer to walk over by myself."

The sun was rising and burned into their skin. When Keereweer had told stories of being in the jungle before the war, he'd called the sun the copper bastard

"In Holland they can't get enough of it. Here you can't get away from it," he'd said.

For over two hours the sun baked them, until finally it was their turn. Keereweer jumped on first. Gijs was next. To his horror, he saw that Paatje was told to go onto the next truck. Gijs halted and turned back, wanting to haul Paatje over, but the guard saw it and slapped him in the face three times. He had no choice but to go back and sit down.

It wasn't a long trip. They were still in Bandoeng, and before he could orient himself, the truck stopped in front of an imposing military building several times the size of the LOG. Keereweer tarried as he got off the truck, and he, too, got slapped in the face and pushed inside. Gijs's fear that the three of them would be separated came true. For the three weeks they stayed at the Fifteenth Battalion, they looked all over for Paatje, but never found him. It was like trying to find a particular ant in an anthill.

"This is beginning to look like the annual cattle show," Keereweer said.

"Cattle show?"

"Yeah. We've been driven together like cattle from all over the place. These are not just *tawanans* from Bandoeng. You ask somebody where they're from and they say Soerabaja, Semarang, Batavia. That tells you something."

"Like what?"

"In the army we always knew something was afoot when they moved us. The Japs have a plan. There's a reason for this."

"Maybe, the war isn't going well for them," Gijs speculated.

After three weeks in the military barracks of the Fifteenth Battalion, they felt as if they'd been living at Amsterdam's Central Station, with trains only coming in and never going out.

"I hope they have a plan for us," Keereweer said. "This is getting too cozy here."

Indeed, they lived in a maze of corridors, and even for an internment camp, it had a temporary feel. Maybe it was because it was a military building.

Two days before Gijs's eighteenth birthday, they were put back on transport. Men who'd lived in the area longer than he had recognized that the trucks drove onto the Grote Postweg that led from Bandoeng to Batavia. They were unloaded in Tjimahi, a small town and military base of the KNIL, the Dutch Indonesian Army. It had housed the Fourth, Fifth, and Ninth Battalions until the war broke out.

"This looks a little different from when I was here last," Keereweer said. He pointed to a fence. "See that *gedek* with barbed wire on top? I think they looped the Fourth and Ninth together."

It was the same routine: off the trucks, their *barang* heaped at the gate, line up in rows of ten, bow, rise, and stand at attention.

The guards took their sweet time calling their names and reconciling them with long lists. When they picked up their belongings outside the gate, it was obvious the guards had rifled through the bags.

"At least they didn't do a body search," Gijs said to Keereweer. But when he unpacked later, he discovered that his last writing book and his three pencils were missing.

The camp was enormous, but at least it wasn't one huge building as big as a city block, like the Fifteenth Battalion in Bandoeng. Wherever Gijs looked, he saw barracks. It made the LOG look cozy in comparison. It wouldn't be hard to get lost here.

Keereweer was quick to notice that the infirmary was next to the Boy's Block. It wasn't just for boys though. Several men were interspersed to keep order.

"Can you stand bunking with me one more time?" Keereweer asked.

"Be my guest," Gijs said.

The barrack was one long building with four shorter ones feeding into it. The outer walls and the floor were made of concrete. Inside, perpendicular to the concrete walls, were wooden dividers. Two rows of cells faced each other with a path in the middle, and each cell had three sides. Against the outside wall, under the window, was a sleeping table made of rough planks. One *tawanan* slept on top, the other below. Against the other two sides was room for a cot. Four people to a cell. Gijs and Keereweer walked down the middle path to find a cell that had room for the two of them, and stopped at one not too far from the entrance. Two gentlemen sat on canvas tripods, a folding table between them.

"May we join you?" Keereweer asked.

"Sure, as long as you pay the bill for this fancy room," the taller one of the two said.

"I'll ask my company to put it on their account. Hello, I am Keereweer."

"How do you do? My name is Ralf Bekker, and this is Nick Weert."

Gijs sized them up as they made their introductions. Ralf Bekker's eyes twinkled and his entire face moved when he spoke. Nick Weert wore spectacles. His sleek dark hair fell over his high forehead.

"Hello there, what's your name?" Mr. Bekker asked, as Gijs stepped up from behind Keereweer.

"I am Gijs Bozuwa, sir," Gijs said, and stuck out his hand.

"Bozuwa? Are you Captain Bozuwa's son?"

"Yes, sir." Gijs could feel the surprise in Keereweer. He'd never told him his father was an officer in the navy. "Do you know him?"

"Sure I do. We went to the Navy Academy together. Your father made a splendid career. I got out of the navy and went to work for a shipping company."

Keereweer asked about the sleeping arrangements. Bekker and Weert used the sleeping table, so Gijs and Keereweer set up their cots against the remaining walls and stuffed their *barang* underneath.

"It looks like the Japs pulled the Fourth and Ninth together," Keereweer said. "I wonder how many of us they plan to put here."

"It has a capacity of ten thousand," Mr. Weert said. "The Dutch and Indonesian POWs were here first, but they've been taken away. Some say to Burma to build a railroad. But that's only a rumor."

"We've been here since the end of January," Mr. Bekker said. "We've seen a lot of people coming since then. When I look around, I think we must be at full capacity, but then another load of *tawan-ans* walk through the gate."

"As internment camps go, this one is well organized," Mr. Weert said. "The Dutch leadership has an outstanding man for its commander. He is from the Dutch Shell. His name is Carl de Villeneuve. A man of character."

Gijs and Keereweer left to take a look around. The first thing that got their attention were seven crosses set in a carefully built bed up against the bamboo fence. The wood of the simple crosses hadn't yet weathered, and the soil looked freshly raked.

"What do we have here?" Keereweer said, and bent down to look at the names. He read them out loud: Rauan, Tetenuka, Sasamu, Tintinoo, Watimena, Umgoh, Dalimba.

"Poor buggers," he said. "These were Ambonese who served in the KNIL and were taken as POWs."

A *tawanun* walked by. "Those soldiers crawled through the sewer to visit their families in town," he said. "They were betrayed. The Japs killed them on this spot with bayonets."

"God damned brutal," Keereweer said in disgust.

"Look here," Gijs said, and pointed to scribbling on the bamboo of the *gedek*. "A request to the next occupants of the camp to take care of this commemorative spot."

"You may think this is a warning," Keereweer said, "but it doesn't apply. They probably thought they would blend in with the townspeople."

"If we tried to escape," Gijs said, "we would stand out like a white rose in a bouquet of tropical flowers."

"We wouldn't get very far, Gijs," Keereweer said.

Gijs had to agree. At each corner of the camp, a watchtower rose high above the compound, an armed guard under the bamboo roofs.

People were everywhere. There was no reason to be lonely. The men came in all sizes and shapes, even nationalities. Gijs noticed that there was a Chinese barrack and one for Armenians, another for subjects of the British Empire. But there was one glaring deficiency: women. More than a year had passed since Gijs saw his mother and sister last. He missed their effervescent spirits. Women were thought about, talked about, and longed for. In the Tjihapit camp, he'd seen teenage boys go after the younger women with zest. That was when they were still well-fed, hormones coursing through their growing bodies. He hadn't turned away from girls his age either. Now at eighteen and underfed, he could not detect in himself any of that urgent attraction toward the other sex, and it wasn't just because they weren't around. He'd noticed it in other men as well, young and old. That part of life was dead. He didn't think or worry about it much. Only one goal superseded all other human drives, and that was to survive.

They hadn't eaten since they'd left the Fifteenth Battalion that morning, and their stomachs rumbled as they watched two boys strain to carry a huge barrel filled with steaming rice. The barrel hung by its handles from a long bamboo stick that rested on the boys' thin shoulders. One boy walked up front, the other behind.

"It's dinnertime. We'd better get back," Keereweer said.

In their room, Gijs opened his suitcase to find equipment to eat with. The small pan his mother had bought for him was a bit banged up, but it still served him well. His spoon he'd strapped to his belt with a piece of leather he'd found at the LOG, so he could have it with him all the time. You never knew when you might come across some food.

It had been a while since he'd stood in line for food. At the LOG he and Keereweer had eaten in the infirmary. A long line of men formed outside the entrance to the barrack. Skinny legs stuck out below shorts that needed belts to hold them together in folds. This was a very serious moment of the day. You had to be sure you got your rightful portion, and for some it was even more important that the man before or behind you wasn't getting more than his share. This made the job of doling out food very unpopular, and the camp leadership had wisely decided to rotate the chore. Everybody got a chance at being accused of not being fair or honest or of giving out favors.

"They've begun to post the menu on the central bulletin board every day," Ralf Bekker said. "Not only that. It lists the exact portion and how many portions are needed that day per barrack."

"Quite an administration with ten thousand people," Keereweer said. "The man from Shell with the fancy name has a job like the mayor of a city."

"Being mayor would be easier," Mr. Bekker said, "because the queen doesn't hit you in the face every time you ask a favor on behalf of the citizens. We don't get to see as much of the guards and the *heihos* because Mr. de Villeneuve does most of the negotiating with them. That's how the Japs want it."

"Until they spring surprise visits on us," Mr. Weert said. "When they're in that kind of mood, they are to be feared."

"I don't want to scare you, Gijs," Mr. Bekker said, "but a British officer was suspected of having a radio in camp, and they put him in a crate that was too small to stand or sit in. We had to walk by him. He looked at us through the slats. One whole day they kept him there."

Gijs could tell from the look on Keereweer's face that he didn't see the need for telling this story.

The exact portion that day was one cup of cooked rice. One hundred grams per *tawanan*. It was measured with a wooden spoon and leveled with a ladle. Not a kernel too much. A server ladled from another barrel a watery soup with leaves of some sort and a tiny piece of meat. The portions were counted down to the last person.

The four of them carried the food back to their room and sat around the folding table on their tripods. It took some self-discipline not to wolf the food down, but they knew they would get more out of it if it were digested slowly. Their concentration was palpable and bespoke their obsession with food. When they were done, they went outside to rinse their plates and spoons at an outdoor faucet. The boys who'd carried the barrels of food to the barrack were now in a hurry to get them back to the kitchen. The bonus for them was to scrape the barrels of any remaining kernels that stuck to the sides and bottom. Not one kernel would be left after they were done with them.

Gijs and the three men strolled around the yard. Above the wall of woven bamboo that surrounded them, the tops of leafy trees waved in the wind, and in the far distance the mighty Preanger Mountains rose above the plateau. The air was cooling, and they went inside.

Chapter 17

"Here's how it works," Mr. Bekker said as he leaned back on his stool.

They were finishing up their *pap,* a sort of porridge that was thick enough to paper the walls with. Gijs looked at Mr. Bekker and clearly saw the navy officer in him. In some ways he reminded Gijs of Vader, except that Mr. Bekker was more jovial, and eager to be at the center of attention. Vader didn't have to work at being at the center. He was the center.

"Every morning," Mr. Bekker said, "our leadership is ordered by the Jap to produce a certain amount of laborers to perform a certain job. That can be anything from chopping wood to tearing down a building. They pay the laborers a few cents per day."

"What can you do with a few cents around here?" Gijs asked.

"They promise to have a *toko* up and running soon, where you can buy all sorts of temptations like tobacco, sugar, bananas, and the like."

"Sounds too good to be true," Keereweer said. "Don't elaborate, please."

"So, if they need, say, one hundred people, then how is Mr. de Villeneuve going to deliver them?" Gijs asked.

"He goes to the block leaders and tells them to come up with volunteers."

"Those kind of jobs are all outside of the camp, right? Are any inside the camp?" Gijs asked.

"Yes, there are food runners, hospital runners. Those are mostly the younger kids. There are also steady crews. One for the kitchen, one for working in the office, but those are tight groups, hard to work yourself into. And then there's the cleaning detail of course. I don't think that's what you want."

Mr. Weert hadn't said anything. Gijs had noticed that he was more given to listening than speaking, but now Mr. Weert had a question for him.

"Were you able to take any lessons at the LOG, Gijs?"

"Yes, sir, I took astronomy and geometry."

"Do you have any idea what you want to be after the war is over?"

"I like that," Keereweer interrupted. "After the war is over."

"I want to go to the Naval Academy, sir."

"That's a boy!" Mr. Bekker said enthusiastically. "That's what I did. Never regretted it."

Mr. Weert looked at his roommate with annoyance. Apparently, he didn't like being put off his train of thought. "There's an effort afoot to get some serious teaching organized. As you can imagine, there are more than a few teachers among the ten thousand *tawanans* here."

"Morning call," the neighbors in the cell across the middle path yelled out to them. "Hurry up!"

They got up from their little table and hastened to the sandy area in front of their barrack. The sun was already warming the air after the cool of the night. It had rained hard, and puddles of water filled the ruts of the road that led by their block.

Only in the nick of time to get themselves into formation, they saw the Japanese guard approach. Two *heihos* with guns slung over their shoulders followed him.

The block leader, whose name Gijs didn't know yet, called out, "*Keirei.*"

Dutifully, every man and boy bowed at the waist and let his head hang low until they heard the leader call, "*Naore.*" Like puppets they straightened up.

Because they were on the late side, they'd been put in front. Keereweer was first and said, "Iti." Ralf Bekker was second. "Ni," he barked, and then Nick Weert said, "San." Gijs was fourth, and he said clearly, "Si you." The person next to him said in a loud voice,

"Go!" Gijs heard soft snickering behind him. It took him a moment to realize that what the two of them had said sounded very close to the English words: "See you go." The guard noticed, but didn't understand and he let it pass.

When all were accounted for, the block leader said, "*Yashme,*" and they relaxed while he asked for volunteers to work at the Tjimindi Farm. Many boys stepped forward. An image of the *toko* with sugar and bananas floated like a balloon into Gijs's mind. If he were ever going to eat any of those goodies, he would need money. He volunteered. They were given time to get a straw hat to protect against the fierce sun. Laborers with sunstroke were of no use.

With a *heiho* on a bicycle in front and another on a bike in the rear, they were marched to the farm. It tickled Gijs's funny bone to see a soldier with a gun, the bayonet prominently sticking out on top, slowly push the paddles of his very Dutch straight-up bicycle. The man looked like a moving corn stalk.

How long had it been since he walked outside an enclosed area? How long had it been since he was in the country with fields stretching into the distance and flowers by the side of the road? He took a deep breath and smelled the special sweetness that comes after a night of heavy rain. Most of his life, he'd been surrounded by sea landscapes, in Holland as well as in Soerabaja, and he'd always thought that he preferred the sea over land. Yet as he looked over the bobbing straw hats of his fellow *tawanans* to the distant Preanger Mountains, even in the haze of the rising dampness, he'd never seen anything more beautiful and heartening.

He savored this liberating moment only until they arrived at the farm, where they were each given a *patjoel* to start hoeing the earth. Gijs had seen *patjoels* being used in the fields a hundred times or more on his family's Sunday outings, but he'd never held one in his hands. Designed by the natives, who were quite a bit shorter than the average Dutchman, it was a stick with a cast iron hatchet set at a ninety-degree angle on one end. It was used for most farm work. Today, they would use it for harvesting peanuts.

Two Japanese guards stood at opposite sides of a field with small bushes in rows. A closer look revealed that the bushes didn't carry any fruit. Where were the peanuts? A man beside him seemed to know what to do. Holding the *patjoel* with both hands, he lifted it up and then smashed it down onto the ground, a little beyond the crown of a plant. When he was sure he had the right angle and was in deep enough, he pulled hard and unearthed strings with pods that had burrowed their way several inches down into the soil. He shook the bush, inverted it, and laid it down again with the exposed pods facing the sky.

"Takes three or four days to dry," he told Gijs.

Gijs was amazed. He would have never believed that the *pindas* he bought on the street in Soerabaja—in a small brown bag—had come from below the earth. Didn't nuts grow on trees? Like chestnuts and acorns?

The *heihos,* their bamboo sticks twirling in their hands, had moved into position on the sides of the field. Under their eyes, Gijs raised his *patjoel* for a first try at working up the peanuts. The metal edge came down too far away from the plant's crown for him to get a good hold of it. He felt the gaze of the *heiho* burning on his hands as he raised the *patjoel* again and swung it down at an improved angle. This time he pulled up a bunch of roots. It was hard work, partly because the *patjoel* was made for men at least a head shorter than he.

He straightened up after he'd worked a whole row, and saw the Japanese guard hitting a boy with the butt of his gun, ten rows up ahead. So, this was what working in the field was like, Gijs thought. Was it worth a few cents to be beaten like that?

"The bastard," the man next to him said in a barely audible whisper.

Gijs looked over at the guard, who seemed to enjoy beating up a young kid. Gijs stooped over again to keep his head down for fear that his disgust might show. *And we have to bow for a man like that,* he thought, *because he is the representative of His Majesty, Hirohito,*

Emperor of the Realm of the Rising Sun, who has been portrayed as our protector, who so kindly provides us with food as if we were his personal guests?

Before the morning was over, four other boys had been whipped with the *heiho's* bamboo stick, while he shouted, "*Lekas, lekas.*" Faster, faster. It was impossible to go faster, couldn't he see that?

Gijs's stomach was growling, his back was aching, and his tongue felt like a leather strap from thirst. They'd worked for five hours. Finally, they were given some water to drink and marched back to the camp in time for the midday meal.

"So, what was your first day as a forced laborer like?" Keereweer asked.

"Brutal."

"Are you going back tomorrow?"

"Well, yeah. They haven't paid me yet," Gijs said.

"If you can get four cents together, you can buy a *sateh* stick. They killed a few dogs last night."

"Oh. Great!" The idea of eating roasted dog meat repulsed him, even if they put peanut sauce over it to hide the deed.

He and Keereweer went outside to stand in line to get their meal.

"Don't forget to get the extra portion they allow for the outside workers," Keereweer said. "You earned it."

"What have you done with yourself all this time, while I was sweating over peanuts?" Gijs asked.

"Oh, I snooped around some. I found out all sorts of things."

"That the end of the war is in sight?"

"Not in sight, but around the corner. Consider this: All internment camps are coming under the authority of the Japanese Sixteenth Army."

"Is that something new?"

"Until now, we were directly in the hands of the *economen*, and only indirectly under the army. They say we all have to be registered. I think they expect an invasion."

"What else did you find out?" Gijs asked.

"That we're supposed to pee into particular bamboo barrels. There are barrels in several locations for this special purpose."

"Special purpose?"

"They make bread from it," Keereweer said, and Gijs could tell he had been dying to pull this over him.

"They turn urine into bread?"

"I know you don't believe me, but this is what I found out."

Providing one thousand people with bread every day, Keereweer told him, required a large quantity of yeast, and there was a shortage of it. Since there were several chemists and engineers at the camp, they came up with the idea of starting their own yeast factory. They knew they could distill ammonia from urine.

"Apparently, that's an important part for making yeast," Keereweer said. "One of the other ingredients they need is bone meal. They make it from the carcasses of the slaughtered cattle. The bones are dried above the ovens in the kitchen, and then they grind them."

"I don't think I'll eat bread here," Gijs said.

"You may want to reconsider when you get hungrier than you are now. Even when you don't eat the bread, you could help others by depositing your liquid gold into the barrel. There's a sign above it: No piss, no yeast, no bread."

When night fell, Mr. Weert suggested to Gijs they take a walk. Their conversation had been interrupted by the roll call that morning, and apparently whatever he had on his mind, he didn't need the wisecracks from their roommates. His earnest look made Gijs feel like he had been called into the principal's office. He slowed his pace as he walked next to Mr. Weert, who was lean but short. A slight breeze played with his dark forelock, and he swept it away absent-mindedly, as if he were swatting a fly. His round spectacles set in a face marked with fine wrinkles created the impression of an intelligent and thoughtful man. These were only casual observations, of course, but they created a feeling of trust. Mr. Weert reminded him of Paatje Hinten.

"What I was going to tell you this morning, Gijs, was that we hope to organize classes in several subjects and then take examinations. We're setting up an administration so that later, after the war is over, you can prove you had proficiency in those subjects."

"Is that possible in plain sight of the Japs?"

"That is a problem, and we have to be careful, but I'm sure we can pull it off. It's important."

"Are you a teacher, sir?"

"I used to be. I taught history. Later I worked at the Department of Education."

"I haven't thought much about studying, to tell you the truth," Gijs said. "Except for the few classes I took at the LOG, the war has wiped it out of my mind."

"That's understandable."

They stopped for a moment to watch the sunset. Streaked with red rays, the sky looked like it was on fire. The orange-red glow changed everything around them, as if somebody had taken a paintbrush to give the ugly barracks a facelift.

Mr. Weert sighed. "There's nothing quite like a tropical sunset, is there? This is such a beautiful country, but its beauty clashes with its brutality."

"Yes, I know what you mean," Gijs said. "I always saw more of the beauty than of the brutality. Now it's the other way around."

The dusk of the evening surrounded them. More people were out and about, trying to avoid the oppression of the barrack for as long as they could. There were only two benches outside in the entire complex, and those were usually occupied. Still, walking outside was better than lying down on a cot and getting bitten by the bedbugs that hid in their blankets.

"It's important, Gijs, that you think about your education, and what is even more important is that you believe in your own future. The circumstances we find ourselves in are not conducive for schoolwork, I know. We're all preoccupied with merely surviving, but we should not give up, or lose hope, especially at your age. There's a life ahead of you."

They'd reached the buildings that were nicknamed The Vatican, because except for the pope, the entire Roman Catholic hierarchy was represented inside, from bishops to lowly priests. As they passed the buildings, Gijs realized Mr. Weert reminded him of Father van Gasteren. Their approach to life seemed to be based on a solid rock. For the priest, that rock had been his faith. For Mr. Weert? Hard to guess, but listening to him was inspiring.

"How did you keep busy at the LOG, Gijs?"

"They needed volunteers at the infirmary when an epidemic of dysentery broke out. That's where I met Keereweer. He taught me a lot, but it didn't come out of a book. He's hands-on. We bunked together in the infirmary for most of the time I was there."

"Hands-on learning is useful, but you have your sights set on a naval career, and that requires credentials to get you into the Naval Academy."

"I know. That's why I took astronomy and geometry."

"Good. Let's set up a schedule to give you a broader base of subjects. Can you meet me tomorrow afternoon?" Mr. Weert asked.

"Yes, sir."

A bugle sounded over the compound, ordering the men back to their *tempats*.

His stomach growling and his back aching from hacking the *patjoel* into the earth, Gijs lay down on his cot and pulled the blanket over him. As the moonlight peered through the cracks between the roof tiles high above, he felt like a drop in a large sea, one of hundreds of men pushed close together. Sleeping behind a curtain with only one other person at the LOG infirmary had been quite different.

Mr. Weert had challenged him to think about his future, a subject he had been avoiding. What future? Thinking about the future always resulted in looking back at the life he'd known. That made him feel so homesick that he quickly turned it off, as if it were a forbidden movie he was watching. Mr. Weert, however, projected a life beyond these walls. His own life. A life he should be preparing for. He was now eighteen years old. It was a bit of a shock to realize that no one other than he was responsible for how that life would be lived. Mr. Weert was right: he should use his head and pump as much knowledge into it as he could, or he would have to call these years the lost years.

He woke up to the same routine of coffee and *pap* for breakfast. Ralf Bekker had a theory that the reason tapioca made up such a large portion of their diet, was that there were warehouses full of the stuff, because it could not be exported. He had been in the shipping business, and he knew that tapioca was used to give cheap textiles more body. He remembered shipping it to Lancashire in England.

"So, we are worth no more than a cheap shirt that needs a little tapioca to give it more body?" Keereweer asked. "Look at my bones sticking out!" He pointed at his ribcage. "Long live tapioca!"

The surprise of the morning call was that they were not going back to the Tjimindi farm. The peanuts hadn't fully dried. Instead, they were told to clean the barrack of bedbugs. Everything needed to be brought outside and put in the sun, especially the cots, sleeping bags, and blankets. Bedbugs, they were told, died in the direct sun. Mr. Bekker and Keereweer busied themselves with trying to catch the bugs and bring them out to a hot concrete platform in the sun.

"Look," Keereweer said, "look at the walls. That's where the buggers hide. The POWs who were here before us killed them by pushing their fingernails on them. You can still see the blood marks. It's as good as painting the walls red."

Next, they took the planks from the sleeping tables outside and shook the bedbugs onto the boiling hot macadam. The bedbugs succumbed by the hundreds.

"I never dreamed," Keereweer said, "that I could count mass murdering as part of my illustrious career."

Pails of water were sent streaming over the concrete floor indoors. The woven bamboo dividers had been placed six inches off the ground so the water could flow underneath. They scrubbed the floors and swept the walls with brooms and got the cobwebs out of the corners. Then they put everything back. It would help for a few days, but the hard reality was that it was impossible to totally get rid of the nasty little beasts. Next week, they would be doing it again, and every week thereafter. Gijs considered himself lucky that the bedbugs didn't seem to like his blood very much. Most people scratched and scratched, especially around their waists. It drove them crazy. Even worse, some of the bites got infected, and malnutrition slowed the healing of the infections.

Mr. Weert made good on his promise to help Gijs. Gijs met with him and some of the teachers, and he was put down for lessons in chemistry and English. Gijs insisted on English because it was the language of the seas. He could already speak it a little bit.

Learning remained a clandestine activity. When a small group of students had gathered in the middle of the barrack, a teacher warned them to be careful.

"This is how we take precautions: take your *botol tjepok* with you when you attend a class. Somebody will stand close to the door to warn if a guard is coming. He will call '*Kyotske.*' This gives you enough time to take your bottle and pretend you're going to the bathroom."

In the Indies it was customary to use a bottle of water after a bowel movement for cleaning up.

Gijs chuckled to himself. Three years ago, he would have laughed anyone out of the room who suggested studying was forbidden, and that to get away with it you had to pretend you were going to the bathroom with a bottle in your hand.

One day after a class he met Frits outside the barracks. He greeted the other boy, and asked if he was taking lessons too?

Frits said no. "I just don't have the energy. I work at the sawmill. That way I make some money. I feel starved all the time. This gets me a little extra food."

"I know how you feel, but we should use our heads. At some point, this war will be over, you know," Gijs said. As he spoke, he felt like a parrot, senselessly repeating the same sentence again and again.

"I hope you're right, but now I think to myself 'better alive and dumb than wicked smart and under the ground.' When the teacher asks which are the five important crops they grow in the United States, by the time I come up with number three, I've already forgotten number one. So what's the use?"

Gijs shook his head.

He was almost back at his own *tempat*, when he heard English being spoken through the open door of the barrack next to his. The Brits' barrack. There was no rule that the nationalities couldn't mix, so he sauntered over and leaned against the doorpost. A group of four was playing cards. From their accents he could tell they were Australians. One of them looked up and motioned him to come in.

"Blond hair, blue eyes, you must be Dutch," he said.

"Absolutely," Gijs said.

"What's up? Are you coming to tell us the war is over?" the Aussie asked.

"Yes, as of this moment," Gijs said, and smiled.

They all laughed, and he sat with them, listening to their banter. He told them he wanted to learn English for when he joined the Dutch navy. Little did he know he would speak English for the greater part of his life, and not on the seas, but in his home.

The peanuts had dried enough to be harvested, they learned two days later at morning call. Gijs grabbed his straw hat and off they marched to the Tjimindi farm. In the field lay the wilted plants with the peanut pods on top, facing the blue sky. The pods had lost the required one-third of their moisture content. This time, they didn't get a *patjoel* to do the work. Row by row. The plants were shaken and the strings with pods gathered in baskets. Gathering the pods was as hard work as digging them out of the earth had been.

Occasionally, Gijs put some in his pocket, looking forward to eating them when he got back to his *tempat*.

The Japanese guard who'd biked behind them on the way to the farm was in a bad mood. He kept calling out words they didn't know, but they assumed they meant hurry up. One young man apparently did something that didn't please the guard. The guard took his straw hat and gave him two *patjoels*. The man had to stand in the hot sun with his arms outstretched, holding on to the *patjoels*, for the rest of the time they were at the farm. It was too painful to watch, and Gijs stayed bent over, concentrating on shaking the peanut pods loose. He scolded himself for not going over to the man and taking the *patjoels* from him. Maybe, he thought, that was the worst part of being a *tawanan*: you were rendered powerless. The Japanese always won. If he followed his impulse, all of them would not get to eat for a week. The guards met every show of rebellion with severe punishment. Mr. Bekker, who liked telling morbid stories, had said last week that a man who'd traded with natives on the way to the farm had been hung by his arms, with his hands bound behind his back.

Back at his *tempat* Gijs emptied his pockets and began peeling the pods.

"Don't eat too many, Gijs," Keereweer warned him. "Your stomach isn't used to eating too much at once."

Gijs thought that if he ate them slowly, he'd be all right, and he ate every one. The result was a whopping stomachache and a night of trotting to the latrine with diarrhea. He went to see the doctor the next day, who told him he would survive, but advised him never to eat raw peanuts again.

The peanut harvesting was over and he received four cents. It wasn't enough to order food at the *toko*. What could he do next? He remembered Frits telling him about the sawmill.

Mr. Roelink was the man who handed out the jobs that could get you extra food as well as money, so Gijs went to see him. He got a sawmill job, but only after he was found to be in sufficient physical condition for the labor. The mill was impressively large. Under a high roof of corrugated galvanized iron, a bamboo structure had been erected to uphold a sturdy platform at man's height. Heavy saw horses on the platform held tree trunks, each about three feet in diameter. One man stood on the platform, another stood below on the ground, and they used a long saw to cut the logs. It was easy to see that the better job was the one on top. The sawdust covered the man below. Since Gijs could not claim seniority, he got the job of pulling the saw down. It was hard work. It made harvesting peanuts seem a lightweight chore. Sawdust matted the hair on his chest and crawled up in his nose. Gritty pieces invaded his shorts and itched his crotch. When they returned to the camp at midday, he headed straight for the faucet.

"Looks like you were not on top of the job," Keereweer said, when he saw Gijs reach for another pair of shorts, one of the three he possessed.

"You could say I was buried by the job," Gijs said.

"Here, hand me those disgusting shorts and I'll wash them out for you. Go lie down and rest up before you have to pump yourself full of chemistry tricks this afternoon."

"I will and thank you."

For three weeks he kept it up, until he had enough money to order a half-pound of sugar from the *toko*. In the mornings, when they drank what might be called tea, he gave his roommates some sugar, and he always gave Keereweer an extra spoonful.

Maybe, he would have worked longer at the saw mill, but a dysentery epidemic broke out, and, just as it had happened at the L.O.G., volunteers were asked to help out in the infirmary, which was close to the Boys Barracks and bigger than the one at the L.O.G.

"What do you think, Gijs? Have we had a long enough vacation from nursing?" Keereweer asked.

Gijs had to think it over. Even though pulling a saw back and forth was hard work, harder than carrying bedpans, it was masculine work. He remembered feeling like a sissy walking through the halls of the LOG in full view of the kitchen crew, which was doing what he considered real work: lifting huge pans, stoking ovens with logs of wood. He said as much to Keereweer.

"Masculine? Those stinkers who fed themselves better than the rest of us? Forget it!"

Of course, he would join Keereweer. It seemed to Gijs as if the universe had a plan for him, and that plan had to do with sick people.

At the first wake-up call the next morning, he got out of bed and walked over to a spot where he could watch the sun rising through high branches of the trees outside the camp. He could only see those topmost branches; the tree trunks were hidden behind the *gedek* and barbed wire. It was cold, and he shivered in his well-worn shirt and khaki shorts. He urged the sun to work itself a foot higher into the sky, so it could send its warming rays above the treetops and chase the cold mountain air away. Other men had come out in their pajamas, and they beat their thin arms around their chests to get their blood running, as he'd seen merchants do in the marketplace in Holland in the dead of winter.

He wanted to think about going back to working in an infirmary. He might have said no if it hadn't been for Keereweer. How could he let his friend down? Keereweer made life behind barbed wire bearable. He never complained, even if he was as hungry as the next man.

Gijs walked back and forth to stay within the range of the sun-rays, which gave off a benign feeling of warmth. What was holding him back? The masculine versus sissy concern was a non-issue, if he was honest with himself. It had to be something else, but it was too elusive to put into words. Images of dying men, of suffering men, floated through his mind. Try as he might, it was hard to make those images go away. He would never get used to having to deal with the end of life.

More *tawanans* came out now. Gijs looked them over and thought what a poor looking lot they'd become. Graying hair, dull from lack of decent soap; thin as rails; enveloped by clothes that had been endlessly patched up by hands that did not know how to sew. He looked at what the Japanese had done to them, and it angered him enough to decide that the best he could do was to defend his own countrymen, even if it meant looking death straight in the eye.

Chapter 18

One evening in July, after they'd downed their meager meal of rice with boiled vegetables, Mr. Weert suggested to Gijs that they take a walk. This, Gijs had learned, meant Mr. Weert had a serious matter on his mind.

"Gijs, did you know there was another camp here in Tjimahi?"

"Yes, sir, Baros Five."

"True, but there is another one yet. On the other side of the railroad tracks."

This was a surprise, and it made Gijs realize how isolated he'd been from his surroundings. He'd arrived in a truck about five months ago and been dropped off at the gate. The only place outside the camp he could identify was Tjimindi, the farm where he'd harvested peanuts. He'd become aware of the existence of the Baros V camp through some lucky boys who went there to join their fathers. But where that camp was located, he didn't know.

Mr. Weert said that immediately after the capitulation, the white women in the Tjimahi area had been put in the homes of the Dutch officers and petty officers. They'd lived there with their children since March 1942. Since the Sixteenth Army took over the authority of Java in April, many things had changed. For instance, Mr. Weert said, there was less opposition now to education. He said he'd given up on following Japanese reasoning, but the most obvious change had been, and still was, the constant transportation of prisoners between camps. The Japanese Army was obviously executing a preconceived plan.

Gijs wondered why he was being told all this disparate information.

"The Japs want to move those women and their small children to a camp in Bandoeng. Sons over the age of twelve have to stay behind. Their idea is to turn what is now called the women's camp into a boys' camp," Mr. Weert said.

"A big camp, like this one?"

"No, it couldn't absorb more than fifteen hundred *tawanans*. Here we're exceeding ten thousand."

Gijs still didn't understand why he was being made privy to this interesting news.

The sun was almost through with the day, and sent its low slanting rays over the tiled roofs of the barracks. A mysterious man, thin and tall as a beanstalk, with flowing white hair and a long beard, walked ahead of them. Gijs had been told this man's hobby was to study the supernatural. He didn't know much about the supernatural, but, Gijs thought, this internment camp might be a good place to study the unnatural.

"Mr. de Villeneuve is working on putting a team together to lead the boys' camp," Mr. Weert said. "He needs people who can deal with fickle Japanese."

"Yes, that would be important. Those kids will need an advocate," Gijs said.

"The boys are raising hell over there at the moment. They steal and fight among each other. The two nuns in charge are at their wits' end."

"Not a pretty picture."

"I've been asked to help set up a program for education. Ten other men are coming along as well, and we need twenty boys your age."

Ah, so that's what this is all about, Gijs thought.

"I would like you to come along," Mr. Weert said.

"I'll think about it," Gijs said, but the prospect tickled his fancy. Six months of living in a huge barrack was quite enough. The only obstacle he could see was leaving Keereweer behind. Mr. Weert had said nothing about him, and Gijs was certain the infirmary wouldn't let Keereweer go. He was too valuable to them.

Mr. de Villeneuve pulled together a group of twelve men and twenty boys. Mr. Schotel, who'd worked as an executive for a Dutch trading company on Bali before the war, would be in charge.

Gijs found it very hard to say good-bye to Keereweer. He'd been like a father to him. If there was any benefit at all to being locked up for a few years, it was meeting a man like Keereweer, a rough diamond that shone even when the low morale all around it tried to dull its glow.

"They'll probably put you in the infirmary over there," Keereweer said. "Just remember the things I taught you. Dr. Wins is in your group. He's a good man."

"I hope he'll let me do more than empty bedpans."

"Oh, if they don't, just remember you can grow tomatoes as big as grapefruits in that lovely brown stuff."

Then Keereweer did something Gijs hadn't expected. The marine gave him a bear hug. Years ago, his parents had told him not to play with the children of petty officers. As he looked into Keereweer's tear-filled eyes, he resolved he would tell his own children that rank didn't equal good or bad. A person's value had nothing to with the insignia he might wear. That's what he would teach them.

He left the barrack in a bit of a daze.

The group was assembling near the gate. It was July 21, 1944. Mr. Schotel, who would prove to be a very competent and courageous administrator, led his group out of the Fourth and Ninth Battalion. The women's camp was a mile away, he'd been told. They were charged with straightening out the boys who were already there and preparing for the arrival of one thousand more boys. Gijs walked at the tail end of the procession, his mind still on the place he had just left.

His leather suitcase weighed about the same as when he'd left home for the Bangka camp. In it were the same three sets of underwear, three shirts, three shorts, and one set of pajamas, well worn, endlessly repaired and patched up, but still the same ones. The bristles on his toothbrush had been worn down to the wood; those on his hairbrush not quite as much, since he kept his hair close to his scalp to prevent uninvited critters from invading. The spoon and the fork, his mug and small pan, they'd all been his trusty companions.

Only the notebooks and pencils Janneke had given him were missing. Oh well, he wasn't the type to write a diary, anyway.

Because he carried his *tikar*, his cot, and his blanket on his shoulders, he saw hardly anything more than his own two feet. When he stepped over the railroad tracks, he knew they were halfway there. Neat rows of decent-looking houses came into his narrow field of vision, between the rolled-up blanket on his left shoulder and his cot on his right one. He hadn't seen a house since he'd left Tjihapit. The camp was divided into two parts by the Barosweg that ran through it.

Everyone left his *barang* on a heap next to the Japanese commandant's house. Mr. Schotel and a few other men went inside. Curious young faces popped up all around them as they stood waiting in the open space next to the house. The boys were not shy. They pushed and shoved each other, but they kept their distance. How would he handle these rampaging critters? Gijs wondered. He didn't have much experience with young boys.

The sun stood high in the sky, and its piercing rays were unforgiving. Instinctively, everyone in his group sought the shade of the tall palm trees. It felt bizarre to be standing on a street with houses on both sides. Even though the entire compound was surrounded by the now familiar *gedek* with a strand of barbed wire on top, the place felt intimate, the kind of atmosphere you'd expect in a small village. The houses were built from a combination of fieldstones below the windows and white painted concrete up to the tiled roofs.

He heard a familiar voice say, "Can you imagine waking up tomorrow morning and not having a thousand men around you?"

Gijs jerked his head around and couldn't believe his eyes. The voice belonged to Pieter Donk. They recognized each other in the same instant.

Everybody looked up when they both cried out, "What are *you* doing here?" Which was a stupid question, of course, but it effectively bridged the one-and-a-half years since Pieter had walked through the gate of the Tjihapit camp, the last time they had seen each other. They shook hands and slapped each other on the back. Pieter was a thinner version of his former self, but although there was less flesh on his body, he still had the sturdy frame of a young man whose shoulders could comfortably carry the whole world. Atlas personified. What had changed about him were his eyes. The look in them was older, wiser.

"There's much catching up to do," Pieter said. "Let's see if they will let us bunk together."

"You know, Pieter," Gijs said, "maybe we've hit the jackpot by volunteering."

"As far as finding you here, I agree. For the rest, it will depend on what the Jap and his guards are like. I don't think they plan to run a sweet nursery school."

Mr. Schotel and the other men came out of the house with the commandant, who didn't look older than his mid-twenties. To judge from the insignia on his uniform, he was a sergeant. The army didn't waste its officers on looking after civilian prisoners. His name, they were told, was Kunemoto Yoshio. Three guards and some *heihos* surrounded him.

"All right," Mr. Schotel said, "we have work to do."

In no time at all, he'd assigned everyone to a task. The first item on his list, he told them, was to reorganize the kitchen. Mr. Nauta would be in charge. A tall, rugged man stepped forward. Gijs's immediate first impression was of a taciturn, tough boss. Beneath a shock of blond hair, his light blue eyes looked at the world with steely determination. He ordered all twenty boys to get their *barang* out of the way and stack them in a house close by where the Dutch leadership would live.

The kitchen was in deplorable condition. Mr. Nauta ordered them to haul outside everything that wasn't affixed and start scrubbing it all in the sun. Inside, they washed the floors and emptied the closets. Some of the food was molded or spoiled. Dirt and leftover food stuck to the counters and chopping table. They scraped it off with butcher knives they found in the drawers, hurrying to get it done quickly. The next meal for over one hundred people needed to be cooked soon. They worked hard, and Mr. Nauta worked the hardest of all. He knew exactly how he would run his kitchen.

As twilight descended, they were assigned to different houses. Two other boys—Rob Binnerts from Batavia and Bart Ament from Semarang—joined Pieter and Gijs. The house consisted of three rooms, plus a kitchen, a bathroom, and a WC. In spite of the cobwebs in all the corners and the grease that stuck to the sink in the kitchen, they couldn't believe their good luck. They put their cots in one room and talked into the night.

Pieter told them that the first internment camp he'd been taken to had been a monastery, Stella Maris, in Bandoeng.

"What did they do with the nuns?" Gijs asked.

"They put them on the first floor," Pieter said. "We slept on the ground floor."

He'd been taken from Stella Maris to the Fifteenth Battalion at about the same time as Gijs.

"You're kidding. I was there too," Gijs said.

Pieter had stayed there longer. He'd come to Fourth and Ninth Battalion in Tjimahi in May.

"Pieter, do you remember when you told me the Japs were thinking of putting all the white people in internment camps? I found it hard to believe at the time, but look at us now."

"Yes, I remember. I also remember that people thought the Americans would take Java back in a matter of months, and here we are in July 1944, with no end in sight."

"What do you know about your family?" Gijs asked.

"My mother and my brother are still in Tjihapit. What I know about my father is that he was interned at the Palace Hotel. Remember that Chinese hotel? I don't know where he is now. Who knows, maybe he's here in Tjimahi. The mail is so slow to get news to each other."

All four boys exchanged the particulars of the various camps they'd been in. Not counting slight differences, it came down to the same experience: horrible food, not enough of it, boredom, and the brutality of guards. They confessed to not having developed a high regard for the older generation. There were notable exceptions, like Keereweer, but for the most part they agreed that the majority of the conversations they'd overheard had revolved around memories of the glorious past and bitter complaints about the present. Not only that. Each of them had seen men they'd looked up to in "normal" life, like bankers and executives, steal food from their neighbors. That had particularly disheartened them.

At morning call they got the task of clearing out the houses on the other side of the Barosweg. Shelves, small tables, and all sorts of knickknacks they threw on a heap. The only things left were heavy wardrobes, and those had to be moved to the homes the Japanese had chosen for themselves. Each weighed well over a hundred pounds. Worse, they needed to be carried uphill.

"This is when you know you're being used," Pieter said.

"Yes," Gijs said. "The Japs don't believe in using their own people or paying natives to do the heavy lifting."

"We're their labor force, and we're free," Pieter said.

"Let's not dwell on it," Gijs said. "We might begin to feel sorry for ourselves."

It took a few weeks to get the job done. More than thirty houses, some bigger than others, had been emptied and cleaned.

Next on Mr. Schotel's list was to set up a decent infirmary. He chose two of the larger officer's homes at the very end of the Barosweg. A billiard table stood in one of them. Kunemoto wanted that table in his house. It felt like it weighed a ton, and it took twelve boys to lift it.

"Billiard tables are made of slate, you know," Rob Binnerts said.

"Hmm. You can write on slate. Wouldn't that be handy?" Pieter said.

"Let's drop it," Gijs boldly suggested.

They decided that when Rob winked, they would drop it.

"Watch out for your toes," Gijs warned.

A Japanese guard had come over with a truck, and they were supposed to lift the table onto its bed. It looked like sheer impossibility, but that fact played into their hands. They groaned and moaned as they carried the colossus out of the house. As they tried to maneuver it onto the truck, Rob winked, and they let go. The green felt that covered the top ripped apart, and the slate underneath broke into pieces as the table hit the ground. The guard was furious. He stamped his feet and smashed the butt of his gun into Rob's ribcage. Pieter was next, and then Gijs, as well as the others. Each got their turn. But Humpty Dumpty couldn't be put back together again, and the guard knew it. He left, looking very unhappy at the prospect of having to tell Kunemoto about the "accident."

With the guard gone, they collected the slate, dropping some of the big pieces on the ground to make them smaller, and stacked it in a shed for later use. If there was going to be teaching, as Mr. Weert planned, they'd need things to write with. A piece of slate would be far less suspicious than paper and pencil.

The food was improving. Mr. Nauta turned out to be a master at making the most out of the little he had to work with. Under his able hands, the volume of cooked rice was almost twice as much as it had been in other kitchens. Pieter could vouch for that, since he'd worked in the kitchen at Stella Maris. He was in awe of Mr. Nauta.

"You know," he said, "the kitchen crews in the other camps fed themselves first and very well. Did you know that in the camp we just left, somebody found out that the provisions that came into the camp did not match the portions we were served?"

"How come?" Rob asked.

"They found the lost food was mostly meat, and it was hanging in the chimneys of kitchen stoves."

"You're kidding. Were they smoking it?" Gijs asked.

"That would be one thing, but the cooks sold the meat at extravagant prices to the other *tawanans*. Mr. de Villeneuve was furious. He dismissed the entire kitchen crew."

"What a corrupt crowd. Is that why we got Chinese food all of a sudden?"

"Yes, and the Chinese did a much better job. I was ashamed of my countrymen," Pieter said.

Mr. Schotel and Mr. Moolenaar set up a comprehensive administration, a task made more difficult by the lack of paper. Everyone who entered the camp had to hand over whatever money he had. That put a stop to the stealing that had been going on. A book-keeping system kept track of what was bought in the *toko*, where the *tawanans* could buy items like soap, sugar, coffee, Indonesian spices, and whatever the camp directors could get their hands on in their negotiations with Kunemoto. Mr. Moolenaar deducted these expenses from their accounts. The money that could be earned by doing chores, like working at the farm at Leuwigadjah, was added to their accounts at a rate of fourteen cents per hour. Doing chores became very popular, not just because they could buy extra food. They also got one hundred grams added to their daily diet.

The new camp was ready. Soon the transports would begin with boys from Bandoeng and Batavia, and even farther away, from places such as Soerabaja, Semarang, and Malang. Gijs and Rob were assigned to the infirmary as orderlies. Pieter became part of Nauta's kitchen crew. Their household was broken up as Pieter went to live in a house with others of the kitchen crew, and Gijs and Rob got the servants quarters behind what used to be an officer's house. They couldn't believe their luck. They had two real beds in a room of their own. The best part was that the house was located at the very end of the street. The guards would not be likely to come that far on their sporadic inspections.

Chapter 19

No matter how well Mr. Nauta organized the central kitchen, no matter how much he was capable of expanding the rice portions, everyone was hungry all the time. It became a matter of life and death to find more food. One way was to cozy up to the *heihos,* who'd been given the job of policing by the Japanese. Most were kindly disposed toward the *tawanans.* They carried messages out of the camp, and an exchange of goods between *tawanans* and *heihos* flourished. When walking between the farm and the camp, the workers also would trade on the side of the road with natives, who were needy as well. They wanted textiles, and gold was always welcome, but it was risky business. The Japanese guards were unmerciful in their punishments if they caught anyone trying to trade through a hole in the bamboo enclosure. Their favorite punishment was to withhold food for a day for the entire camp. It was painful, but it didn't stop the trading. Hunger drove the *tawanans* to take ever-greater risk.

Another way to get food was to grow it. Behind each house was a little plot of land. Java's extraordinarily fertile soil offered an abundance of nutrients, and there was no lack of moisture. Often at the end of the afternoon, the sky would darken with heavy, low-hanging clouds. The world went very still, the birds stopped singing, and a mantle of anticipation fell over everything. The first drops that pounded the dusty roads raised a heavy earthy smell that hung over the landscape for just a few minutes. Then the rains poured down in a noisy concert of gurgling drains and roofs that clattered like drums. The downpours were voluminous and rapid. A low mist hung over the land afterward, the air pregnant with moisture. This created the ideal conditions for growing sweet potatoes, called *oebie,* and tomatoes. Gijs and Rob dug a trench behind the officer's house and emptied into it every bedpan they had taken from an infirmary patient. Their tomatoes were of spectacular size, as Keereweer had predicted. They also attracted thieves like honey, but the location of their house at the end of the Barosweg protected them somewhat.

Frogs were another favorite. A brook ran behind one part of the camp, and the boys became clever at catching and skinning the frogs. The only problem was that after a while, there were no frogs left.

One Sunday, when they didn't have to work, Pieter, Rob, and Gijs concocted a plan to catch a chicken. They could hear chickens cackling and scratching for food behind the *gedek*. The *kampong*, where the natives lived, was on the other side. Pieter had taken a handful of rice kernels from the kitchen. Gijs made a small hole at the base of the *gedek*. Rob rigged a trap. They laid a trail of kernels and spent much of the day waiting for a daring chicken to follow the rice trail. It finally worked. A hen stuck her head through the hole, and the next and last thing she knew, a straw hat fell on her. It had been a fatal move. Pieter knew how to do the rest. They had an excellent meal that evening.

It was rumored that dogs were lured into the camp, and then killed and eaten, but this happened more toward the end of the war, when the prisoners were literally starving. Still, any animal that innocently strayed into the camp had a death sentence written on its fur. Sometimes they found food in surprising places. Gijs had the fright of his life when he walked to the outhouse in the middle of the night one night, sat down, and sprang back up because he felt something soft underneath. A big snake had curled itself on the seat. He cried out, and Rob came running from their house..

"Where is it?" he asked, when Gijs told him what had happened.

Gijs couldn't care less, but Rob grabbed a *patjoel* and killed the snake. They ate it the next day. It tasted like eel.

Mr. Schotel tried to discourage trading and stealing, because the punishments enacted by the Japanese affected the entire camp population. He hoped that by organizing a camp police from his own people, apart from the guards and the *heihos*, he could prevent the worst youthful transgressions. Stealing was not a good thing, of course, but he knew the hunger made it somewhat understandable.

Mr. Schotel chose the strongest young men he could find. Two of them, Koning and van Onselen, lived in the same house as Pieter, so Gijs heard all about their investigations. As the police began to make regular rounds, they became suspicious of a certain gentleman, who'd come over from the Fourth and Ninth Battalion to help with the teaching and other tasks. Mr. Kok was his name, a small man with untrustworthy eyes, as if the devil lived behind his forehead. Besides his eyes, what was suspicious about Kok was that he was extremely well fed. In a camp of hungry prisoners, plumpness was a dead giveaway that something illicit was going on.

Kok had wormed himself into a group of twenty-five permanent workers who went daily to the farm at Leuwigadjah, where they grew vegetables and tended pigs. He set up relations with the two Japanese supervisors there, who had the keys to the storage bins of corn, rice, and sugar. The corn was for feeding the pigs. The rice and sugar was for the extra ration the workers got for their labors. Kok had made a deal with the Japanese, whereby he could take a small bale of rice or sugar in an empty drum and bring it to the camp. Every prisoner was inspected upon return from the farm, but the guards never inspected what was in Mr. Kok's drum, which made the camp police suspect that Kunemoto himself was involved in the swindle. Kok paid one hundred guilders for his wares, and then turned around to sell the food at a stiff price to his fellow prisoners, and he did this at least once a week.

The camp police were furious. Not only did he collect money, Kok also lent money at rates that would make a profiteer blush. When they were sure of their case, they decided to teach him a lesson he would not forget. They chose Koning and van Onselen, the two strongest men, to carry it out. After the bell had sounded for lights out one evening, they sent a *heiho* to warn Kok that he had to present himself at Kunemoto's house, while they hid in the bushes. When Kok walked by, they pounced on him and gave him a drubbing like he'd never had before.

Of course, Kok went directly to Kunemoto to complain. He said he had not recognized his perpetrators, so Kunemoto ordered everyone out of bed and lined them up outside of his house for an unusual night roll call. Who had done this terrible act? he demanded.

Koning and van Onselen immediately stepped forward. Kunemoto may not have expected such a quick confession, and probably hadn't expected that the perpetrators were the two strongest men of the camp police. He hesitated, and then decided not to make too much of a show of punishing them. They each got a couple of hard whacks in their faces.

Kok may have thought that was the end of it, and he would have to do no more than keep out of sight, but the camp police were not through with him yet. Pieter told Gijs that the next time people had to be moved back to the big camps to make room for another shipment of boys from Batavia, Kok would be on the list. Best to take a rotten apple and put it where it can't spoil the rest. Kunemoto, who had the last word in these matters, didn't object.

At 10.30 AM, the "travelers" had to assemble in front of the kitchen for morning call. Since they wouldn't leave until two, Kok had left his *barang* behind. Meanwhile, as normal procedure, a group of boys had the task to clean the houses that were being vacated. The mattresses were the property of the camp and had to be collected and taken to the *goedang*. Kok, however, had planned to take his with him. He had sewn all his money, promissory notes, jewels, and other valuables inside the mattress. Kok was horrified when he returned to his room and found that some boy had taken his mattress to the *goedang*. To everyone's amusement, Kok ran all over the camp to find the boy who'd done this to him, but without result. In despair, he offered Mr. Schotel five hundred guilders, which he had on him, if he would allow him five minutes in the *goedang*.

Mr. Schotel, who had a reputation of being incorruptible, took the money, put it in the general fund, and allowed the crook to sort the mattresses out. When Kok came out of the *goedang*, he was a poor man, just a regular *tawanan* like everyone else. He hadn't found his loot. Nobody knew what had happened to it.

Pieter, who'd watched the course of events from close by, came over to the infirmary that day after his kitchen work was done. Everybody was talking about Mr. Kok and what an unpatriotic, miserable man he was to suck money out of his own countrymen. They couldn't get over it, how low this man had stooped to save himself, and to make money off other people's suffering.

"How many bastards like that are there among us, you wonder?" Rob said.

"Of course there are others," Gijs said. "This isn't the first time we've seen grown-ups take the low road. Being an example for boys like us doesn't seem to be foremost on their minds."

"I wasn't planning to follow their example," Pieter said. "There must be better examples to follow."

"Let's think of men we would be proud to emulate. That may cheer us up a bit," Gijs said. Paatje Hinten and Keereweer immediately came to his mind, and he told the others how those two men had inspired him.

"Well, I have limitless admiration for Jonkheer de Villeneuve," Pieter said. "He has blue blood in his veins, and maybe that helps, but that man was given an impossible task to keep order among ten thousand *tawanans*, and he dealt with it honestly. What a man!"

"I didn't meet anybody like that in Batavia," Rob said, "but if we survive this war, I will hold the camp leadership here up as my heroes. Mr. Nauta, Mr. Schotel, and Mr. Moolenaar are incredible people in my view. Do you realize these men all volunteered? They're paid for their good work with beatings by the Japs. They take it on the chin for us."

They sat around, smoking cigarettes that Pieter had bought at the *toko*.

"Remember, Pieter," Gijs said, "when you told me back in Bandoeng that you thought the Japs would just as soon drive us all into the ocean?"

Pieter looked at the crinkles of smoke that rose from his burning cigarette. "Yes, I do, and I think they still would, but they know they can't get away with it."

"Starving us is a better tactic for them," Rob said. "At least they'll be able to say they didn't kill us. We just died."

"That's morbid," Gijs said.

"I know. Not the kind of thought that carries you through the next day."

"What will?" Pieter asked.

"When I was at the Bangka camp, I slept next to a young priest," Gijs said. "I was in bad shape, because I didn't want to eat rice. I hated rice, can you believe that?"

They laughed.

"This priest," Gijs went on, "told us not to let the Japanese break our spirits. Rise above the humiliations and love one another. It made an impression on me. I don't know if I believe in a God, but from what I've seen so far, love accomplishes more than hate."

"True enough," Pieter said. "It's just that the percentages are wrong."

"We simply have to believe that the small percentage is stronger and wins out," Gijs said.

"Let's hope so," Rob said.

It was dark now. They were barely visible to one another, as they sat in the grass beside the infirmary. Sweet smells rose from shrubs and flowers that had been soaked by the last downpour. The 10:30 PM bell would soon sound over the camp. It meant lights out and quiet. Pieter got up to get back to his own *tempat* before it was too late.

Mr. Weert, true to his word, set up a curriculum for the boys. It was a haphazard organization, and in no way did it resemble school. What Mr. Weert had to work with were teachers without textbooks and pupils who had not sat on a school bench for two-and-a-half years. The boys who'd been sent up from the women's camps had received no education at all. Apart from these setbacks was the poor physical condition of both the teachers and the pupils. They were hungry, and they wanted to be on work details, not in school, so they could buy extra food at the *toko*.

There were six times as many boys as men in the camp. Twelve hundred boys and two hundred men. Among those men were teachers, and even men who hadn't been teachers volunteered to share their knowledge. Older boys, like Pieter Donk, also helped out, mostly with younger boys. The broken pieces of slate came in handy, and some textbooks had been smuggled in over time and gathered into a small library. Kunemoto turned a blind eye to these happenings.

Mr. Schotel had successfully brought order out of chaos by creating a steady routine. Every *tawanan*, adult or boy, knew he had to get out of bed at 7:30, get his porridge, go through morning roll call, and have his room clean by 8. Work detail was until 11, when the lessons started for a two-hour period. At 1 they could stand in line for their cooked food. At 4 they got a piece of bread and, with a bit of luck, a banana. The evening meal was at 6, evening call at 7. All the lights went out at 10:15, and after 10:30 on the dot there had to be absolute silence.

By making a tight schedule that everyone could count on, it was possible to plan lessons, although Mr. Weert's window of opportunity was only two hours. In the evenings, the boys did their homework and the teachers prepared the lessons for the next day, but several times the pupils found that their teacher had been taken ill and was in the infirmary. It took tremendous determination for the boys to finish schoolwork and take exams. Their exams were graded, and they were given a piece of paper that verified that they had completed the course. Boys with forethought had concluded that if the war ever ended, they did not want to go back to the class they'd been in when the Japanese had closed the schools in April 1942. They got as much schoolwork done and over with now.

All it would take to end the classes was for Kunemoto to declare them illegal. To be on the safe side, the classes were conducted in small groups and always inside a house.

In October, Mr. Weert landed in the infirmary with a severe case of dysentery. Epidemics of the dreaded disease seemed to come in cycles. Gijs had seen it happen in every camp he'd been in.

"You know, Gijs," Keereweer had said to him, when the dysentery epidemic broke out in the Fourth and Ninth Battalion, "I am of a good mind to cut a hole in each cot and put a bedpan on the floor beneath it. That would save a lot of hassle."

And so he did. Gijs suggested it to Dr. Wins, who agreed it would be a good idea. Rob and Gijs got some butcher knives, cut round holes in the canvas in a number of cots, and placed a pail underneath. It was crude but practical. This way, they saved the patients the agony of having to get up, or of being too late, or of lying uncomfortably on the steel rim of a bedpan. Gijs and Rob turned the patients over several times a day to wash them. It was the best they could do under the circumstances.

Gijs was sitting behind his desk in the large room that once had been the living room of an officer's house, when Mr. Weert stumbled in. Behind Gijs were the cots filled with patients. Mr. Weert looked washed out, as bad or worse as Mr. van Dam had when he came to the infirmary at the LOG. Because he'd had a bad case of dysentery himself, Gijs knew exactly how his former roommate felt. He placed him on a cot directly behind his desk.

After a few days, Mr. Weert's condition worsened. His bowel movements were bloody, and Gijs became alarmed. To make sure his patient wouldn't dehydrate, Gijs helped him drink water, as much as he could get into him. Dr. Wins was not impressed with the tea enema routine that Keereweer had used, when Gijs mentioned it. Bacillary dysentery needed something more potent to kill the bacteria, he said. They both knew what that something was: Cibasol, the sulfa wonder drug. There was only so much of the drug to go around. The Japanese military doctors, as Gijs knew only too well from his previous experience, kept it for their people. It was a dilemma. Dr. Wins knew what to prescribe, but he also knew the prescription could not be filled.

Gijs told him how he had lucked out at the LOG; how a Japanese doctor had given it to him, and that maybe not all Japanese were cruel. Dr. Wins thought it over and went to the military hospital on the other side of the railroad tracks. It was used by all the internment camps in Tjimahi, as well as by the Japanese military. Dr. Wins was just as concerned about Mr. Weert as Gijs was. He'd seen too many men die from the disease, especially when it combined with hunger edema.

Dr. Wins got what he wanted, and when he returned he told Gijs he had been right. Not all Japanese were cruel.

It took a week for Mr. Weert to get over the worst, and another week for him to get his strength back. When he begged Gijs to close a before-the-war magazine with ads of luscious food and lavish restaurants, which Gijs had found in a closet and sat reading at his desk to pass the time between chores, he realized Mr. Weert had come through. They began to chat a lot.

"It baffles me," Gijs said at one point, "how the guards can force us to bow for them, even hit us when we don't. I know it's to honor their emperor, but we certainly honor our queen and we don't expect foreigners to bow for every Dutch soldier, officer, or whoever represents our queen. Can you explain that, Mr. Weert?"

"That's a far more complex question than you realize, Gijs."

"I was afraid it would be."

"The easy answer is to say that the emperor is a deity, because he is the descendant of the Goddess Amaterasu. This belief is rooted in their original religion, called Shinto, which worships nature and the spirits of their ancestors. In essence, Shinto is a primitive tribal religion, but it remains an essential part of the Japanese culture."

"So, are we really expected to see the Japanese emperor as a god, and not as an earthly ruler?"

"The Japanese would like you to think that way, yes," Mr. Weert said. "Sixty-five years ago, in 1889, they wrote it into their constitution. Even though the constitution allowed for freedom of religion, it made Shinto officially an institution of the state. What that really means is that patriotism is the only true religion for every Japanese citizen, and what goes hand in hand with this worship of the emperor is a feeling of superiority. A Jap's view of the world is suffused with the certainty that, because of his extraordinary heritage, he is more courageous, more virtuous, and more intelligent than other peoples. Japan is destined to rule the world. That's how they see it."

"They're certainly acting on it," Gijs said, and laughed.

"Their world view is called 'hakka ichiu,' which means the eight corners of the world under one roof. All countries form an organic whole, with Japan as the brains. It will grow and develop under the exalted virtues of His Majesty, the emperor. They see it as their divine mission to bring the Japanese national structure to the rest of the world."

"So, that's why we sit here in an internment camp, at the receiving end of their divine mission!" Gijs said.

He decided not to press Mr. Weert for further enlightenment that day. There would be another time. Meanwhile, he formulated the questions that the conversation had raised for him. Mr. Weert was a history teacher, and it would be interesting to philosophize with him about how rulers seemed to use religion toward their own end.

When he brought it up in their next conversation, Mr. Weert chuckled.

"Gijs! You're touching on one of the fundamental problems that faces humanity: the desire for power, greed, territory, the riches of the earth, the differences in race…We struggle and struggle to engineer a world we can share equitably, but it is so hard!"

"I've noticed," Gijs said.

"If you want to find answers, you will have to study history."

And that was the thought Mr. Weert left Gijs with as he left the infirmary.

Chapter 20

Gijs thought he should wash his blanket. It was early December, the rainy season. He reasoned that wringing soap out of a blanket, even the poor quality soap he'd bought in the *toko* that hardly foamed, would not be easy. Better let the heavy downpours do the final rinsing for him. He took the blanket to a concrete platform with a faucet and a drain that was the designated place for doing laundry. Clotheslines were strung nearby between the trees.

A Japanese soldier walked by as Gijs hung the blanket on the line to dry. It was heavy with water and dripping. The soldier stopped and walked over. He examined the blanket and fingered it. With sign language and in broken Maleis he made it known that he wanted the blanket. Gijs shook his head. The soldier repeated his wish to have the blanket. Since it was the only blanket Gijs had and one of the few things he'd been allowed to bring to the camp, he wasn't willing to part with it. He shook his head again. No!

The soldier got angry, shouted, and whacked him in the face with his flat hand. It stung, but it wasn't enough to make him give up his one and only blanket. He looked the soldier in the eye and shook his head. No!

The soldier viewed Gijs's refusal as insubordination, even though the soldiers had no right to take the essential possessions of a *tawanan*. Another hard slap in his face. Gijs dug in his heels. He knew he was on the right side of the rules. The soldier tried another tactic. With his fingers he indicated that he would pay for it. Again, Gijs shook his head. No!

After another round of hard slaps, Gijs began to reconsider. If he had to part with his blanket, he would charge an outrageous sum. Fifty guilders. It was impossible to win an argument with a Japanese soldier, but at least he could make it worthwhile by getting a good sum of money.

The soldier didn't think long about the offer. He turned on his heel and walked away.

Would this be the end of the incident? Gijs wondered. Back at the infirmary, Rob took one look at his swollen face and asked what had happened.

"The Jap wanted my blanket."

"He didn't get it, I see," Rob said.

"Right. I finally told him he could have it for fifty guilders."

"That's a lofty sum. Did he bite?"

"No, he walked away."

Rob looked concerned, but he didn't give voice to his worries. In the evening, a *heiho* came to the infirmary and brought Gijs to the guard post next to the camp's gate. A guard, Minamihara, was waiting for him. He accused Gijs first of refusing to sell his blanket to a Japanese soldier, and then of charging a scandalous price for it.

During the four months he'd spent in the boys' camp, Gijs had never been inside the guard's building. He'd heard plenty about it, though, and what he'd heard didn't give him much comfort as he stood before the man who had been widely nicknamed, for reasons unknown to Gijs, "the Indian boy." Minamihara was infamous for his sadistic streak. The stories about his brutalities were legion, and Gijs could only hope they had been grossly exaggerated.

The Indian boy was shouting and carrying on in broken Maleis, making it clear that Gijs should sell the blanket to the other soldier for less. A price was not mentioned. Gijs refused. A deep anger at the injustice settled in, and words his mother had once spoken streamed into his mind. "We cannot let ourselves be brought down to the same level of insanity. See it as a test." She had said this after receiving the news that Vader's ship had been attacked, and they'd wondered if the world had gone crazy.

"This is my test," Gijs mumbled to himself as the first blow from Minamihara's sheathed saber landed on his head.

This is my test, he thought when he was brought outside and made to stand in the pouring rain with only his shorts on while the blows from the saber continued to fall on his head, his shoulders, his back. Occasionally, he was asked if he would sell his blanket, but he kept refusing.

The night turned into dawn. The blows never stopped, except for the repeated question: was he willing to sell his blanket. His answer remained the same.

The ordeal ended suddenly at six in the morning, when a cart with vegetables appeared at the gate, followed by a Japanese petty officer. Gijs was let go. He staggered back to the infirmary, where an anxious Rob awaited him. When he saw Gijs, whose head was bleeding and swollen, his arms and body covered with lurid bruises, welts, and scrapes, he immediately called Dr. Wins. The doctor, in turn, called Mr. Schotel to witness the result of the guard's handiwork. Mr. Schotel was appalled.

Gijs's head wounds and other scrapes were treated and bandaged, and Dr. Wins admitted him to the infirmary. Pieter came by, having heard from Mr. Nauta and Mr. Schotel what had happened.

"My God, Gijs, you look like you've been in a car wreck!" Pieter said.

"That might have been better," Gijs said with a wan smile.

"Do you still have your blanket?"

"Oh, yes!"

After he'd spent twenty-four hours in the infirmary, Minamihara summoned Gijs. Again! Dr. Wins told the messenger that his patient was unable to come, but that made no difference to the soldier. Rob and another orderly carried Gijs to the guard's building on a stretcher. Minamihara was waiting for him, obviously not satisfied with how his "negotiations" with Gijs had ended the day before. This time he would do better. He called in the *heihos* and had them beat Gijs up in the style of the native boxing art, called *pentjak.* The *heihos* took turns slapping him in the face with the sides of their right hands. His head bandages flew off. Minamihara sat on a chair, watching. As if this were not enough, he got out handcuffs; fastened them around Gijs's wrists, and made Gijs kneel before him. As Dr. Wins came in to see how Gijs was faring, and to plead with Minamihara to forgive Gijs, he was treated to the spectacle of the brute raising his sheathed saber and bringing it down on Gijs's head. Minamihara refused to forgive.

Dr. Wins went directly to Kunemoto, who intervened.

Gijs could hardly stand up straight. Blood poured from his face and from a mean gash on his left shoulder. Dr. Wins ordered Rob and Pieter to get a stretcher for the trip back to the infirmary. Dazed and bandaged up, he lay down on his cot. Rob covered him with Gijs's own blanket, which he'd rescued from the line and hung out to dry in his room.

The next day, Rob panicked when he saw a Japanese soldier walk into the infirmary. Oh no, he thought, not again. The soldier carried a big wooden box and asked to see Gijs Bozuwa. Rob wondered if he should allow the visit. But what means did he have to keep the soldier away from Gijs? He was not an expert at reading a Japanese face. Emotions between the two extremes of very angry and very happy were locked up behind a mask that could not be easily removed by a European. Yet, Rob decided, since the Jap stood before him with a flat box and not with a stick, he might have better intentions than Minamihara had shown.

Through the slit in the bandages that enveloped his head, Gijs watched the soldier approach. It was the one who'd wanted to take his blanket. He felt defenseless and without any fight left in him, but the man's presence sparked his curiosity, and he tried to sit up. The soldier said nothing, just took the lid off the box. Rob, standing behind the soldier, gasped when he saw a dozen pastries inside. The man smiled and handed the box to Gijs. Then he turned and left.

On January 12, 1948, Minamihara Koshoku, born in Korea on October 13, 1923, stood trial before the Temporary Court Marshall in the building of the Supreme Court of the Dutch East Indies, in Batavia.

He was accused of war crimes on six counts, all of them having taken place in the Baros Six Camp (the boys' camp), in Tjimahi.

Nine witnesses testified under oath. Among them were Gijs, Mr. Schotel, Dr. Wins, Mr. Nauta, and Mr. Moolenaar. Gijs, back in Holland, made his legal statement under oath at a court in The Hague on August 7, 1947.

Minamihara was accused, among other war crimes, of "gruesome mistreatment of the boy Bozuwa."

He received a sentence of fifteen years in prison.

Chapter 21

The bandages muffled the sounds of the outside world. What did he look like? Gijs wondered. An Egyptian mummy? Did he care? His head throbbed. His whole body ached. Rob had put him on the cot behind the desk, but Gijs was hardly aware of his comings and goings. He let his fingers run over his blanket, his own blanket. Had it been worth it, to get beaten up like this? He wasn't quite ready to assess whether he should label the struggle a defeat or a victory. Not until he could walk out of the internment camp, alive and with his blanket on his shoulder, could he call it a victory. And that day seemed far away.

In the stillness of his bandaged head, Gijs tried to make sense of what had happened to him, and not only in the last two days. He counted the months since he'd left the Houtmanstraat in the Tjihapit camp in Bandoeng. Twenty-two months! That was how long it had been since he'd seen Moeder and Janneke. How long since he'd seen Vader? Two years and eight months! Where was everyone at this moment? The boys who'd recently arrived from the camps in Bandoeng had told him their mothers would soon be put on transport to somewhere. A week ago, a long train had traveled through Tjimahi with women on their way from Bandoeng to Batavia. Workers at the farm in Leuwigadjah had heard shouts coming from the train. The women knew they were passing the Tjimahi camps where their husbands and sons were.

Moeder and Janneke might have been on that train. It worried him that they might be in Batavia. Even though he'd been born there, he had no memory of the place, but Moeder had often told of how hot and muggy it was in the capitol. If they were put in a camp like the Fourth and Ninth Battalion with thousands of other women and very young children, they would have a much harder time to endure. In the Houtmanstraat, even with a full house, they had at least been with friends and in a bearable climate. A postcard he'd received in October from them had been written in Maleis and had obviously been censored. Six months it had taken to get from Bandoeng to Tjimahi. It was his most up-to-date information about their whereabouts.

He'd never heard from Vader again after the reassuring note that he'd survived the shipwreck. It was hard to guess what could have happened to him. Gijs preferred not to dwell on the possibilities.

Thoughts like these had been easier to keep at bay in the day-to-day life he'd carved out for himself. Flat on his back, uncomfortable with bandages in odd places, he had plenty of unwelcome time to ponder the changes. Being a part of a family where decisions were made for him, playing sports, traveling around freely, eating what he liked and going to school, these were all things of the past. It was even hard to remember what it had been like to sail on the ocean with his father, or to kick around a soccer ball with him after school. Sitting in a chair at a table covered with a linen cloth and eating with a silver fork and knife, or opening a drawer and finding a clean set of underwear, these things seemed like stories in a book. In his new life it counted most to feed himself as well as he could with whatever he could find. That was task number one. Task number two was to live by the rules. These were the new criteria he lived by.

"Hey, Gijs, can you hear me?" It was Pieter's voice.

"Yes. Don't shout, I have a headache."

"I wonder why! I want to thank you for the pastry. Boy, did that taste good."

"I'm glad you liked it," Gijs said. "Wasn't that a neat surprise, to get a box full of goodies? I thought Rob would faint when the soldier opened the box."

"I've been trying to figure out why he gave them to you," Pieter said.

"He didn't say anything, so it's hard to know."

"Rob and I think he felt bad when he found out what had happened to you. He wanted the blanket, but not at that cost."

"Could be," Gijs said. "Any news?"

"Yes," Pieter said, and he lowered his voice to a whisper. "There are persistent rumors that the Americans have landed with a big army in the Philippines."

"Let's hope that's true."

"We think the Japs here know it and that's why they're so tough. The war isn't going well for them."

"I wonder what we should hope for," Gijs whispered. "That the Americans make a quick move and we're liberated, or the Japs win and they won't be quite so hard on us?"

"Are you serious?" Pieter whispered back. "Did Minamihara knock your good sense out of you? Of course, the Americans should win. Mark my words, they will."

Gijs smiled. One of Pieter's many gifts was that he had the power of conviction. If Pieter made a statement, you believed it, or at least you wanted to.

The day before Christmas, Gijs was released from the infirmary. Dr. Wins said he could not come back to work for at least another week. Christmas at the LOG had not been remarkable, but this year it would be different. Since the Japanese Sixteenth Army had taken over the authority, rules about education and religion had relaxed. It was one of the signs Pieter used to convince Rob and Gijs that the war was not going as the Japs had hoped.

"Just think of it," Pieter said. "Right after the capitulation, our culture had to be erased. The quickest way was to forbid the Dutch language in schools and churches."

"True," Rob said.

"Then they wanted to humiliate us by putting us out of sight."

"Not before they'd caused a spectacle," Rob said. "I remember scenes in Batavia of the natives lining the streets while we walked with our *barang* on our shoulders on our way to the Tjideng camp. The natives couldn't believe their eyes."

"Yes. I remember open buses with white women and crying children driving through the streets," Gijs said. "But they didn't get the response from the natives they'd hoped for."

"The boys who've arrived from all over the place," Rob said, "tell horrible stories about how they sat on straw in closed cattle cars, traveling for days. Little guys, twelve years old! No more showing of their circus animals before the big circus show."

"So, you see," Pieter said, "they're giving up on trying to root out Western culture. They're preoccupied with the war. To me, that is the clearest sign it's going to be over soon!"

"Shall we make a bet on when the war will be over?" Gijs asked.

"What's the prize?" Pieter asked.

"An evening out with a beautiful girl," Rob said.

Gijs was not surprised. After listening to Rob's stories, he was convinced their room would have been plastered with posters of pinup girls if they were available.

"I don't know if I could deliver that, Rob," Gijs said. "I am a bit out of touch with the social scene."

"How about you, Gijs? What kind of prize would you like?" Pieter asked.

"I would like to sail with my father on the North Sea."

"You will," Pieter said.

"How about a motorcycle for you, Pieter?"

"Wouldn't that be nice? Preferably my old trusted DKW."

"Let's keep dreaming," Gijs said.

On Christmas Day, a religious service was held on a grassy knoll between two white houses, which were on the same side of the camp as the infirmary. Since anyone could attend, Gijs walked slowly over the gravel road to join. He stood behind the small crowd, leaning against the rough concrete wall of one of the houses. The Protestant minister didn't talk about dreaming. He talked about hope. Without hope, he said, there is no life. "Light has come into the world. Place your faith in the child that came to save the world." Gijs knew he had hope. He'd never given up hope. The part about the child saving the world he wasn't sure of. He envied the minister who evidently believed it was possible.

In the afternoon, everyone was herded into the large building where, before the war, cavalry horses had been shod. Recently, it had been reopened to use the huge foundry for making *patjoels* and other articles the Japanese needed. Two hundred *tawanans* had been brought in from the Baros V camp to work in it, but today it was the domain of a group of boys, who had initiated a Club for Recreation. They'd already given several performances. Even Kunemoto had attended.

Long lines of boys and men flowed like an unfurling ball of wool through the groupings of small houses toward the blacksmith school. They'd washed their clothes for the occasion, which was a chore they tried to avoid, because it was such a hassle without a sink, and because they never had the satisfaction of declaring them clean. The soap was ineffective. Their before-the-war cotton fabric was a wrinkly mess, but they didn't have irons to flatten the clothes, and it was debatable whether they'd know how to use them if they could find them. Camp was not a happy place for neatniks. For the Christmas 1944 festivities, this was the best they could do.

A crudely constructed stage inside the blacksmith school served as a field for the shepherds. Something that resembled a hut leaned precariously against a wall, and a curtain hung to the side of the podium.

Kunemoto appeared in civilian clothes, smiling broadly. The Catholic priest spoke briefly. The boys' choir sang, accompanied by two violins and a guitar. It never ceased to amaze Gijs how some things, even as big as a guitar, had made it into camp. Neither a violin nor a guitar had been on the list of allowed articles.

The pageant was short but effective. Three shepherds appeared. They hardly looked like shepherds, but the audience understood that the pillowcases pulled over the backs of their heads identified them as such. As they sat on the rough wooden planks of the stage, they complained about their poor living conditions. Pieter elbowed

Gijs and whispered, "Good thing Kunemoto doesn't understand Dutch." Suddenly, a fourth shepherd burst onto the scene, confirming rumors about the coming of the Messiah. He invited the other three to follow him. The curtain fell away, and a backdrop of small houses in Bethlehem appeared, artistically drawn on a large piece of paper. Gijs wondered where the paper had come from; no one seemed to know. A light fastened to the top flicked on a transparent star. The choir picked up the cue and sang, "*Eere zij God* (Glory be to God)."

One of the shepherds asked the audience to turn around, and there they saw a large Christmas tree, beautifully decorated and topped by a lit star. It was stunning. How had this happened? Gijs wondered again. Where had the decorations come from? The questions were answered with secretive smiles. Better not ask, they seemed to say.

As everyone trooped outside after the performance, each *tawanan* received a paper bag with four onions, three ginger cookies, some favorite Indonesian spices, and, best of all, a large fondant in the shape of a Christmas bell. Coffee candy! Gijs looked at Pieter as he opened his present.

"Who made this?" he asked.

"Nauta," Pieter said.

On New Year's Eve, Mr. Nauta outdid himself again. Every *tawanan* received the traditional Dutch *oliebol,* fried dough.

A new year was on its way: 1945. As the minutes ticked by, they wondered if they were entering the last year of the war, but for too many it would be the last year of their lives.

Chapter 22

The New Year did not start out well for Pieter. Somebody in the kitchen knocked over a pan with hot oil, and the boiling liquid landed on top of his right foot. He ran over to the water faucet and stuck his foot under the cold stream, which helped, but he was left with a mean burn on his instep. Dr. Wins lanced the blister.

He was a sad sight, hobbling around with only his left foot in a sandal, because he could not tolerate the strap of his sandal over the instep of the other. Predictably, the burn turned into an ugly, infected wound. Dr. Wins said this had a lot to do with poor nourishment. Wounds had a hard time healing when the body had little defense against invading bacteria. He admitted Pieter into the infirmary and told him to stay off his feet until the wound was healed. There was no magic medicine. The healing process would have to take its own course.

It fell to Gijs to bandage his friend's foot twice a day. Slowly and carefully, he would lift off the old bandage, clean the wound, and cover it with a cotton square soaked in Burrow's Solution, a disinfecting solution that would keep the wound clean and wet. Then he wrapped Pieter's foot in a tightly woven yellow cloth called *taft*, which prevented the solution from leaking out. Lastly, he wound a bandage around the ankle and foot in such a way that it wouldn't slip off.

"So, you don't just empty bedpans," Pieter said, as he watched Gijs carefully apply the bandage, twisting it after each completed circle around Pieter's foot so it wouldn't sag, a trick he'd learned from Keereweer.

"Thank God for that! I wouldn't have lasted long as an orderly if that was all I did in a day," Gijs said.

"I thought that the helpers in the kitchen were the hardest working people in the camp, but now that I see what Rob and you have to do, I'm not so sure."

"Yes, there's a lot to do here. Laundering the sheets is the hardest part. The soap we get is lousy, and it's a constant hassle to get soap in the first place."

"How about the bandages?" Picter asked.

"There's no such thing as new bandages. So we use the ones we have over and over. We boil them every night." Gijs thought he wouldn't tell Pieter what a stinky job it was. Drying them was another difficult trick. The wind would knot them together as they hung on the line to dry. Looking at Pieter, Gijs had an idea.

"Hey, Pieter, since you're just lying about, would you like to use this gadget here to wind the bandages up after I wash them?"

He showed him a table-sized mill with a handle and a few thin dowels that kept the bandage material in a straight line. The mill changed the bandage from an unorganized ball, the way it came off the line, into a neat roll.

"Sure. Anything to save me from boredom," Pieter said.

The infirmary steadily became busier. That people suffered from dysentery was nothing new. Every *tawanan* seemed to get his turn eventually, and often more than once. The patients Dr. Wins had recently admitted were adults with childhood diseases like measles and chickenpox. The doctor said he could see what three years of stress and hunger had wrought.

"At first," he said, "most men benefited from a different regime. They had lived the good life with a generous amount of alcohol, too much food, and not enough exercise. That first year they didn't have to perform any labor, and the food wasn't all that bad. Now they do hard labor and get less to eat. Their natural resistance has broken down."

Every bed in the infirmary was taken. Gijs and Rob were busy all through the day, keeping the patients clean and making sure they got enough water so they would not dehydrate.

Pieter saw it was impossible for them to help feed every patient. Without asking, he went over to a patient who showed no appetite. From the corner of his eye, Gijs saw how the man leaned forward to allow Pieter to put a spoonful of cooked rice into his mouth. When he looked again, the plate was empty. Pieter got more involved. He wasn't allowed to walk, but he wasn't sick. Gijs would find him, at any time of the day, sitting next to a bed, talking to a patient or straightening his bedclothes and rearranging his pillow.

Not every patient who walked in walked out. That was the hard part. Washing sheets, emptying bedpans, bandaging wounds, administering the few medicines they had available, helping people drink and eat, all of it was work, but dealing with the end of life touched a nerve.

One early morning, when Gijs came into the ward, Pieter called him over.

"I have to talk to you. Mr. Enkeling died last night."

"Rob told me."

"I sat with him," Pieter said. "The last thing he said was 'Why?' It's haunting me."

Gijs looked at his friend and thought back to when he'd first met him in Bandoeng. Handsome, in control, impressive on his motorbike, those had been the first impressions, but what had made him feel comfortable with Pieter was his thoughtfulness. Pieter would not take the ending of a man's life lightly.

"It brings you to the core, doesn't it?"

"It sure does. You can reconcile the ending of a long, fully lived life," Pieter said, "but one that's cut short? It's really sad when you have to sum up your whole life with one word: Why?"

"It's unanswerable," Gijs said.

"What bothers me about Mr. Enkeling, poor guy, is that he left this earth wondering what his life had been worth, and I think to myself, what right did the Japs have to cut his life short?

"I always wonder," Gijs said, "how we put a value on someone's life. If a life is fully lived, it seems to have a value we can understand, and that makes it less hard to part with."

"Who or what determines the value of anyone's life? And what right does one man have over another man's life? That's the real question."

"Yes, I suppose so. What I've learned so far in camp is that there's no life without death, and there's no death without life."

"That's deep," Pieter said.

The morning porridge was delivered. Gijs had to go back to work. He left Pieter lying on his cot in deep thought.

Gijs celebrated his nineteenth birthday in bed. Dr. Wins had no difficulty making the diagnosis when Gijs presented himself with complaints of a sore throat, high fever, and fatigue. Dr. Wins just looked at his yellow face and said, "You have hepatitis A. What you need is rest and glucose to correct the hypoglycemia."

Gijs wasn't sure if the doctor was joking. He didn't know what hypoglycemia meant, but he did recognize the word glucose.

"Sugar, right?"

"Yes, and lots of it."

"That's a tall order, doctor. I don't have any sugar left over from this month's rations."

"Let's see what we can do about that."

Sugar equaled gold. The island of Java grew tons of sugarcane, but that was before the war. What had happened to those prosperous sugar plantations? Many *tawanans* hypothesized that the *econo-men* had failed to master the technique of the sugar cultivation. Others said there were warehouses bulging with the stuff, available to the Japanese but not to the *belandas*.

When Rob and Pieter came by to congratulate him on his birthday, Gijs was in bed in the servants' quarters. They said they wouldn't sing *"Lang zal hij leven,"* because they assumed he had a headache. But they had a big present for him. A bag with two pounds of sugar.

"Thank you, but how in the world did you get hold of that much sugar? Am I now complicit in stolen goods?"

"It's all on the up, Gijs," Rob said. "Dr. Wins said you needed lots of sugar to get better, so we put our rations together and asked for some extra at the *toko*. Doctor's orders, we said."

"It worked!" Pieter said. "So, don't worry about it, just eat it. They need you at the infirmary."

One thing about an internment camp, Gijs thought as he let himself fall back on his pillow, was that you got to know people through and through. Not all men were jewels, but these two were rocks you could build on.

By March, Gijs was back at work. He'd missed being in the infirmary. Not the part about doing laundry and emptying bedpans. What he had missed was waking up in the morning and knowing he had a destination. Being around sick people was something he'd gotten used to. A few weeks of high fever and generally feeling lousy had made him doubly aware of the state of mind the patients were in when they were down and out, lying on their cots, staring at the ceiling. He'd noticed that it took little effort to get them out of their funk. Just dropping a cheerful line in passing seemed to move their barometer up to fair weather.

"Gijs," Pieter had asked him during one of his frequent visits when he was sick, "are you still on course to become a navy officer?"

"Funny that you should ask. Mr. Weert asked me the same question the other day. I haven't been able to take classes lately. I've spent too much time in bed!"

"I heard he has a hard time keeping the education program going. It's no wonder, really. Everybody wants to work to get extra food, and after work they're too exhausted. What was your answer to Mr. Weert?"

"That I am wavering."

"I'm not surprised. Ever since I saw you at work, I've thought you'd make a good doctor."

"Make that an orderly. I like taking care of people," Gijs said.

"Well, okay, an orderly then. Would that be too much of a switch from being in the navy, like your dad?"

"You know, Pieter, I think I liked the life my father led. It was adventurous. It was always exciting."

"And you didn't think about what it would be like in wartime, I bet," Pieter said, and he laughed.

"I wasn't thinking along those lines then, that's true," Gijs said. "You have to wonder what's left of the Dutch Navy."

"We'll soon find out. You know, between you and me, I think somebody in this camp has a radio."

"What makes you think that?"

"I walked by Mr. Schotel's house late one evening, and I swear I heard a newscast in English. I stopped and listened. I am quite sure of it."

"The man will get shot if they find out."

"Don't worry, they won't hear it from me. Not from you either, I know."

"Right. Do you think the news is good or bad?" Gijs asked.

"The Allies are hard at work, but the Japs are stubborn. They're holding out."

The rumor mill was working with more grist. Where the grist came from was anyone's guess, but news that the Allies were making significant advances was persistent. One sign that it was not a rumor was that the military hospital, where three camps sent their sick, needed to be emptied out. The Japanese military command needed the entire building to take care of their wounded in case of an invasion. In April, the Dutch hospital staff moved into the lower part of the boys' camp with all their patients. The boys who lived down there had to move in with those in the upper part of the camp. It was getting very crowded. Rob and Gijs praised the day they had been assigned to work in the infirmary and given the servants' quarters to live in by themselves.

Workers at the Tjimindi farm told of trenches they had to dig. Trenches for fighting? Could it be true then? Would the Allies invade and liberate them? It was tempting to believe in that scenario over the one the pessimists proclaimed, which was that the trenches would become their own graves. All the Japanese had to do, they reasoned, was to line them up, shoot, and ditch them before the Allies could reach them.

Pieter came over to the infirmary with news. Mori, a North Korean, was replacing Kunemoto as the camp commandant.

"Is that good news or bad news?" Rob asked.

"I'll let you know," Pieter said.

It was bad news. Mori was fanatical about hygiene, and he was none too gentle in policing new rules. He demanded that every prisoner had to hand in twenty dead bedbugs at every night call. Twenty bedbugs filled four matchboxes. Mori had various ways of punishing if he suspected not enough had been caught. If a section of the camp handed in too few, he had everybody line up in pairs and forced them to beat each other up. When he felt they weren't hitting hard enough, he walked in between the rows with a bamboo stick and did the hitting himself. The boys returned to their bunks with bruises and welts on their necks and upper bodies.

Pieter, who was closer to these happenings because he worked in the kitchen, reported one day that something awful had happened. Mori had discovered that roof tiles were missing on several buildings. He was determined to have them replaced. How many are missing? he asked Mr. Schotel. Three thousand, Mr. Schotel said off the top of his head. He had learned that the Japanese expected immediate answers. Mori ordered the tiles and the roofs were repaired, but they were several hundred tiles short. Mori declared that someone had stolen them. Who was guilty? he demanded. Nobody was, because Mr. Schotel had asked for too few tiles.

"You know what the bastard did?" Pieter said. "He put Mr. Schotel, Mr. Nauta, Mr. Moolenaar, and thirty-one section heads in a small storage closet and left them there from ten o'clock at night till one in the morning."

"You mean in that little building without windows?" Rob asked.

"Exactly. Can you imagine? Thirty-four men in a closet without ventilation. Mr. Nauta said they couldn't sit. They had to lean on each other, and it got unbearably hot in there. He said he'd rather get beat up than endure that again. The sergeant of the guard let them out against Mori's orders."

"What a beast," Rob said. "It's time we get out of here."

"If only we could," Gijs said.

Two deaths a day. Less food. Pig entrails for meat. Guards meaner than ever. How much longer? These were the thoughts Gijs woke up with one morning in early August, and they repeated themselves over and over in his mind, like a mantra.

He worried more than ever about his parents. The older adults were the ones at greatest risk. He saw it around him every day. Of course, in the back of his mind he'd worried about them all the time. It had become the mental backdrop to life in prison. However vague, those worries were always there, but he'd discovered that the more he explicitly worried about his parents and sister, the more he missed them.

From all he'd heard from prisoners who came from other camps, the boys' camp was Valhalla. It was certainly an improvement over the other camps Gijs had lived in. This was largely due to the excellent leadership of Mr. Schotel. Stories about the Tjideng camp in Batavia sounded like descriptions of hell, and that was where Moeder and Janneke were. The main strikes against it were the oppressive heat, the high humidity because they were on the coast, and the incredibly crowded conditions.

At least he knew where Moeder and Janneke were, but where was Vader? He could be anywhere, but certainly not on Java. Rumors had it that many POWs had been taken to Burma to work. Another rumor was that the top brass had been imprisoned separately, but where was unclear. He assumed that Vader was with the top brass, and he liked to think that the Japanese would be a little gentler with them for fear of retribution by the Allies after the end of the war. What worried him most was the chance that Vader had been executed for having destroyed the naval airfields on Java. This was a recurrent thought, but it came to him only in his darkest moments.

Gijs looked at his own body. His ribs stuck out; his ankles were swollen with edema. That was what lack of protein did to a body. Some *tawanans* had so much edema, they couldn't walk anymore. If he looked this badly while in a relatively "good" camp, in what condition would he find Moeder, Janneke, and Vader?

If he was going to get through, he told himself, he'd better put those thoughts out of his mind, or he would fall into a big hole of longing and self-pity. Since it was not within his power to change his family's circumstances, he had to move on with his own life and see to it that he survived. He was quite sure that's what they were trying to do.

Chapter 23

"Something is afoot," Pieter said to Gijs and Rob later that day. He'd walked into the infirmary after he was through working in the kitchen. The smell of chopped onions still surrounded him.

"Don't tell us if it's bad. We've had enough of that," Rob said.

"I think it's good, or at least it's going to be," Pieter said. "We haven't seen Mori for a few days, and you know how he likes to make the rounds to see if he can stir up trouble? All of a sudden, he's nowhere to be seen. And another thing. We don't have to hand in bedbugs anymore."

"Is that how we tell the war is over?" Gijs asked. "No bedbugs and no Mori?"

"Well, it's something at least. The real news isn't official yet. A new kind of bomb has been dropped on Japan. The thing was so powerful, they think it will bring the Japs to their knees."

"Sounds like radio news."

"It is. Enough said."

"Okay. I can't wait for the next edition," Gijs said.

Did they dare think the war could be over? It felt like waking up from a bad dream that still has a hold on your mind.

On August 15, the boys who regularly worked at the hospital were told to dig trenches instead. On the sixteenth, all the pigs at the Leuwigadja farm were slaughtered. On the seventeenth, the work in the foundry stopped. On the nineteenth, the boys and men who worked in Tjitjalenka building a railroad came back and told of amazing scenes: the Korean guards took down the Japanese flag and danced on it. They even urinated on it.

For a week the camp lived in a sort of twilight zone. Mr. Schotel, who later admitted that he indeed had a radio, knew about the atom bombs being dropped on Hiroshima and Nagasaki. He also knew that the Japanese emperor had told his people in a radio address, on the fourteenth, that he had ordered his soldiers to lay down their weapons unconditionally. Unlike in Europe, where the Allies conquered territory and freed the oppressed citizens, there was no liberation army on Java. Mr. Schotel wondered what would happen next. There was no official word from the camp's commandant, because he'd disappeared. In the guards' building several Japanese soldiers were getting themselves royally drunk. He worried that if they became violent, the *tawanans* would have to defend themselves. Mr. Schotel decided not to make any official announcement, but knowing that everybody already assumed the Japanese had lost the war, he asked for disciplined behavior. It was not clear how the Japanese would react if the *tawanans* suddenly started celebrating.

Finally, Mr. Schotel was called to the office of the Japanese officer who ruled over all camps in Tjimahi. Mr. de Villeneuve and Mr. Bos, the other two Dutch camp commandants, were present as well. The emperor, the officer told them, in his infinite wisdom, had ordered the end of the war to spare more bloodletting. The word capitulation was not used. The officer said the prisoners were free, but emptying the camps would take some time. Meanwhile, their food rations would be doubled. Everybody was free to move outside of the camps, but he warned that they should return in the evening. The Japanese were now their protectors and responsible for the safety of the *belandas*.

When Mr. Schotel walked back to his camp, he could see a large crowd from far off.

"The war is over!" he shouted.

The Dutch red, white, and blue flag was raised and rippled in the breeze. Nobody knew where it had come from. Spontaneously, the national anthem was sung, hesitantly at first, and then emotions burst loose.

"*Lang leve de Koningin, Hoe zee!*"

Chills went down the spines of old and young alike. After the evening roll call, Mr. Schotel gave a speech. He asked for one minute of silence to remember those who could not be part of this celebration, and for the Allies who had fought and died for them. Then he sternly warned they must still obey the Japanese guards.

It was the beginning of a rather bizarre time. The Japanese army had lost the war, but there were no liberators to restore order. The *tawanans* were free, but they could not leave their internment camps. All wanted to know if they still had families, houses, and jobs, but they didn't know how to find out. After years of too little camp food, of hunting frogs and eating rats, they ate too much food, in spite of doctors' warnings that their stomachs couldn't take it.

Trade with the natives on the other side of the fence thrived. The Japanese guards, who'd beaten them unmercifully before, now smiled benignly as items traveled in both directions over the *gedek*. What the natives desperately wanted was cloth of any kind. One boy traded his worn-out underwear for a bottle of oil.

"Gijs, do you have something to trade?" Rob asked. He'd just exchanged a handkerchief for chocolate.

"I sure do! A blanket!"

"I thought you would hold on to that for life. The symbol of your triumph over Minamihara!"

"I don't need a symbol," Gijs said. "I need an egg for breakfast."

He traded his blanket, which was still in decent shape in spite of the brutality of the last few years, for a dozen eggs, a box with cookies, and a basket full of bananas. The next morning, the patients who were still in the infirmary each had a duck egg for breakfast.

After a few days, the temptation to step out of the camp and see the world on the other side of the bamboo fence, perhaps see old friends in the camps on the other side of the railroad, overwhelmed them. Rob, Pieter, and Gijs decided to slip out and walk over to the Fourth and Ninth Battalion Camp. The Japanese guard looked the other way, and they quickly walked out of the gate, straight through a corn field, and through *kampongs,* where the natives cheered them and shouted "Perang habis (The war is over)!" The natives looked almost as shabby as the boys did themselves. They weren't underfed, but it was clear that the war had taken a toll on them. No wonder they traded food for textiles. Their garments looked gray from wear.

Gijs wanted to see Keereweer, to find out how he had fared since Gijs had left the Fourth and Ninth. He checked in the infirmary first.

"Gijs, you're still alive! You even grew an inch or two," Keereweer said, as he clasped Gijs's hand.

"How have you been, Keereweer? You've shrunk around your waist."

"Yeah. This is not a fat farm, you know. What can I say? I survived. There were times I wondered."

"Did you get sick?" Gijs asked.

"Yes. A bad infection on my leg. A Jap kicked my shin."

"What did you do to deserve that?"

"I sent a message out of camp to the relative of a patient. The message was found and traced back to me. Kicking my shin was only part of the punishment. But, you know, that's all over now and I'm here to tell you about it!"

"Right. We can put it behind us," Gijs said.

"I don't know. The Japs, yes. But now we have Soekarno to contend with."

"What do you mean?"

"Soekarno and Hatta declared the 'Republic Indonesia' a week ago. I don't think we will return to the life we knew."

That bit of news registered only briefly with Gijs. It didn't sink in that some natives had different plans for the future of the nation than the colonialists. At the moment, all he cared about was to be free.

"I came to thank you, Keereweer. You've made an orderly out of me."

"My pleasure. Now you can practice giving injections to an orange!"

They shook hands. Keereweer smiled and went back to the infirmary. As he opened the door, he turned around and called, "Good luck, kid."

On the way back, the three boys talked about leaving camp. They'd had enough. What kind of liberation was this if you couldn't get out of your prison, even if the food got better? But where to?

Pieter had just found out that his father and younger brother were still in the Fifteenth Battalion camp in Bandoeng. His mother, like Moeder and Janneke, had been transferred to Batavia from Tjihapit. The Red Cross, he'd learned, was trying to reconnect families.

"Congratulations, Pieter" Gijs said.

"Thank you. I'm very relieved. Now I'm wondering what happened to our house."

"That's one thing I am sure of," Gijs said. "I don't have a house to go back to."

"How about you, Rob?" Pieter asked.

"My parents are divorced," Rob said. "Mother went back to Holland, just before the war. My father worked for the government and traveled a lot, so I lived with an aunt and uncle in Bandoeng. My father was in a prison camp in Soerabaja, but maybe he was transferred."

"It sounds as though all three of us should try to get to Bandoeng somehow," Pieter said.

"I wouldn't know where to stay," Gijs said. "I only lived there, outside of the camp that is, for a few months. I don't know anybody in Bandoeng."

"I have an idea!" Rob said. "We can stay with my aunt and uncle. My uncle is a doctor and I know for sure that he was allowed to stay out of the camp. They are the nicest people in the world."

"Are you sure you can show up with two strangers?" Gijs asked.

"I have no doubt," Rob said.

"We'll be considered deserters, you know," Pieter said. "Mr. Schotel told us we should stay in the camp, and the Japs are supposed to see to that."

"Will that hold you back?" Rob asked.

"No! I'm just mentioning it. We should pick a good moment to step out unnoticed."

"I know," Gijs said. "We should leave during the celebration for the queen's birthday, on the thirty-first."

"Brilliant," Rob said.

To prepare for their escape, Gijs sorted through his possessions. Was it worth carrying underwear that had been worn to threads? He decided they were not worth taking. He would wear the best of what he had and pitch the rest in a trashcan. When he looked at the shoes he'd worn when he walked into his first camp, he thought he could walk out on them as well, but the soles were like cardboard and the upper leather inflexible. He soaked them in cooking oil. For almost three years, he'd worn sandals made from rubber tires. His cot and *tikar* he would gladly leave behind. Most important to keep were the small pieces of paper that certified that he had passed exams in English, biology, astronomy, and chemistry. Altogether, it wasn't enough to put in his leather suitcase, so he left that.

Deserting the infirmary weighed on his mind. What would Dr. Wins think if Rob and he didn't show up? Yet he couldn't tell the doctor about their plans. Repeatedly, warnings were sounded against leaving camp. He didn't understand what people were worried about, but that was beside the point. His guilt about leaving the infirmary was assuaged when Mr. Schotel told them the infirmary was closing, and to bring the patients to the lower part of the camp where the hospital now was. With relief, Gijs and Rob transported the few who were still their charges.

The queen's birthday was four days away. It allowed barely enough time for them to get into condition to walk the ten miles to Bandoeng. They ate as much protein as they could put their hands on to reduce the swelling in their legs from edema. Physical exercise was not the problem. Their muscles had been put to the test every day of their camp lives.

Finally, Queen Wilhelmina's birthday arrived. Her Majesty had requested that her birthday not be celebrated with too much exuberance, out of respect for the victims of the war. That might have been easier to comply with in Holland, where they'd been liberated back in May. In the Dutch East Indies, it had hardly been a week, and it didn't even feel that way, surrounded as they were by fences and Japanese guards.

The day started at the square near the gate and the guards' building, where all the *tawanans* and even the guards gathered. First, several men gave speeches recognizing the great leadership Mr. Schotel, Mr. Nauta, and Mr. Moolenaar had demonstrated at the boys' camp, and documents, written on whatever pieces of paper they had been able to find and illustrated by the boys, were handed to them. Every *tawanan* had signed them. The three men were deeply moved by the gesture. "Thank you, boys," was all Mr. Schotel could manage to say.

Mr. Schotel had the Japanese guards raise the Dutch flag, while the national anthem, "*Het Wilhelmus,*" sounded over the internment camp. Gijs, Rob, and Pieter had positioned themselves in the very last row. It was only a short walk from there to the gate. Everyone's gaze was fixed on the flag and on the podium, where the Catholic priest and the Protestant minister were going to speak. Everyone, including all the guards.

Gijs elbowed his friends. They turned and walked out the gate. They didn't have money. Only the clothes they wore.

Chapter 24

As they reached the bottom of the hill, they turned around to take a last look.

"I don't know about you," Rob said, "but I hope to never see that place again."

"We may want to wipe it out of our minds, but I wonder if we can," Pieter said.

Gijs kept his thoughts to himself. Somewhere deep down, he knew imprisonment had changed him and set his life on a different course. Some of what he'd experienced he wouldn't ever want to go back to, but he didn't feel bitter as he walked toward freedom. There had been good days and bad days, good people and bad people. It could have been far worse. "Your spirit is not for the Japanese to break," Father van Gasteren had said, and Gijs knew he had heeded the warning.

"No sense going to the railroad station," Pieter said. "We don't have money to buy a ticket."

"Besides," Gijs said, "the place will be riddled with Japs. Not exactly what we want."

The best route to take, they decided, was to walk the ten miles over the railroad bed. That way they could avoid traffic and stay clear of the Japanese, who were ordered to keep them inside the camps.

The streets of Tjimahi were full of potholes. Paint on the buildings was peeling. Shrubs had been allowed to grow wild. Not much attention had been paid to any repairs.

"I don't think people outside of the camps have had an easy time of it," Pieter observed.

"We will probably hear many stories about that," Rob said. "A lot must have happened that we know nothing about."

They searched their way through the periphery of Tjimahi till they found the railroad bed. The distance between the railroad ties didn't match their stride, so it made for hard going.

"I'm glad I pulled on all the socks I own, holes or no holes. I feel every pebble through my shoes," Gijs said.

"Maybe we'll figure out a way to adjust our stride so we can just step on the wood," Rob said.

"Don't look down at the pebbles, Gijs," Pieter said. "After a while you'll forget about them."

The sun had reached its zenith and poured heat over the flat rice fields on both sides of the tracks. With the Preanger Mountains in the far distance, the fields seemed as endless as the sea. Straight lines divided the fields into patches, turning the landscape into a checkboard. They hadn't seen anything this orderly and luscious for years.

After an hour of walking, they found shade under a cluster of palm trees next to the tracks. It was very hot. Their shirts stuck to their chests, but they knew better than to take them off.

"Boy, are we out of shape!" Rob said.

"Maybe we need a *heiho* with a bamboo stick to keep us going," Gijs said.

"Amazing what those guys could make us do, if you think of it," Pieter said.

"I'd rather not," Rob said.

Behind them were the noises of a *kampong*. As they turned around, they saw natives, who stared at them as if they were white ghosts. What were *belandas* doing outside a camp? they were probably thinking. Gijs wondered if they knew the war had ended.

Rob, who spoke fluent Maleis, talked to them. Indeed, they didn't know the Japanese had lost the war. They started to shout and sing. A bit later, some women in sarongs offered the boys sliced fruit and water. Rob told them they were on their way to Bandoeng. One woman left, returning a little later with some bananas. They thanked the women profusely and went on their way.

The air was getting heavy. This was the hour for the daily siesta, not for walking over an open railroad bed under a blasting sun. Yet freedom beckoned, and they'd seen worse. They passed several small *dessas,* and in one a Dutch flag hung from a pole, but the blue part had been sheared off. A sign had been fastened to a small house with the word *Merdeka* in bold letters.

"*Merdeka* means freedom, if I remember correctly," Pieter said. "It's the slogan of the Nationalists."

They stopped and peered under the trees to see more of the small village. It wasn't encouraging. As friendly as the natives in the previous village had been, unfriendly scowls greeted them here. For the first time, they understood what Mr. Schotel had been hinting at. Some natives were not of a mind to be put back under colonial rule. Rob, Gijs, and Pieter resumed their walk in silence.

It was twilight by the time they reached the outskirts of Bandoeng. A brilliant sunset had settled over the city. Hanging over the horizon of rooftops, the sun looked like a fireball in a blood-soaked sky.

"The Empire of the Rising Sun is sinking," Pieter said.

It was pitch dark by the time they reached Dr. Kuylman's house.

"I think you better go in alone, Rob," Gijs said. "It might be a bit overwhelming to have three skinny guys barging in on them."

Pieter and Gijs could hear shouts of recognition and jubilation inside the house. Minutes later, Rob returned with his aunt and uncle. They couldn't have been more gracious. Rob had been right. Dr. and Mrs. Kuylman were extremely nice people.

"We don't look very presentable," Gijs said. "This is the best we could do."

"Those days are over, when we worried about being presentable," Mrs. Kuylman said. "You're alive and free! That's worth a party, and you don't need a black tie to celebrate."

Gijs was grateful for Mrs. Kuylman's welcome. She was a tall woman, reminding him of his mother, very Dutch with blond hair and blue eyes. She was the first Dutch woman he'd laid eyes on since the internment. Dr. Kuylman was equally tall, but his hair was graying and sparse.

Even though moments before they had felt as if they couldn't take one more step, they perked up as they were led to the dining room. Mrs. Kuylman told a *kokkie* to prepare something to eat, and in no time they found themselves sitting on real chairs with soft cushions, plates piled high with steaming *nasi goreng* in front of them.

"This is amazing," Rob said. "We've seen enough rice to last us a lifetime, but not with chunks of meat and all these wonderful spices."

It felt absurd to be holding a silver spoon and fork, to handle a real knife, to have a pressed white linen napkin and a table covered with an embroidered tablecloth, and fresh flowers in a shiny crystal vase.

Dr. Kuylman and his wife had opened their home as well to a friend, Mrs. de Quant, and to her son from a previous marriage, Karel Vogelesang. Their house was apparently large enough to provide each of their guests with a bed. Gijs sensed they did not have children of their own.

It was simply sensational to lie down on a real bed with smooth cotton sheets. Gijs felt enveloped by luxury when he pulled the covers over his tired body, which hadn't been treated this well for a long time. It promptly responded by curling up like a contented cat, and he fell into a deep sleep.

Rob woke him up the next morning with a fluffy towel, a bar of soap, clean underwear, a pair of shorts Dr. Kuylman had lent him.

The next week they spent getting themselves back in shape. Mrs. Kuylman saw to it that they got enough protein to get rid of the edema. They felt better every day.

For various reasons, Dr. Kuylman, his wife, Mrs. de Quant, and Karel had been able to stay out of the internment camps. Mrs. de Quant's husband, who was the garrison commandant in Bandoeng when the war started, had been taken away as a POW. The other four only knew what life in the camps had been like through rumors. Rob, Pieter, and Gijs had to answer many questions, but they had difficulty compressing their experiences into a plausible story. It sounded almost too fantastic to talk about eating snakes, dogs, and frogs; too sensational to tell about the beatings they had suffered at the hands of their captors. How do you convey what it's like to sleep on a cot for almost three years, to wash your clothes in cold running water without soap, to be hungry all the time? How do you talk about the constant fight against bedbugs, or how fed up you became with the adults who did nothing but play bridge and complain? They knew it wasn't right to generalize. It wouldn't be fair. They did not get beaten up all the time, and not all adults had been boring. So, they doled out snippets of their experiences.

Living outside of the camps had not been easy either. Dr. Kuylman was weary to the bone. He was an ear, nose, and throat specialist. There had been a constant lack of skilled nurses in the hospital, and the same was true for medicines. When Gijs heard that Karel helped Dr. Kuylman in his practice, his ears pricked up.

"Dr. Kuylman, I am enjoying your hospitality and I would like to do something in return. I was an orderly for most of my time in the various camps. Could I be of help?"

"You most certainly can."

Gijs considered one week of doing nothing quite enough, and was happy to be back in a familiar setting, assisting a doctor. This time in a hospital. The size of the place made a difference, but the work was the same.

Rob didn't join. He went to Soerabaja to find his father. Gijs didn't see him again until several years later in Holland, where both of them were studying medicine, but at different universities.

Pieter left to see if he could put his family back together. His father and brother were indeed in the Fifteenth Battalion and in reasonable shape. Their home had been plundered by rampaging youths. *Pemoedas,* they were called. For Gijs and Pieter this was a new word. *Pemoedas* were native boys, in their teens or twenties, who went around with bamboo sticks, taking the law into their own hands. They drove around in trucks, harassing people, and not just the whites. Their trucks were hung with banners that proclaimed *Merdeka!* The vacuum that had been created by the capitulation of Japan and the lack of Allied troops to restore order gave them an opening to push their nationalistic zeal. Soekarno and Hatta—two politicians, who had studied in Holland and who started the nationalistic movement for which Soekarno had served time in prison under Dutch rule—had wanted to negotiate with the Dutch government before declaring the Republic Indonesia, but the *Pemoedas* deported them and put them under heavy pressure. Finally, Soekarno gave in to their nationalistic zeal, and on August 18 he declared the Republic Indonesia. Meanwhile, he had lost control over the rampaging youths, and he didn't have an army at his disposal to bring them back in line.

One day in the hospital, a colleague of Dr. Kuylman, Dr. Poortman, approached Karel and Gijs and asked if either of them could drive a car.

"Sure," Gijs said.

"Sure," Karel said.

"All right then, I have a proposition. I can commandeer a Red Cross ambulance. My mother is in a hospital in Batavia, and I want to bring her here. Do you think you can drive a big ambulance like that?"

"Sure," Karel said.

"Sure," Gijs said.

"We'll leave tomorrow morning at eight."

Karel and Gijs looked at each other after Dr. Poortman had left the room.

"Have you ever driven a truck?" Gijs asked.

"No, and I bet you haven't either!"

"True. I learned to drive from our chauffeur in my father's car."

"So did I."

The Red Cross ambulance was a square box on wheels, painted the typical green army color, with a red cross in a white circle on top and on both sides. It was impressive. Gijs and Karel glanced at each other with their eyebrows raised, but they stepped inside the cabin, trying to look like pros.

"You're the oldest, Gijs. You go first," Karel said.

Gijs took a deep breath and tried to remember how to start a car. It had been a long time since the time he'd driven with Soepardi on that fateful day in 1942. The starter knob was on the floor and he pressed it hard with his foot while he held the choke out. The engine roared.

"All aboard?" he called, acting more confident than he felt.

The steering was heavier than he remembered from the Chrysler, but this was a truck, after all. Also, his view was limited, certainly more limited than driving a car with the top down. He'd never learned to drive with an eye on the side mirrors, but despite these sweat-provoking thoughts, Dr. Poortman seemed to have supreme confidence in him. The doctor leafed through some documents as Gijs maneuvered the ambulance through the streets of Bandoeng, under its magnificent tall trees and along its wide boulevards.

Soon they were on the *Grote Postweg* that would lead them past Tjimahi on the way to Batavia.

"This is a little easier than walking over railroad ties, I bet," Karel said.

"Quite."

It seemed ages ago, like in another lifetime, that he was a prisoner. He'd left that status behind. His mind was now set on finding Moeder and Janneke in the Tjideng camp, and trying to discover where Vader was.

The distance they had to travel was one hundred and eight miles. It led them over bridges and tunnels, through the Preanger Mountains and beyond. In the valleys underneath the steel bridges, they saw elaborate terraces of rice. Having been starved for so long, Gijs had forgotten how fertile Java was. It would be impossible, in normal times, to starve on this island, even if you were dirt poor. The volcanoes had fertilized the land many times. Anything that was planted into this soil would thrive. He'd seen that with his tomato plants. No, they hadn't been starved for lack of food, but because the Japanese had hoped they would eventually succumb. Starving them to death would look better than shooting them. Scandalous!

Karel took the wheel after they'd gone through the mountain passes and given the ambulance some time to cool down its over-worked motor.

The closer they got to Batavia, the hotter it got, and Gijs grew even more anxious about the condition he would find Moeder in. The main reason, apart from the adventure it presented, that he'd volunteered to drive the ambulance to Batavia was that he wanted to find his mother and sister. But where should he begin his search? All he really knew was that they had been taken to the Tjideng camp. On which street did they live? Tjideng comprised a large section of the city.

Dr. Poortman knew Batavia well and had no difficulty finding the hospital. They parted company, agreeing to meet again at three in the afternoon to start the trip back. Gijs had two hours to find his family. Maybe he could get a lift, he thought. That would be quicker than traveling in a *bedja*. He hadn't stood in front of the hospital for long when a military vehicle stopped for him.

"Where are you headed?" the man asked. It didn't take Gijs more than a second to realize that he wore the uniform of the Dutch Naval Air Force.

"To Tjideng, sir. The camp, I mean."

"Trying to find your relatives?" the officer asked.

"Yes. I know my mother and sister are there."

"What's your name?"

"Gijs Bozuwa, sir."

"I just saw your father in Manila. Captain Bozuwa, right?"

"You did? Are you serious? Yes, that's my father. He's in the Philippines?"

"Didn't you know?"

"I haven't known where my father was since they took him pris-oner on Sumatra right after the capitulation."

"Does he know where you are?"

"I don't think so. The Red Cross may have lost track of me, because I walked out of the camp I was in, in Tjimahi."

"You know, Gijs, I can't contact him here on land, but once I'm in the air I can do what I want. I'll contact the Philippines and leave a message for him."

He swung his car in front of the Tjideng gate. Gijs thanked him profusely and the officer smiled.

"Good luck finding the rest of your family," he called as he drove away.

The good news that Vader was alive and the coincidence of getting a ride from a man who knew Vader was more than he could digest right away. His heart burst with happiness.

Gijs entered the guard building and asked for Mrs. Maria and Miss Janna Bozuwa. The clerk looked up the names in a thick book. Around fifteen thousand people had been stuffed together in the Tjideng camp.

"Laan van Trivelli, number one," the clerk said. "It's the house on the corner."

My God, Gijs thought, as he walked through the streets. It was like a ghetto. It stank to the high heavens from open sewers. Later, he was told that the Japanese commander had refused to empty the septic tanks. The women had to do it themselves. The women he met on the street were terribly underfed. He had become used to men with sunken eyes and legs thick with edema, but to see these signs of malnutrition on women was somehow worse. It was already three weeks since the capitulation. He wondered what the women had looked like back then.

He saw the house on the corner. People were gathered on the veranda. A woman, as tall as he remembered his mother to be, was dealing out rice to a group of women and children. He recognized her curly hair.

"Moeder!" he shouted.

He jumped over the concrete wall, ran across the lawn, and took her in his arms.

Chapter 25

This would probably be the only time in his life that Gijs would see his mother lose control of her emotions. As he held her tightly, he felt her body give in, as if she no longer had to hold herself upright in the face of immense fears and worries. That wordless response to him made Gijs feel loved and appreciated. Then he held her away at arm's length. His mother's eyes were wet with tears, but they looked as blue and determined as he remembered them, and although her face was thin with hollow cheeks, she remained a beautiful woman. A week ago, she had turned fifty-three.

"Gijs!" Janneke shouted, and ran over to him.

He let go of Moeder and embraced his sister. Every woman and child, who moments before had stood in line on the veranda to receive a portion of measured rice, stood as if struck by lightning. Moeder's task was taken over by someone else, and soon the Bozuwas found themselves alone.

"I didn't recognize you, *jongen*," Moeder said, sitting on the edge of the low concrete wall that enclosed the veranda. "You have grown taller and you're, I don't know how to say it, you're just not a boy anymore!"

Her legs were badly swollen, and he'd felt her ribs under her faded cotton dress. She weighed only a hundred ten pounds, Janneke said, who also looked grossly underweight.

"Vader is in Manila," Gijs said.

"He is?" Janneke and Moeder cried out. They looked at him as if they didn't dare believe him.

"Yes, and soon he will know I am alive and well, because the pilot will radio a message to him." He told them of his drive with the navy pilot.

"Oh," Moeder said, "that is such good news. It's almost hard to believe after worrying about him for so long."

"Janneke, have you heard from Jan?" Gijs asked.

A painful look flashed over her face. "Yes, I have. Unfortunately, the message was that he died."

"Oh, my God, that is terrible, Janneke. He died?"

"His ship was torpedoed. He was on a troop transport from South Africa to England. This was back in 1942. Not far from the coast of England, the Germans sank the ship. I didn't hear about it until at least a year later."

"Bastards," Gijs said. He didn't know what else to say. This horrible fact was too hard to deal with in words. Janneke's status in life had changed drastically. At twenty-four years old, she could have been a happy young bride. For two years she'd know Jan had died, and the immediacy of the pain had faded. For Gijs, it was a shock to realize that Jan, who had been a hero to him, was gone for good.

" I have one hour left to get to the hospital for the ride back to Bandoeng," he said. "I talked with Dr. and Mrs. Kuylman before coming here, and they said that I bring you to Bandoeng. You can stay with them."

"You're joking!" Janneke said. "How big is their house that they can put so many people under their roof?"

"Big," Gijs said. "But more important, they're very hospitable. I sense they want to do what they can for people who were interned, partly because they were able to stay on the outside."

"That's a very, very generous offer. Do you feel we can accept it, Gijs?" Moeder asked.

"Yes, I think it's safer for you to be in Bandoeng, and we will take it day by day," he said. Suddenly Gijs was aware that he was in charge.

He came back for them ten days later. He had to get a permit to travel, because Lord Mountbatten, the supreme commander of the Pacific area that included Indonesia, had proclaimed that all prisoners had to stay inside the camps for their own safety. The Japanese troops were ordered to protect them against the Nationalists, who'd become more threatening by the day. Mountbatten apparently didn't have enough troops under his command to secure Java and the other islands. The *tawanans* inside and outside the internment camps, however, angrily claimed that the British were in no hurry to come to the aid of the Netherlands, their archrival for centuries, to help it retain its colonies. In any case, Lord Mountbatten didn't provide what was needed: protection from the *Pemoedas*.

Gijs would be forever grateful that he'd walked out of his camp on August 31. With Mountbatten's much stricter order, it was very difficult to leave an internment camp now. The Japanese guards held back those who tried. Their orders, they said. It took persuasion for Gijs to obtain a pass to travel from Bandoeng to Batavia, and it would be equally hard to get Moeder and Janneke out of the Tjideng camp and onto a train. But if he'd learned anything at all from the war, it was persistence. You do what you must.

Moeder and Janneke stood ready to travel, each with a backpack. Whatever else was deemed worthwhile they'd stuffed into a suitcase. Their farewell to the women they'd shared the war years with was charged with emotion. Gijs noticed the children called Moeder *"Ou,"* which was a bastardization of the Dutch word *Mevrouw*, which meant Mrs. She must have been the respected leader of the house, he thought, and it didn't surprise him.

After the formalities of signing out, they walked to the train station. Banners with *Merdeka* in big letters on them caught their attention.

"What does that word mean?" Janneke asked.

"Freedom," Gijs answered.

"Whose freedom?"

"The natives of the Republic Indonesia."

This was news to his mother and sister. The happenings in the world had bypassed them.

"Who declared the Republic Indonesia?" Moeder wanted to know, and in her voice Gijs detected indignation.

"Soekarno and Hatta."

"Those two? They collaborated with the Japanese! Soekarno and Hatta saying so doesn't make it so," Moeder said, as if that would be the end of it.

An open truck with teenage native boys in it drove past them, the boys screaming loudly and threatening pedestrians with bamboo sticks. Signs with that new word, *Merdeka,* hung on all sides of the truck. Gijs wished them away with his whole being. It was discouraging to free his mother and sister from prison camp, only to have them confronted with a new threat.

Pandemonium reigned at the station. More passengers than the train could carry stood on the platform. Thank God Moeder and Janneke didn't have too much *barang*, although less would have been better. About fifteen minutes after they got there, everyone was ordered off the platform. It needed to be cleaned. All the passengers crowded outside the station, loudly complaining. It was a hassle to get back in. All passes were checked. The authorities in charge of the station were obviously trying to reduce the number of passengers that could get on the train. They used any excuse to deny a ticket, but Gijs managed to get the three of them into a first class compartment. It was filled with Japanese officers. For the first time he felt safe in their company, as he watched one of them kick back a *Pemoeda* who wanted to enter the compartment. Moeder and Janneke looked with fright at the angry face of the young native. This was an entirely different world than the one they'd known. Gijs doubted that they had envisioned, on the first day of their regained freedom, that they would be sitting in a train compartment with the very people who had kept them imprisoned and underfed, and would see hate for their white skin in the eyes of a young native man.

Bandoeng didn't present quite such an angry picture, and their fright abated as they basked in the warm hospitality of Dr. and Mrs. Kuylman. Janneke dropped into an armchair and exclaimed, "A chair! What a marvelous invention! Paintings on the wall! We haven't seen a painting or anything decorative in ages!"

Like Rob, Pieter, and Gijs, they delighted in the first meal at a table with silver cutlery, the first feel of cotton sheets in a real bed, the first shower. They were in heaven.

They'd hardly been the Kuylmans' guests for a week, when Mrs. de Quant heard that her old home, the official residence of the garrison's commander, had been made available to her again. She promptly invited Moeder, Janneke, and Gijs to come live with her and her family. The house was spacious, she said, and each of them would get a room to themselves, an unheard of luxury. They accepted at once.

Moeder, who had just heard that their stored belongings had gone up in flames during a bombardment in Soerabaja, said, "We have twelve silver teaspoons to our name, that's all. But we have found something far more valuable: hospitality."

Gratefully, they picked up their backpacks and their one suitcase and installed themselves in the spacious home of the family de Quant. The *kokkie* and *djongos*, who'd served the family before the war, came back to help out their *Nonja besar*.

Gijs left every morning with Karel for the hospital. Moeder was utterly amazed that her son had an interest in medicine. A Bozuwa male who voluntarily surrounded himself with disease and suffering? That was something new to get used to, but she listened to his stories with interest. Not much could throw her off balance after what she'd seen in camp.

"This morning," Gijs told her one day, "I had to help Dr. Kuylman with a tonsillectomy. The patient was a seven-year-old boy. He was a squirmy little fellow. I put him on my lap, crossed my legs over his in a sort of vice. I folded one arm over his chest and gripped his hands, while I held his forehead back with the other."

"Didn't he get anesthesia?" Janneke asked.

"No. Dr. Kuylman thinks that's too dangerous. It might make the patient choke on the stuff when they inhale, and that could result in pneumonia. If they cough as a reflex, it goes away from the lungs."

"It sounds brutal," Janneke said.

"I know, but it's better to have a live patient the next day."

"You're beginning to sound like a doctor," Moeder said, but he detected a certain pride in her voice. Convincing his father that he wanted to become an orderly would be a different matter.

One day, Mrs. de Quant received a message that her husband would be coming home from "very far away." A week later, Colonel de Quant arrived, a tall handsome man, in spite of the poor physical shape he was in. Janneke and Moeder kept their distance as the colonel greeted his wife, but then he turned to Moeder and said, "I assume that you are Rietje Bozuwa? I bring you greetings from Gerard."

As Moeder stared in surprise, he went on. "Your husband asked me to bring you his greetings and gave me the address in the Tjideng camp, but when I got to the Laan Trivelli, Ton Perks told me you had moved to Bandoeng. When she gave me the address, Merdika Lio, number ten, I asked her, 'Are you sure? That is my own home address!'"

Colonel de Quant had spent the war years in the same POW camps as Vader, the last one being in Manchuria. The Russians had freed them.

Gijs came home to a firm handshake from the colonel, who said to him, "You can be proud of your father. He had a leading role in the camp. The English and Americans couldn't get together on choosing a leader, so they chose a Dutchman, and that was your father."

It was October by then. There was unrest in the *kampong* across the street. The *Pemoedas* still had enormous influence, and they forbade the older natives to serve white people. The loyal *kokkie* and *djongos*, who had returned to work for the de Quants of their own free will, weren't allowed to work for a white family anymore.

Colonel de Quant's hands were tied. The British were in charge. They forbade the members of the Dutch military who had returned from various POW camps on foreign soil to reorganize. The Brits used Gurkhas from Nepal, well known for their bravery, to keep some order in Bandoeng. The Brits installed cannons on the front lawn of the de Quants' house, and the Gurkhas lay on the grass next to them. With their impressive turbans and colorful clothes, they were a picturesque sight, and at the same time scary enough to keep the agitated young natives at a safe distance. But things went from bad to worse in the city. The *Pemoedas* got bolder, stealing cars and plundering houses. They even chopped off a man's head from inside a tram while he bicycled next to it.

Traveling through the streets of Bandoeng on his way to and from the hospital, Gijs saw evidence of growing tension. One day he watched as some Japanese soldiers flattened a bicycle under a tank. The bicycle had carried a tiny red and white flag of the new republic. He noticed shops with boarded windows. In the paper he read that young hotheads had threatened restaurant owners and storekeepers if they served Europeans. Most of the merchants yielded to the *Pemoedas'* demands, but they were angry about it. Not serving Europeans decimated their income. Finally, British troops arrived, and they were soon engaged in street fighting. Shots were heard around the city. Going out of the house became dangerous.

A new war had started.

Early in December, an officer of the Dutch Navy came by to say they had to prepare for a trip by airplane to Batavia, because Captain Bozuwa had arrived there from the Philippines. On December 5, Saint Nicolas Day in Holland, an army vehicle drove into the yard. A marine put their backpacks and suitcase in the trunk and waited for Moeder, Janneke, and Gijs to say another emotional farewell.

The army bus had barely traveled two miles on its way to Andir, the airport outside of Bandoeng, when it came under fire. Several *Pemoedas,* hidden in the ditch alongside the road, were shooting at them. The marine ordered his passengers to get down on the floor. With their noses on the floor planks, they heard the bullets whistle overhead and the motor revving as the chauffeur pushed hard on the gas to get them out of range. Adrenaline rushed through their bodies. Gijs could taste it on his tongue. What should they do? Keep lying down?

The marine told them to get up and take their seats. "They don't aim very well," he said. "Don't worry."

A young Dutch Navy officer met them at the airport, where they boarded a huge transport plane. When they arrived at Kemajoran Airport in Batavia, Moeder discovered her rucksack had been stolen. The escorting, young officer was very disturbed and apologetic, but Moeder said she couldn't be bothered. She would see her husband in a matter of hours.

Gijs wondered, as they were driven to the harbor, how it would be to see his father again after forty-four months. In his first camp at the Bangkastraat, he could not get Vader's face into focus. He remembered how deeply that had upset him. He still couldn't recall his face. Vader had become an aching feeling instead of a person.

The army vehicle swung onto the tarmac of the wharf where the *ss Plancius* was moored. The navy had requisitioned the large passenger ship so returning navy officers and their families would have a place to get reacquainted. The Dutch officers were not allowed to disembark, because the English "liberation" authorities forbade them.

There, looking thinner than they'd ever seen him, was Vader in a khaki American uniform, pacing up and down, waiting to be reunited with his family.

Chapter 26

As a family, the Bozuwas were not given to dramatics, but this moment of reunion was as demonstrative of their emotions as they would ever allow. The worries about one another, the longing, the aches of separation, the endurance it had taken to survive, had accumulated to a point of explosion, sparked by the immediate recognition of one another. No matter that each of them had shrunk and wore ugly scars of malnutrition, the essence of what they meant to each other was palpable in the way Vader ran with open arms to the army vehicle. Moeder stepped out first. Gijs had never seen his parents embrace passionately, but they did now. Tears ran down Vader's cheeks as he let go of her and put his arms around Janneke, hugging her hard. Gijs got out last, taking his father by surprise. *Maybe he doesn't recognize me,* Gijs thought. They were of equal height as they stood before each other. Always the officer, Vader shook his son's hand, gave him a jovial slap on his shoulder, and then held him at arm's length to take in this strapping young man who was his own son.

"Gijs!" he said, but he could say no more.

As they walked up the gangplank with their shabby luggage, they, in effect, left the Dutch East Indies. Once on deck of the *Plancius*, they were on Dutch soil, protected by the red, white, and blue flag that proudly flew from the stern.

The welcome on board by the navy personnel was heartwarming. Officers rose to their feet and applauded when they entered the lounge. Tea and cakes were served. Anything they asked for they were served by a steward.

As they sat around a table drinking their tea, Gijs blurted out that he didn't want to become a navy officer after all, but a medical orderly instead.

"An orderly?" Vader said. "Well, we'll see about that later."

That was not a good move, Gijs thought. There were more important things to discuss.

After dinner at the Captain's table, they were assigned three cabins. They spent the evening in the biggest one, telling tales into the wee hours. Their individual stories bore resemblances: brutality from the Japanese guards, malnutrition, poor accommodations and unsanitary conditions, boredom, difficulty living in close quarters with strangers and complainers. Vader's story, however, contained high drama, and the hours of that first evening and night were devoted almost entirely to his account of what had happened to him since he'd last seen his family.

Vader, who could be taciturn, was an excellent storyteller. With the accuracy of a military officer, he described events as if he were making an official report, but he laced them with humor and perceptiveness, so it wasn't hard to conjure up the images that went with the facts.

"You know that I got on the *Poelau Bras* and that it was sunk?" he began.

"Yes, but we don't know any of the details," Moeder said. "Really, all we know is that you survived it, landed on Sumatra, and were taken prisoner. The last we heard was that you were in a POW camp in Manchuria."

"A lot happened in between," Vader said.

"We were on board the *Poelau Bras*, headed for Ceylon, with two hundred and forty people. Ninety of those were crewmembers. The rest were navy and army brass, and civilians who were essential to the oil production the Japs were coveting. When we were almost in neutral waters, a Japanese reconnaissance plane flew over. I was on the bridge with the captain at the time, and we said to each other, "They'll come back with bombs." Of course, we'd gone through a drill with the life vests and lifeboats the night before. It wasn't long before nine planes, in formations of three, came at us, firing their machine guns. I could feel shudders going through the steel frame and heard water gurgle in underneath me. You can imagine the panic that ensued! The planes kept coming back, raining bullets over us. I raced into the lounge to direct passengers to the lifeboats, and I saw people, who moments before had sat with a glass of lemonade in their hands, staring at the ceiling with glassy eyes."

Only three of the lifeboats made it into the sea, Vader said. The others had been rendered inoperable by the bullets. The Japanese kept coming back, mercilessly strafing the lifeboats and swimmers.

"A bad situation. To the left and right of me I heard pistol shots. Some officers committed suicide. I decided to jump overboard. The ship was rolling and pitching, and the sea was rougher than it looked from the railing. I swam as fast as I could to get away from the suction. The *Poelau Bras* was sinking fast. Her bow pointed to the sky, then she slid backward and disappeared. I will never forget that moment. In some strange way, it was awesome to watch."

Vader took a deep breath and let it out slowly before he went on. Nobody interrupted.

"The Japanese planes finally stopped coming. What I saw around me was a seascape dotted with bobbing life vests holding alive and dead bodies. A Ping-Pong table floated among the debris. I held onto it with another man, a sailor, for a long time, hours probably, gathering my wits and my strength. The sailor gave up and slipped away. At a distance, I saw the three lifeboats. The lucky ones aboard were struggling to keep the boat from sinking. Water poured in through the bullet holes. I spurted over there. I told them to pull me in, but they wouldn't. They said the boat was leaking badly. I told them that I was Captain Bozuwa and that I knew how to fix the leaks. One of the marines saw the insignia on my wet shirt and recognized me. He'd once served under me. That was my lucky break. He pulled me in."

Vader had bailed out the water with the only tool at hand: a tropical helmet. The wood around the holes tightened up just from being in the water. They put up the twenty-foot mast, fastened the main sail and jib. The prevailing wind, he knew, would take them to

Sumatra. A few men argued about this course, offering the wishful thinking of going to Australia, but logic and reason prevailed. At four in the afternoon, five hours after they'd been torpedoed, they were sufficiently organized to start the trip.

"Unfortunately," Vader went on, "the bullets had also shot holes into the water tanks. One tank was empty, the other half full. Every six hours everyone got a half-cup of drinking water. Water was what we needed most and had the least of. For food we had ship biscuits, but they only made us thirstier and they tasted like sawdust."

The group found six oars. Two men pulled on each oar. Every shift of twelve rowed for half an hour. After four days of rowing, they laid the oars on the bottom of the boat to make a platform so they could stretch their cramped bodies. Each passenger got two hours to lie down. The wind propelled the boat.

"The wood of the boat got so hot," Vader said, "we burned our skin on contact. Then there were the doldrums to deal with. In the morning the wind would die down completely, and the ocean looked like a piece of glass. But in the evening, the wind would pick up again and rage over us with sprays of salt water that made us shiver with cold."

Vader stopped for a moment. "Can you stand it, Rietje?" he asked.

"Barely," Moeder said, but he continued.

"It was tempting to cool off and jump overboard, but we could see sharks circle the boat. We were scared to death of sharks."

By the fifth day, the lack of water, the heat, the blinding sun, the monotonous seascape, began to crack minds. One man had waved his pistol and cried, "Give me water, or I'll shoot." Someone grabbed his pistol and threw it overboard. Another man wanted to toss all the life vests overboard, because they reminded him of the ship sinking. Yet another, for no good reason, started to laugh uncontrollably.

On the sixth day, they saw a bird, but the bird flew away and no land was spotted. Very early the next morning, they saw land. They heard waves crashing in the distance. They smelled sweeter air, and in the morning the sun didn't rise up from the sea. It rose slowly from behind a dark smudge on the horizon. As it came closer, they saw a white line in front of green hills. Jungle!

"Finally, we could drop anchor on the seventh day of our journey. We swam through the surf and threw ourselves on the beach. Palm trees, loaded with coconuts, swayed overhead. We found stones to crack the coconuts open with and drank the milk till we burst. Under the shade of the palm trees, we spread out and fell asleep."

"What a story!" Janneke said, her legs dangling over the side of a bunk. "I'm grateful we didn't know."

"What happened after you woke up?" Gijs asked. He'd been listening breathlessly. His father was a hero. That was unquestionable.

"Well, bliss never lasts forever," Vader said with a smile.

"You can imagine what we looked like. Our skins were salty, a week's worth of beard on our faces, the women's hair uncombed. I tell you, we were a sight! One of the men had Indonesian blood, and he climbed into the palm tree as defily as a monkey to throw us the coconuts. He found a footpath from the beach into the jungle. We concluded that people must live nearby. Two men went with him to investigate. Almost immediately, they found many people watching them. The oldest man among them asked the obvious question: 'Where did you come from?' Our people were able to communicate with him in Maleis. They told him what had happened, and that there were more of us back on the beach and that we were in desperate need of rice."

The man had said his people were very poor, but he sent a little girl to her mother. Some time later she came back with a round-bellied pot full of cooked rice. They ate the rice with banana tree leaves. They paid the older man for the rice and pumped him for information. First, where were they? The southern tip of Sumatra, he told them. They looked on the map they'd found in the lifeboat and saw a lighthouse. Balimbing, on the Cape of the Vlakke Hoek.

It wasn't too far away. We could sail over there, the man said. Maybe they would know there if the other lifeboats had landed.

"In the boat, in spite of squabbles," Vader said, "we had one purpose: to get to land. But once we had solid ground under our feet, the unity fell apart. The crewmembers wanted to go back to Java, to their families. They saw no danger. We told them the Japs would probably intern them, but they thought that idea was ludicrous. The Japs could not run the country without the whites, they reasoned, and the natives hated the Japs and would not cooperate.

"But several of us faced certain imprisonment and even the death penalty. For us there was no way back to Java."

"They must have ended up in camps, like the rest of us," Moeder said.

"Yes, I would imagine. It wouldn't have been too hard for them to get back to Java, if they managed to charter a small boat from the local fishermen. Well, anyway, we found the lighthouse. A young native told us that nine men had built a hiding place in the jungle not too far from the lighthouse. We paid him to take us there. Not an easy trip. We were covered by bloodsuckers, which fastened to our skin. If you pulled them off too early, they left wounds, which inevitably got infected.

" What we found was amazing. Men of the BPM, the Dutch oil company, had built houses on stilts, held together with palm leaves and liana. They had taken enough food with them to last for two years, but then they were invaded by the thirty-two people from our lifeboat, and later by another nine from one of the other lifeboats.

"I still had the money in my breast pocket, Rietje," Vader said, "that you gave me on the day I left. We put our money together and decided to see if we could buy a *prauw* large enough to sail us to the Mentawei Islands, about three hundred miles north of the coast. With a seaworthy vessel, we could have reached Australia from there." He paused. "Maybe it was all madness," he said, as if he'd spent the years since wondering how he could ever have thought he would reach Australia in a small sailboat.

They walked for days through the jungle, from one *dessa* to another. They saw droppings of elephants and heard strange hissing noises and branches breaking nearby. For men of the sea, this was quite an unnerving experience.

"We got the *prauw* and paid for it. The night before we were to board, the natives betrayed us. The Japs had become aware that three lifeboats of the *Poelau Bras* had landed on the coast of Sumatra, and that a total of one hundred and thirteen survivors were roaming the island. The natives had to choose sides. That is the end of the ship-wreck story. Are you ready for the rest?"

"We need a break," Janneke said. "Let's order some coffee."

Vader struck up a cigar he'd been given as a welcome aboard. Bluish smoke circled around him, veiling his thin but tanned face. After what he'd been through, he looked remarkably fit for a fifty-five year old.

"I was brought to a prison in Palembang by train. I'll spare you the details. I traveled a lot these last few years, on foot, in the back of trucks, in cattle cars, and in the bowels of ships. Anyway, all Dutch residents in the area, plus all the survivors of the *Poelau Bras*, were driven to Palembang. After a few days, the Japs figured out who I was and that I was responsible for destroying the naval air force bases on Java. They condemned me to death."

"And yet here you are," Moeder interrupted.

"Yes, thank God. I told the lieutenant in charge that he would have to give me the status of a POW first and bring me before a military tribunal. I also reminded him that I outranked him, and that he could not execute me there and then."

"Did he accept that?" Gijs asked.

"Yes. Rank and order mean everything to the Japanese military. They would bring me to Singapore, where higher placed officers would try me, they said. It turned out that they were in the process of collecting the American, British, Australian, and Dutch top of government and military in Singapore. They called this assembly of colonels and generals 'The Special Party,' but it didn't mean we got special treatment. Oh no! Although the Japanese government did not ratify the Geneva Convention and refused to honor it, they were sufficiently cognizant of its stipulations that they didn't want to mess too much with us. They kept threatening me, but obviously, they didn't execute me. Looking back, I think the Japanese higher-ups in Tokyo hoped we would succumb to the treatment they had in mind for us. Then they could safely say they hadn't killed us."

"It was somewhat like that in the civilian camps," Moeder said.

"So I heard. They really wanted to wipe us off the Pacific map."

The steward knocked on the door and brought in the coffee. Moeder had no difficulty with switching back to her role of housewife. She arranged the cups and poured the hot coffee.

"Do you still take it with sugar and cream, Gerard?" she asked.

"That would be a treat," he said.

"What happened after Singapore?" Gijs asked.

"I was taken to Taiwan by ship with a group of British generals. I can't give you all these events blow by blow, but the essence is that we ended up in a camp called Karenko, previously an American mission. We arrived there on September 8, 1942."

In February 1943, the Governor General, as well as what was left of the Dutch-Indonesian Army and the Dutch Navy's top officers, who had been held in Batavia, arrived at the camp. The Special Party was now complete, four hundred and five men, of which one hundred thirty-six were military caretakers.

"Imamura was the commandant, a very unfriendly man," Vader said. "The first thing we were ordered to do was take off our shoes. As replacements, we were given wooden sandals, a size too small, so we couldn't escape. The wooden shoes were stowed in a closet and could only be worn when we worked outside. We were told that we would get a monthly salary and had to work on a farm, with vegetable gardens and animals to tend. The idea was that we could keep the vegetables and meat we raised, but it turned out to be a hollow promise. In the end they took most of it for themselves. The

Governor General was the goat herder! If he did something wrong in the eyes of the Japs, the guards hit him in the face, just as they did to us. The GG had stipulated that he didn't want to be treated differently from the rest of us. He was amazingly cool and collected, a true example for everyone. It was hard to see him being treated as if he were a naughty boy. And to think that this man had ruled over seven million people and was the representative of the queen! It was jarring."

"Yes, that must have been hard," Moeder said. She was a great admirer of the GG.

"The wind was always blowing in Karenko. It rained a lot and the sun seldom came out. But in June, we were transported to another camp: Shirakawa. Here we were in a swampy area with flies and mosquitoes. Rats were also frequent visitors. We lived in drafty barracks and we slept on bare floor planks. It was Spartan. The sanitary conditions were abominable. We were forced to dig a fishpond. Of course, we didn't knock ourselves out, and we let it be known that we considered forced labor a breach of the Geneva Convention. We had been told to write about how we thought we were being treated, and we added our objection to forced labor to the composition. We were very aware that the Japs might use our words after the war. The commandant was so angry about our answer that he designed two lists. One read at the top: 'The undersigned wants to work voluntarily.' The other: 'The undersigned does not want to work voluntarily.' Everyone had to sign. Two Australians, one Brit, and five Americans signed the first list. Three hundred forty-four signed the second list.

"It was not without consequence. We got a long list of orders as punishment. I'll give you an example. It was forbidden to lie down on cots or on the floor between morning call and evening call. We were no longer allowed to play cards or play musical instruments. No more food was forthcoming from the farm. The guards would hold several inspections in the barracks. Saluting fellow POWs was forbidden. The extra food we got as laborers in the farm's fields was taken away. That's just a few on a long list. We felt like potted plants or dogs in a kennel."

"Unbelievable," Moeder mumbled. Gijs and Janneke were transfixed by their father's story.

"By the end of September 1944, it became obvious to us that the war was not going well for the Japs. Air raid warnings were sounding regularly. That was a new development. Apparently, the Allies were considered close enough to strike Taiwan. We were moved again, and I have to say that this was the worst part of the whole POW ordeal. We were informed that we would travel by ship to Japan between October nine and twelve. We were allowed only as much luggage as we could carry. Many of the instructions indicated we were going someplace cold, but we had no idea where.

"A beautiful passenger ship was moored in the harbor of Keelung. Finally justice, we thought. But no. There were two hundred and sixty of us—the GG and some generals had left earlier by plane—and we were brought downstairs, below the afterdeck, to a half-dark, watertight compartment. The ventilators didn't work. It was unbearably hot, and the portholes had to remain closed. We lay down packed together on wooden sleeping platforms against the hull, like sardines in a can. Really! I can't think of a better comparison. It was impossible to lie down fully stretched. The interpreter announced that our food would be brought in pails. Each pail served twenty men. The only times we were allowed on deck was to clean our plates and to visit the *benjo*. Those were cubicles that served as our WC.

"We had boarded on October 9. On October 12, the first American air raid happened. The doors in our watertight partitions were closed. A mouse could not have escaped. Six bombing missions that day, and we could hear the near-misses fall in the water close to the ship. The next day, more air raids. When we were finally let out, we saw a big crater on shore about thirty yards away. The Japanese passengers had been taken ashore and stayed in a hotel. At evening call we were allowed to stand on the deck for ten minutes.

We had not been able to wash ourselves, and on the sixth day we were ordered to come to the wharf, naked, with a towel and a bar of soap. A Japanese soldier in plain sight of Japanese soldiers and geishas, who enjoyed the unusual spectacle, sprayed us with a fire hose.

"Suddenly, on October 22, the ship started to move, and we left Taiwan for good."

"Good God, Vader, what did you do all that time in the bowel of that ship?" Gijs asked.

"We decided we might as well play cards. In the middle of the area we stayed in was an opening where we could sit on the floor."

"I think we are ready for another round of coffee," Janneke said. "I have to unclench my jaws. Even though you are sitting here telling us the story, it seems hardly possible that you survived it all, and you haven't brought us to Manchuria yet!"

The steward brought in a tray with fresh coffee and more cakes.

"That'll keep me going!" Vader laughed. "And I will tell you all this only once."

He kept his word. Gijs and Janneke could later remember only very few times that Vader discussed his war experiences.

"We were not given life jackets for the trip, unlike the Japanese passengers who walked around in them from the beginning to the very end. The anchor was dropped near Moji on the north side of Kyushu. Like drunks, we walked off the ship, exhausted, dirty, and hungry. We were in Japan, the country of our enemy! We could tell that the enormous Yawata Steelworks were barely operating, and the evidence of Allied bombing was everywhere. Men, women, and children were digging trenches. We wondered if they feared an invasion.

"The trip to Manchuria was very, very long. The train trip along the coast was beautiful. We were put on a ferry from Japan to Fusan on the southeast coast of Korea. A Japanese journalist, who visited us there, told of heavy fighting in the Philippines. He thought it would result in a big victory for Japan. The final leg of the trip was by train along mountain ridges, through fields and villages. We crossed the Yaloe River between Korea and Manchuria. The temperature dropped precipitously, and we noticed every lake and river we passed was frozen solid. We arrived on November 14, 1944, in Cheng Chia Tun, a small town on the eastern side of the Gobi desert, about one hundred twenty mile from Moekden. It had taken the Japs more than a month to transport us from Shirakawa on Taiwan to this place.

"It was bitter cold. Each of us received six cotton blankets and even a sheet, but we had to put newspapers in between the layers of blankets to keep warm. It could get so ungodly cold there that when I smoked my pipe, my exhaled breath froze into icicles that hung from the stem! For the rest, it was the same as before, as it must have been for you. Lack of food, lack of medicines, brutal punishments, deteriorating physical conditions for many, and the feeling this war would never end. What was so hard was to live without free will, to do only what you were ordered to do. You could never realize your own ideas. Men of our rank weren't used to that."

Moeder chuckled.

Although they had some sources of information, there was so much they didn't know. A few could speak fluent Japanese and translate the Japanese newspapers they found here and there. That helped. The war in Europe was going badly for the Germans, but they knew nothing of Stalin's promise at Yalta to participate in the war with Japan once the Germans were defeated. Stalin made good on that promise two days after the first atomic bomb fell. On August 8, 1945, he declared war on Japan, and on the ninth he invaded with no less than ten armies. The prisoners did not know this, but they did notice great agitation among the guards. Once again, they were moved to another POW camp outside of Moekden.

Vader said, "A Russian captain arrived on August 20 at our camp. He said, 'Gentlemen of the Allied Prisoner of War Camp. In the name of the Red Army, I declare that you are free as of this moment.'

You can imagine our reaction! The Japanese officers who stood next to him looked beaten. One of them cried."

The Russians disarmed the Japanese soldiers in front of the prisoners with great ceremony. The Japanese were ordered to put their weapons, swords, ammunition, and leather straps on the ground. The Russians picked up the guns one by one and handed them to American soldiers, who'd come with their officers as caretakers and been turned into guards by the Russian captain. The swords were handed to the Japanese officers, according to an event in 1904, when Russian officers received their swords back after the fall of Moekden.

Bidding the American General Parker farewell, the Russian captain said to him, "Do as you wish. You Americans are far too easy with these guys. Take it strictly with them."

"It was a veiled license to kill," Vader said, "but we made the Japs clip the grass on their hands and knees."

It had been quite a task to get the prisoners out of Manchuria. They could not leave until September 11. First by train to the harbor of Dairen, in northeast China. A huge American hospital ship, aptly named *Relief*, brought them to Okinawa.

"I can't begin to tell you how wonderful it felt to sleep in a real bed with sheets. On our pillows we found a pair of pajamas, toilet articles, cigarettes, and matches. We had our first meat, vegetables, and potatoes in a long time. You must have gone through the same emotions when you finally came out of camp."

"We sure did," Janneke said. "I never realized what a privilege it was to sleep on a mattress and under cotton sheets!"

He looked at his watch. "I think it's time for a nightcap," he said. "Would you believe it is three o'clock in the morning?"

"Am I allowed to drink alcohol?" Gijs asked.

"You look like a man. Act like a man!" Vader said, and sent a tender look toward his son.

A servant brought a tray with several bottles. They could choose between cognac, Drambuie, triple sec, and crème de menthe.

"The time in Manila was hard in different ways," Vader said. "We were frustrated we were not allowed to reorganize and restore order on Java. It was a political game, but that's for another time. Let's celebrate that we are here together, come what may!"

The stateroom was not large. There was barely room for the four of them. Moeder and Vader sat in comfortable armchairs, but Janneke and Gijs had to sit sideways on the bunk beds. They'd hardly noticed the awkwardness of their cramped positions, though. With only one porthole to look out from, the stateroom felt like a bubble that could keep the outside world at bay. The perfect space for a reunion after their family had been broken up by world events.

Gijs gingerly took a sip of cognac from the traditional cognac glass, with its wide belly and narrow opening. So often, before the war, he had watched his father and his friends swirl the gold-colored liquid around in the glass and then sniff the delicious aroma. It was an after-dinner ritual in their living room, with officers in dress uniform and civilian men in black tie. Gijs looked at the four of them sitting in the stateroom, stuffy from Vader's cigar smoke. Janneke and Moeder in worn and faded dresses. Vader in a battle dress uniform of another nation. Himself in borrowed clothes that were too big.

Cognac was potent stuff, he thought, as the small sip of liquor burned its way down. It had immediate effect. After the second sip, he was filled with warm feelings for his family. After the third sip, he wondered how he was ever going to convince his father, this man who'd proven to be so astute and strong, that he wanted to become an orderly. It would not be easy, but he was determined to stay the course he'd chosen for himself.

Chapter 27

It was the morning after the long night of storytelling. Debriefing would probably be a more apt description, Gijs thought, as he stretched out on his bunk after a few hours sleep. He was exhausted. The seemingly interminable period of not knowing had ended, a dense curtain lifted. Four people, who had not seen each other for three and a half years, had finally shared what had happened to them. *We will never get to the bottom of it all,* Gijs thought. *We know most of the facts now, but what about the emotions?*

As always, the future wore a veil. He tried to penetrate its opacity. How would each of them adapt to new realities and new roles? That Janneke's life had changed was clear. She'd lost the man she loved to the sea, but she was young enough to go on, and from what he'd observed in the past two months, Janneke would not let life beat her down. Her scars were invisible, because she was clever at directing attention away from herself by always doing for others. Although he was sad for her, he didn't deeply worry about her.

He tossed under his smooth cotton sheet—still such a delight— as he contemplated the changes his parents undoubtedly would face after this time of reunion. In spite of the physical hardships she had suffered, Moeder had thrived in her role of leader and mediator in the camp. With her innate sense of fairness, she had ruled with authority in the house that was packed with women, living there against their wills. How was she going to fit back into a marriage with an equally authoritarian spouse? Would she find employment for her honed skills as a mediator and a leader?

His father had his own challenges. As part of a defeated navy that had lost most of its fleet, he would find less room at the top. The officers who had fled to Australia before the capitulation were still on active duty. During the time Vader was in Manila, he had been less than impressed with their understanding of what the POWs had gone through. Bitterness might be Vader's lot before the course of his career got sorted out.

Gijs felt comfortable projecting his own future. Convincing his father of his plans might present an obstacle, but he was determined to win the argument. The war had put him on a certain course.

After breakfast, Gijs asked his father if he knew how to get a telegram sent out.

"A telegram?" Vader asked. "Why do you ask?"

"Because I have to send one."

"I will ask the radio operator. It has to be important, of course."

"It is. I made a good friend. His name is Pieter Donk. I didn't have time to say good-bye to him."

"Do you have an address?" Vader asked.

"Yes. Just before we left, I heard his family had reoccupied their house in Bandoeng."

"Okay. Write it down and I'll see to it."

Gijs found a piece of paper. On it he wrote Pieter's address and a note: "Our family reunited in Batavia. Return to Holland. Thanks for everything. Gijs."

In spite of the excitement of the last few days, Gijs already missed Rob and Pieter. Nobody he would meet from here on in would understand, in quite the same way, what the past three years had been like. He'd been lucky to have them as friends. He'd survived the beatings and hepatitis, because Pieter and Rob had shared their own food. They had acted outside the norm. Their friendship would become the touchstone for his future relationships. Gijs met Pieter again, a few years later, at a rowing regatta in Amsterdam where Pieter studied law.

"We have to go to Australia in order to return to Holland," Vader told them at lunch after a few days on the *Plancius*. "The ss *Kota Gedek* is moored in the harbor of Melbourne, waiting for repatriates."

"How will we get to Australia?" Janneke wanted to know.

"With a Catalina," Vader said. "Eight other passengers will join the four of us."

The Catalina was a seaplane, like the one Vader had tried to escape in during the final days before the capitulation. It offered close quarters for twelve people, who sat on benches on each side of the plane. Gijs was told to sit on a wooden trapdoor that covered a bubble made of a transparent material. In time of war it was used as a machine-gun post.

On the third day of their island-hopping, via Borneo and Celebes, they landed on truly free soil in Port Darwin, the most northerly harbor of Australia, where they were given the first milk they'd tasted in years. They traveled from there to Sydney. Almost as soon as they got to their hotel in Sydney, the electricity went off because of a labor strike. The next morning, the hotelier told them he couldn't serve breakfast. The electric bread-cutting machine didn't work, he said. Moeder and the other women they'd traveled with stormed into the kitchen and told the chef that they had spent three years in internment camps, and that if he could hand them a few knives, they would cut the bread for him. The chef was taken aback, amazed at these skinny women in their faded cotton dresses, who took over his domain and served breakfast to all the guests in the hotel.

Melbourne was the final destination. That was where the Dutch Navy had made its headquarters since the capitulation in 1942. Everyone on the Catalina was excited, knowing that many old friends and colleagues would be there to greet them, another beacon on the road to normalcy. But it almost didn't happen. Their landing in Melbourne's harbor was dramatic.

During the approach, Gijs removed the trapdoor he'd been sitting on for five days and lay down in the bubble so he wouldn't miss any of the arrival. He saw a big crowd on the shore. Excitement coursed through his veins when he recognized the white officers' caps of the Royal Dutch Navy among the people standing on the quay. Suddenly the plane took a nosedive toward the water. He heard his father shout a heartfelt curse.

"God Almighty, what is he doing? This is a stupid maneuver!"

The bubble Gijs was lying down in was surrounded by gurgling water, and he lost sight of the shore. Fish swam for their lives underneath him, and above him he heard panicked voices and his father cursing the pilot. Somehow, the pilot managed to pull the plane up and steady it on the water, but the damage to the plane was great. The passengers crawled out and were fetched by a motorboat that had been at the ready to transport them to land. Loud cheers rose from the crowd.

Classmates of Jan Schippers formed a special welcoming committee for Janneke. In that moment, Jan's death came into sharp focus for Janneke. It flashed into an even starker reality than when Moeder, in prison camp, had told her that Jan was lost at sea. The sight of their dress uniforms brought back memories she'd held at bay, when survival had been the goal in her day-to-day life. But Janneke would not be Janneke, Gijs thought, as he watched her struggle with the sudden rise of wrenching emotions, if she didn't force herself over the threshold from a dark tunnel into the light of the future. She regained her composure, and Gijs admired her inner strength.

Arrival in Melbourne

The passengers were brought to a hotel that the navy had rented in its entirety. Over the course of the month they stayed there, the dining room was witness to many emotional reunions. To learn how the war had wreaked havoc in human relationships, one just had to look around the Hotel Gatwick in St. Kilda.

They needed new clothes badly. Vader had received back pay, and the family set out to shop. Vader and Gijs went to the Navy Depot and both came out in battle dress, a novelty to them, Vader with the proper insignia while Gijs's uniform was bare. He wore it proudly, and in time he would impress his classmates back in Holland with it.

Moeder and Janneke had more fashionable clothing in mind. Feeling self-conscious in their well-worn clothes, each longed for a colorful, cheerful dress. Since everything they owned had been worn to its last thread, in a large department store they selected panties, bras, slips, camisoles, and stockings, and asked for a dressing room. They stripped themselves of what they had on and luxuriated in the fine fabrics against their skin. The salesclerks brought a variety of dresses to try on. The transformations were so stunning, they felt like strangers to themselves when they looked in the mirror. Their old underwear and dresses they left in a heap in a corner of the dressing room. "You can throw those away," Janneke told the astonished salesclerk.

After their month of recuperation, they took a sixteen-hour train trip back to Sydney to board the *Kota Gedeh*, a cargo ship that had been used for troop transports during the war. The passenger accommodations had been remodeled to fit in couchettes for the women. Below deck, the walls were stacked with wooden bunk beds for the men. Had they known what was in store for them, they might not have set foot on the *Kotah Gedeh*.

The ship stuck to the south coast of Australia, but it soon ran into a horrific storm. Its masts were shorn off; all the china, pots, and pans got smashed; and the captain broke his arm. The passengers lay strapped to their cots. Gijs braced his feet against the footrest and held onto the sides so he wouldn't fall down from the top bunk. Moeder and Janneke were so terribly seasick, they didn't care whether they survived or not.

"After all these years of misery in camps, and now we perish after all," they said to each other.

The captain came by with his arm in a sling to say the ship was sitting out the storm on a course to the South Pole. For two and a half days the *Kotah Gedeh* bobbed up and down in the high seas. Thoroughly battered, it steamed into the harbor of Perth, where an enormous crowd of people, who'd heard of the ship-in-need over the radio, welcomed them. It took a week to clean, reload, and repair the damage. Once again, they were brought to a hotel. There was no other way to get back to Holland, so Moeder and Janneke swallowed hard and returned to the *Kotah Gedeh*.

The crew was a rough bunch of Australians, who'd spent the war years on troop-transporting ships. The captain didn't trust them with liquor, and he sought out Gijs and a young man named Hans Sandkuyl to tend the bar. They told the captain they'd both served as orderlies in the camps. If they'd managed to wipe grown men's behinds, they said, they could cut off sailors before they got too drunk. The captain liked their pluck.

A long trip was ahead of them, at least a month, and the barkeepers struck up a friendship in between filling shot glasses with Dutch *jenever*. They had their age and height in common, and they'd both stayed in the Tjimahi camps. It wasn't hard to find common ground. Behind his strong prescription glasses, Hans's eyes exuded intelligence. His voice was throaty, his smile charming, and his laugh hearty.

"Do you have any idea where you're headed after we return to Holland?" Gijs asked.

"Staying with family, I suppose."

"I meant, do you know what you will do?"

"Going back to school to get a high school diploma. After that I want to go into medicine."

"Your father isn't a doctor, is he?"

"No," Hans said. "He's with the Dutch Shell."

"And you don't feel compelled to be in oil yourself?"

"Not after the camps. I liked being an orderly."

"Me too," Gijs said. "When you say you're going into medicine later, what do you mean by that? What I liked about being an orderly was finding ways to make people more comfortable. The doctors couldn't do much for the patients, because they didn't have the medicines to do the trick. In the end, I think my friend Keereweer did more for the patients than the doctors. They would come in, look at the chart, and spend little time with the patients themselves."

"True, but think what they could have done if they'd had the tools and drugs they needed."

"A lot more, I suppose, but the orderlies were the ones who were with the patients all the time."

"It doesn't need to be that way," Hans said. "It would be more challenging to find other solutions. So, I lean toward studying medicine and becoming a doctor."

His conversations with Hans gave Gijs a lot to think about before talking to his father about his future.

Every late afternoon, he poured shots of Dutch gin and glasses of sherry for the repatriating passengers. The crew came from "before the mast" to get their portions, and, truth be told, Hans and Gijs felt like grown men when they told the crew off, after the sailors tried every trick in the book to get more booze.

Together with Hans, Gijs corralled two attractive girls, with whom they spent many leisure hours in a lifeboat on the top deck. How better to spend idle time than in the company of the other sex, which had been invisible to them for so long? With enough protein aboard, their juices were running. Not freely, because Vader came to check on them every now and then. Gijs suspected Moeder sent him on inspection tours. But he and Hans swore that all they did was soak up the sun and talk about what it would be like back in Holland in winter after years in the tropics. In fact, out of sight in the lifeboat, they were delivered from the endless debates going on in the lounge and on deck about the world's political situation.

Gijs was aware that Vader and Moeder were giving him time to have the kind of fun he'd missed. But as they approached the Mideast, Vader thought it was time to have a serious talk with his son. One day he brought Gijs on deck, and they leaned against the railing, as they'd done on the way to Java when Gijs was fourteen. Then Vader had pointed out the stars and constellations, telling his son how important it was for a navy officer to know them well. He'd proven the point by sailing a lifeboat to Sumatra, never losing the way.

"Have you thought more about your future, Gijs?" Vader asked.

"Yes, Vader, I have. I always thought I wanted to follow in your footsteps and join the navy. I even took astronomy in camp. But I've changed my mind. Working as an orderly for several years has had a big influence. Hans Sandkuyl went through the same thing. We've talked a lot about it."

"You know what I think about hospitals, and doctors and sickness. It's hard for me to imagine that anyone could be attracted to a profession in that field."

"I know that, Vader."

"Being an orderly may not give you much satisfaction in the long run," Vader said. "The compassion you have felt for your fellow *tawanans* may wear off, and you will be bored. By that time, it may be too late to start another career."

Gijs could see where this line of reasoning was going. Vader had given it thought.

"You would rather see me become a doctor, right?"

"In my mind, although I couldn't even imagine becoming one, it would be more challenging."

Gijs thought of the conversation he'd had with Hans. In between pouring drinks and having fun with the girls, he'd thought about the choice.

"I just don't know, Vader, if I can get into university," Gijs said, as he leaned over the railing and watched the calm sea wash up against the steel of the ship.

"It will be hard. No question. Your schooling has been haphazard, and not just because of the war. I bet you can't count on one hand how many schools you've attended." Vader laughed. "I am the guilty one, hauling you back and forth over the ocean."

"I learned other things from that!"

"It will be hard, Gijs, but you have a good mind, and I think that if you really, really want this, you will get there. It may take more time than you like, but you can do it."

Did I just hear Vader say that? Gijs thought. *Would he really support the idea of me becoming a doctor?* He looked into his father's face, with the deep wrinkles and steady eyes under the balding head with its ring of graying hair. His father's father had been a contractor. Vader hadn't followed in his footsteps. He'd chosen the sea. Now his son chose medicine.

"Okay, Vader, I will try."

"Good luck, son!" Vader said, and slapped his shoulder.

Chapter 28

Holland veiled herself in an icy fog on the morning of March 1, 1946, as the *Kotah Gedeh* steamed up the Maas River. The hoarse boom of a foghorn warned of poor weather, and from somewhere in the invisible distance, the sound of chugging motors reached them. Suddenly, the squat and muscular forms of several tugboats rose up, swarming around the steel hull of the big ship, getting into position to push and shove it to its ultimate destination: a dock in the harbor of Rotterdam.

Snowflakes twirled in the air as Gijs emerged with his father from below deck. Seen from the railing, the contours of the landscape were unrecognizable in the early darkness. For six years, they'd lived close to the equator, where the day and the night were dealt twelve hours each. Here, closer to the North Pole, and it being winter, the days were short and the nights very long. Through their knitted mittens, the iron railing felt like an icicle to their hands, and they pulled up the collars of the winter coats they'd received from the Red Cross in Aden, at the mouth of the Suez Canal on the Indian Ocean side. The Red Cross had been thoughtful and well organized in doling out shoes, underwear, and warm clothes to the repatriates before they entered the Mediterranean Sea and sailed toward colder weather.

"It couldn't be more Dutch," Gijs said. "Cold, dark, and enough snow to cover up its imperfections."

"I love the smell," Vader said, and he sniffed the air as if he were preparing to taste a good wine. "It reminds me of when I was a boy in Dordrecht. Most of my free time was spent at the river and the docks. I think it's the smell of tar mixed with diesel fumes that bring it back."

"Is that how you thought of going into the navy?" Gijs asked.

"I suppose so. The harbor fascinated me, and I was not interested in joining my father's business. It was at the time of the First World War. He had lost his fortune in worthless German money. Going into business then was not a viable option."

"War influenced your choice of profession, and it looks like it will do the same for me," Gijs said.

The sight of Rotterdam was shocking. They'd known, of course, that the Germans had bombed it relentlessly at the start of the war to force Holland's surrender, but they weren't prepared for the still visible devastation. Even with the good face the powder-sugar snow put on its facade, the city could not hide its scars. As he surveyed the disturbing gaps in the cityscape, Gijs thought about how going home had been an abstraction, born out of a hankering for familiarity. He needed to make some serious adjustments in his thinking. Caught up in his own war story, he hadn't allowed for what had happened here.

His aunt and uncle—Moeder's brother and sister—stood behind barriers to welcome them, but Gijs and his family couldn't do more than wave back. All navy personnel and their relatives were whisked away to a navy base, where administrative details had to be taken care of. Eventually, they were brought to the doorstep of a house in Dordrecht, where Vader's two sisters lived on the Hallincqlaan, their temporary address until the future got sorted out.

His two aunts, Tante Jo and Tante Cor, one widowed and the other never married, opened their arms and their home on that wintry day. The day was as cold as it had been years earlier, when they had stood on the platform of the railroad station in Rotterdam, huddled in their fur coats, waving them farewell on the start of their trip to the Indies, two months before the war broke out in Holland.

The aunts pulled out all stops to celebrate their younger brother's safe return. Everything they offered was, as they repeatedly said, saved from before the war. A cigar for Vader, a dry sherry from

Spain, a fine Bordeaux with dinner, the embroidered linen table-cloth, all of it had been lovingly saved for their return, for the day they could all say they'd survived the onslaught of war at two ends of the earth.

It was festive and exciting, but only for a day.

As Gijs sat in an armchair, his fingers playing over the plush upholstery as he listened to more war stories, a panicky feeling took hold of him. Was this their ultimate destination? After all they'd been through, it came down to this? Living with two elderly ladies, sweet but set in their ways, in a provincial town in a cold and somber country? The walls of the living room, lined with heavy pieces of mahogany furniture and darkened by the winter twilight, crashed in on him. It was as if life in a camp had never happened, as if he'd never known people like Keereweer and Pieter Donk. How could he make them come to life in this stifling atmosphere? It seemed nonsensical even to bring up their names. These old aunts could not possibly understand how much his life had evolved because of those men.

Tante Cor told Vader that when they'd looked into schools for Gijs, she'd discovered that the principal of the high school had played soccer with Vader. Vader paid the man a visit and got Gijs admitted to the senior class. Donned in his battle dress uniform that he'd received in Australia, and with a pack of Camel cigarettes tucked in its breast pocket, Gijs went back to school. Two weeks earlier he'd turned twenty, somewhere on the Indian Ocean.

It was absurd to sit on a school bench and listen to a teacher explaining organic chemistry, when Gijs had no clue what the man was talking about. He did better in history and geography classes, and he had no difficulty with English, but it quickly became obvious that he would not be sufficiently prepared to take the final exams in July. There was just too much catching up to do. Teachers showed little understanding when he explained what conditions in an internment camp had been like. They suggested he was exaggerating when he told about doing homework on a piece of slate. It seemed impossible for them to relate to the secrecy that surrounded lessons for a group of no more than four students; or how he could be so tired after a day of hard labor that he had no energy left for putting his nose in a textbook—assuming he'd been lucky enough to get his hands on one. If he used the word hungry, they came back with stories of the horrible hunger Holland had endured one winter, and that usually ended the conversation.

Particularly discouraged one day, he walked home by way of the harbor, remembering his father's remarks about how he used to spend his free time on the docks. Watching the busy traffic of boats braving the choppy waters on that cold day, he wondered if he should change his mind, forget about reaching for a high school diploma that would get him into a university. He could choose the sea for a career. *You don't need to know about organic chemistry,* he thought, *to steer a ship.* But deep down he knew he wasn't serious.

The evening meals were no help in dispelling his downcast mood. His aunts' culinary skills had grown around the plentitude of fish in their city, and it meant that they did not believe in cooking fish fillets. Oh no! They boiled the whole fish, head and tail, and that was how they presented it, on a large china platter with a mustard sauce in a sauceboat on the side. The fish's dull, extinguished eye stared at the ceiling without focus, and looking at it made Gijs feel extremely uncomfortable. Small metal bowls were clipped onto the dinner plates, to be filled with the bones of the carcass. It was very hard to watch his aunts chew bites of fish and spit out the tiny bones. Revolting, Gijs thought, and for years he didn't touch a haddock or any other kind of fish. When he mentioned it to Janneke, she agreed it was disgusting, but it made culinary sense, she said. Fish tasted better cooked with the bones left in.

Every morning for two months, Gijs got himself to school, dressed in his uniform, and always with a pack of Camels in the breast pocket to bolster his courage in the face of overt ignorance. The other students, three years younger, were in awe of him, but not his teachers. What should they do with this young man, he knew they wondered, who hung back in the last row in the classroom? Taking the final exams in July, as unprepared as he was, could not amount to more than a desperate leap into the dark.

One day in May, he picked up the newspaper after he'd come "home" from school, and a small article caught his eye. The Secretary of Education extended *Het Londens Besluit*, which amounted to granting students who had returned from the Dutch East Indies a diploma that would enable them to study at a Dutch university. The same was granted to students who'd been caught up in the war and had not been able to attend school in Holland during the German occupation for various reasons. The Dutch government, in exile in London, had initially decided this. But there was a caveat: the students had to meet certain criteria. That small sentence sent chills up Gijs's spine. Yet the article would not leave him alone. Suppose he would get it, if he tried?

When Vader came into the livingroom, he brought it up.

"I don't give you much of a chance, Gijs. I think you have to buckle down, study, and do the final exams."

"Would you lend me some money for a return ticket to the Hague, so I can find out the details? I'll pay you back if I return empty-handed."

With ten guilders in the pocket of the American suit he'd received from the Red Cross, Gijs set out early on a beautiful spring day to The Hague. Meadows, dotted with Friesian cows, rolled by his train window. It was Holland at its best. The intense green of the luscious grass lifted his mood. Spring had brought new life. He could almost hear the grass being clipped and chewed by the cattle in the fields.

He reached inside his suit jacket to make sure the envelope was still there with the all-important pieces of crumpled paper, all the proof he had that he'd passed certain exams in Tjimahi. He repeated to himself what his line of reasoning would be in front of the civil servant who would decide his fate today. All he could hope for was that the man would have some empathy. It was not a given.

He walked up the stairs of the massive building that housed the Department of Education. A clerk behind the information desk pointed him toward a long corridor lined with wooden benches, where students waited their turn to make the same case Gijs was hoping to make. For every student who went in for an interview, a new one took a seat on the benches. It turned into a long wait, and at some point, Gijs had to go to the bathroom. He asked a man in a gray dustcoat, walking by with a tray of coffee cups, where the men's room was. As he walked down the hall, he looked for familiar faces among the waiting students, but he didn't see any.

In the men's room, he picked the one urinal that was not in use. While relieving himself, he was aware of the intense gaze of the gentleman to his right. It felt a bit uncomfortable. Before he could look up, he heard, "Gijs!"

For a moment he was totally confused.

"Gijs, fancy meeting you here!" the man said.

He looked into the face that belonged to the voice. "Mr. Weert! I didn't recognize you with a suit and tie on! This is amazing!"

While washing their hands at the sink, Mr. Weert asked what he was doing there.

"I'm trying to get the special high school diploma that I read about in the paper," Gijs said.

Mr. Weert looked into his eyes and whispered, "I am the one who gives those out."

"What?"

"All right, follow me."

Gijs walked behind Mr. Weert down the long corridor, still lined with waiting students. Looks of envy burned into his back. Once in his office, Mr. Weert motioned him to sit down in a chair across from him.

"This is more comfortable than sitting on the edge of a cot, isn't it?" Mr. Weert said. "Tell me, Gijs, what has happened in your life since I saw you last?"

Gijs told him of walking out of the camp, being taken in by a wonderful doctor, and working for him in the hospital. About finding his family, flying to Australia and almost drowning there, and about going back to school in Dordrecht.

"Do you find it hard?" Mr. Weert asked.

There was no sense denying it. "Yes, sir."

"What are your plans, Gijs?"

"I want to study medicine."

Mr. Weert got up and seated himself behind his desk. "I'm not surprised. If you promise me that you really will become a doctor, I will give you the paper you need to enter medical school."

He pulled out a printed form, filled in Gijs's full name, signed it, and walked around the desk to hand it to him.

"I wish you all the luck in the world, my boy."

"Thank you, sir," Gijs said, and shook his hand.

With the money left over from the return ticket, he bought a cigar for his father and tucked it in his breast pocket, next to the unopened envelope with his Tjimahi testimonials and the brand new diploma.

He was on his way.

Bali – Indonesia – 1972

Outside the Ngurah Rai Airport on Bali, Gijs asked a taxi driver to recommend a place he could stay the weekend. Afterward, he wondered how the man had sized him up, for the driver brought him to a small hotel in an obscure neighborhood where he was handed, first thing, some pornographic pamphlets. Oh well, he was tired. A good night's sleep was all he needed. He transferred to a hotel with a more decent reputation the next day.

The people at Care-Medico headquarters in Djokjakarta, Indonesia, had warned him that after two weeks he would need a break. Gijs, with only one month to give away as a volunteer, objected. At home he worked seven days a week, he told them. Why not here? But practicing medicine in a small town in America was not comparable. Here he'd been traveling from hospital to hospital, giving lectures about congestive heart failure to doctors and nurses. Moreover, he'd left New Hampshire in its mud season, and the switch from cold to hot weather had been as wearing on him as upgrading medical care in Indonesia's rural areas. So he had agreed to take a break, and he'd chosen Bali.

The island of Bali had always had a mythical ring to him. His parents vacationed here, sometime before the war, and they'd brought back a replica of a boat made entirely of cloves, right down to the small figures holding the oars. The boat stood on a shelf in his office, and he let his patients smell it if he wanted to distract them from their ills. Amazing, they would say. After all these years, it still smells of cloves.

Before he had reported for duty at the Care-Medico headquarters, he'd stayed in Batavia, where his host lent him a car plus chauffeur to visit Bandoeng. They'd stopped in Tjimahi, at what once had been the boys' internment camp and was now a military base of the Indonesian Army. From the car window, he looked up at the white-painted concrete walls and the tiled roof of the guards' house, where Minamihara had beaten him. At first glance all of the buildings seemed unchanged, but they bore no resemblance to what his mind told him they should look like. A building was just a building, a place just a place. It was as if he was staring at the name of someone he'd known well, chiseled in marble with the correct dates of birth and death, but with no connection to who that person had been in life. Without the shouting Japanese guards, without his growling stomach, without his buddies, these buildings did not hold the same gravity.

What had he expected from visiting Tjimahi? Was he there to verify a fact of history? That it really happened? That, indeed, he grew from adolescence to manhood among these small houses, neatly spaced along a winding road? Had he expected to find the old Dutch East Indies back? Bygones were bygones. He told the driver to keep going, and relegated the memories of life in prison back to where they belonged, inside the capsule that sat neatly tucked away in the far reaches of his mind.

Once on Bali, Gijs took his mother-in-law's advice: that the quickest way to orient himself in a strange place was to take a bus ride. It wasn't hard to find one, since Bali's main source of income was tourism. Gijs folded his long legs into the seat that had been built with smaller people in mind and toured the island. The tour guide called attention to Mt. Agung, an active volcano. It had last erupted in 1963. In whatever direction Gijs looked, the brightest, most fertile color green surrounded him. It lay over the hills and the rice paddies like a quilt made of lush vegetation, with the sea and the sky making up the trimmings. Soepardi used to drive his family through country like this. What he saw now clicked with what he remembered, as if he were sitting in the old Chrysler with the open roof, his parents in the back, Janneke and he on the jump seats. *Djalan, djalan,* they called this roaming around on Sunday afternoons. Vader would be in civilian clothes, wearing a Panama,

Moeder a fashionable straw hat with a wide rim to keep the sun out of her eyes. How he wished he could tell his father about being here, but Vader had died in 1965. Janneke was married to a judge. Moeder was a widow, living in a modern apartment in Rotterdam, with running hot water and central heating.

Gijs Bozuwa in 1972

He had wanted to return to the Indies after he graduated from medical school, but it had not been a good time. Holland's government and Soekarno's republic were at odds. A week ago in Djokjakarta, he'd been introduced to a Dutch schoolteacher who'd lived on Java before the war, during the war, and after the war, which meant she'd seen Dutch colonialism, Japanese occupation, and the struggles for independence. With her blond hair and blue eyes, she was undeniably of Dutch colonial stock. Besides, if he'd had any doubt, her modest home gave away her heritage with the Friesian clock on the wall.

"The Bersiap phase was bad," she told him. "Soekarno had a hard time controlling the rampaging youth right after the war."

"I remember it well," Gijs said. "They shot at us on our drive to the airport. We were glad to get out."

"Soekarno depended on support from the communist party. When a coup was attempted, the communist party was thought to be behind it, and the party was outlawed."

They were walking through the center of Djokjakarta, since the teacher had offered to show him the sights. She led him onto a bridge and stopped in the middle.

"The attempted coup happened in 1965. A violent anti-communist purge followed." She leaned over the iron railing and pointed to the rapidly streaming water below. "More than half a million people were killed. Dead bodies floated under this bridge, day after day. I saw them with my own eyes."

"And you stayed? After all the violence you've seen in this country?"

"I was born and raised here. Never went to Holland. I love this country and I love its people. It's what I know. Tell me, is there a perfect place in this world?"

"Maybe there is one, but human nature, being what it is, can turn any God-given place into hell," Gijs said.

"True. Heaven and hell live side by side. The trick is to believe you're in heaven while you're in hell."

The teacher was living proof of what she believed.

The tour bus drove into Ubud, Bali's cultural center. The American tourist in the seat beside Gijs poked her elbow into his ribs.

"Look at those women," she said. "Isn't that cute, the way they walk with baskets on their heads? Makes for great posture. They should send our models over here for training!"

He got off the bus, followed the Balinese women into the Hindu temple, and watched them place the fruit they'd carried onto the altar. Offerings to please their gods.

Someone in a hurry brushed him gently aside and apologized. The face Gijs looked into was ghostly white, covered with a thick paste and painted with dark lines going in all directions. The eyes, dark as coal, met his own briefly and unnerved him, but he followed the creature to an open area within the temple where a dance was being performed. In the middle stood the ugliest woman he'd ever laid eyes on. Mostly nude, unshapely with sagging breasts, claws, and long, unkempt hair. The temple guide explained that she was Rangda, the demon queen, who leads an army of evil witches against Barong, king of the hosts of good. The man with the white face was Barong. The sword in his right hand was the symbol of strength. Gijs observed that it was smaller than the sword the Japanese guard had used on him.

On Sunday afternoon it was time to go back to work. At the Bali airport, a group of Japanese stood to the side of the ticket counter while their tour leader argued with the clerk behind it. The sounds of the Japanese language, especially raised in anger, sent chills up his spine. Gijs stood in line, waiting his turn, until he realized with a shock that he'd fallen back into the pattern he'd acquired in the internment camps: when the Jap shouts, you obey or duck. He raised his eyebrows and made eye contact with the clerk, who motioned him to come forward. The Japanese tour guide was annoyed, but stepped aside. When Gijs showed his ticket, the clerk said he was sorry, but the plane was overbooked and he would have to wait till tomorrow for the next plane. Gijs reached into his jacket and produced a document with impressive seals and stamps, provided by the Care-Medico people. It proved he was a guest of the Republica Indonesia. "This will get you out of any pickle, or get you to the front of any line," they'd said.

The clerk studied the document and immediately understood that he could not ignore it without some unpleasant consequence. He gave Gijs a boarding pass.

As Gijs picked up his small suitcase to walk to the gate, the Japanese tour guide resumed his shouting, only louder. He had been outmaneuvered. Gijs shrugged and kept going.

Glossary

atap – roof of bamboo leaves
aubergine – eggplant

baboe – maid
bami – noodles
barang – luggage
bedjah – bicycle with passenger cart
belanda/blanda – Caucasian/white
botol – bottle

dessa – small village
djongos – male servant/butler

Econoom – economist. Plural: economen

gedek – fence of woven bamboo strips
goedang – storage shed/pantry
goela-djawa – dark brown sugar from cane
goeling – long pillow

heiho – Indonesian soldiers used by Japanese army

Indo – half-blood

jenever – Dutch gin
jongen – boy
Jonkheer – nobility title

kali – river
kampong – city neighborhood where natives live
kebon – gardener
klamboe – netting over bed
koelie – laborer
kokkie – cook
kyotske – bow (Japanese)

laboe poetih – green vegetable

Maleis – Malaysian
merdeka – freedom
Mevrouw – Mrs.
Moeder – Mother

nasi – fried
nonja besar – lady of the house

pasar – open market
patjoel – hoe
pentjak – Indonesian style of boxing
pikoelan – bamboo stick to carry merchandise with
pinda – peanut
pisang – banana
prauw – type of ship used by the native fishermen

rijsttafel – elaborate rice meal
rotan – furniture made of woven reeds

sarong – wraparound native dress worn by men as well as women
sambal – strong spice
sateh – barbequed
sawah – rice field
slendang – cloth to carry baby in
ss – steamship

tamarind – a type of tree
tempat – place
tempeh – yeasted soybeans
tikar – mat to sleep on
toko – store
tuan – Mr.

Vader – Father

Waringin tree – also called Banyan tree

Sources

Op Reis met de 'Special Party,' by Generaal-Majoor P. Scholten, A.W. Sijthoff's Uitgeversmaatschappij N.V.

Vaarwel, tot Betere Tijden, by J.C. Bijkerk, Uitgever T. Wever B.V.

Je Denk, Ken Niet, Maar Ken!! Samengesteld door Hans Liesker, Stichting Jongens Japanse Kampen Tjimahi/Bandoeng 42'-45.

In Naam van de Keizer, Samengesteld door Theo Lavaleije en Gerard Weijers, Stichting Jongenskamp, Tjimahi.

Jongenskamp Baros 6, Tjimahi, 1944-1945, Dick van Engelenburg, Stichting Jongenskamp Tjimahi.

Jongens in de Mannenkampen te Tjimahi, Samengesteld door H.A.M. Liesker, N.H.M. Liesker, L.G. Woortman, G. Weyers, Stichting Jongenskamp Tjimahi.

De Laatste Tempo Doeloe, by Hein Buitenweg, N.V. Servire.

Bandjir, Een Indische Kroniek, 1935-1950, by T.Y. Hobma-Gastra, Uitgeverij Lunet.

De Kracht van het Lied, by Helen Colijn, Uitgeverij van Wijnen.

I often consulted the *Encyclopedia Britannica* as well as the Dutch *Winkler Prins Encyclopedie*, Elsevier.